Towards 2000

Towards 2000:
The Future of Childhood, Literacy and Schooling

Edited by

Ed Marum

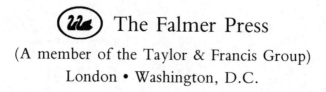 The Falmer Press

(A member of the Taylor & Francis Group)
London • Washington, D.C.

UK   The Falmer Press, 4 John Street, London WC1N 2ET
USA   The Falmer Press, Taylor & Francis Inc., 1900 Frost Road, Suite 101,
Bristol, PA 19007

First published in 1995

**A catalogue record for this book is available from the British
Library**

**Library of Congress Cataloging-in-Publication Data are
available on request**

ISBN 0 7507 0420 9 cased
ISBN 0 7507 0421 7 paper

Jacket design by Caroline Archer

Typeset in 10/12pt Bembo by
Graphicraft Typesetters Ltd., Hong Kong

*Printed in Great Britain by Burgess Science Press, Basingstoke on paper
which has a specified pH value on final paper manufacture of not less than
7.5 and is therefore 'acid free'.*

Contents

Contents

Acknowledgments

The contributors would like to thank colleagues, students and children who have worked with us and helped us define and articulate our views about and feelings for the importance of literacy in society.

Parts of Chapter 5 in Section 2 first appeared in *Children's Literature in Education* (1991), published by Human Sciences Press, New York, and in *Children's Books in Ireland* (1994), published by the Children's Literature Association of Ireland, Dublin.

Material from the National Curriculum is Crown copyright and is reproduced by permission of the Controller of HMSO.

Where other sources have been identified, acknowledgments are made in specific chapters.

Summary

Ed Marum

Many people in the education profession would agree that Britain in the mid-1990s has seen a period of more than usually overt national governmental control of the school curriculum, accompanied by a centralization of power to that government, a radical diminution in the role of local authorities, and an explicit politicization of educational issues for non-educational ends. Having arrived in 1995, the 'post-Dearing' era, a central concern for all those involved in and committed to state educational provision, is the contemporary character and nature of our schools, both as they are shaping in the years following the introduction of, and amendments to, the National Curriculum and as we collectively anticipate the close of the second millenium.

Central questions which need to be addressed include the nature of future 'schooling' in our education system, our current definition of 'childhood', and the directions in which, as professionals, we wish educational provision to develop. Given the cultural and social importance ascribed to 'literacy', this book seeks to examine the current situation of the curriculum in English and to offer practical suggestions for ways in which teachers may move positively forward in both planning and work, involving pupils more actively in the educational process as they do so.

The book's contributors share a common perception that the future quality of classroom teaching remains of central importance in our society. We believe that now is the right time to begin to reappraise the developments of recent years, to assert some new positions based on that reappraisal, and to offer the hope that a new partnership of parents, pupils and teachers can effectively and constructively look forward with confidence to what the future holds. In many respects we believe this progress and development must be achieved despite, rather than because of, the requirements of the revised National Curriculum proposals for English. We are also keenly aware that a critique of the current state of English teaching will not *of itself* be of help to those thousands of teachers in schools who have the daily job of teaching that curriculum. Rather, we see a critique as a necessary if partial element in the articulation of our position, as the basis from which a contemporary rationale for the teaching of English may be more fully developed.

Following the 'Dearing' review, the revised orders for English in the National Curriculum are to be implemented incrementally from September

1995. All primary and secondary teachers of English will need to respond and adapt their practice to take account of the new requirements. We hope, above all, that this book offers teachers some positive and practical suggestions which they will consider and find useful as they grapple with the challenges posed as education moves towards the year 2000.

The first millenium brought many expectations of the ending of the world and the second coming of Christ. In the extending irrationalities of our own time, many of them flourishing in the most developed centres of advanced industrial civilization, we can already see some signs of this happening again, as the arbitrary date approaches. The danger of nuclear war is widely described, within an old scheme and vocabulary, as the threat of 'apocalypse'. Orwell's *1984*, a numerical inversion from 1948 when he was writing his book, has become a date with tyranny. And beyond those who believe or half-believe in these arbitrary numerical significances, there is the deep habit of using some mark in time — a new year, a birthday, a millenium — to reflect and to look forward, to try to see where we are. (Williams, 1983)

But here on Millbank there were only ex-children shuffling to work. Further up, just before Parliament Square, was a group of licensed beggars. They were not permitted anywhere near Parliament or Whitehall or within sight of the square. But a few were taking advantage of the confluence of commuter routes. He saw their bright badges from a couple of hundred yards away. This was their weather and they looked cocky with their freedom. The wage earners had to give way. A dozen beggars were working both sides of the street, moving towards him steadily against the surge. It was a child Stephen was watching now. Not a 5-year-old but a skinny pre-pubescent. She had registered him at some distance. She walked slowly, somnambulantly, the regulation black bowl extended. The office workers parted and converged about her. Her eyes were fixed on Stephen as she came. He felt the usual ambivalence. To give money ensured the success of the government programme. Not to give involved some determined facing away from private distress. There was no way out. The art of bad government was to sever the line between public policy and intimate feeling, the instinct for what was right. (McEwan, 1987)

Don't you know that the dream has come true?
Don't you know by now the dream has come true? (Collins, 1990)

References

COLLINS, J. (1990) *Fires of Eden*, CBS Records Inc. (Malaysia).
McEwan, I. (1987) *The Child in Time*, London, Jonathan Cape.
WILLIAMS, R. (1983) *Towards 2000*, London, Chatto and Windus.

Introduction

Ed Marum

Until the middle of the eighteenth century, literature and literacy meant almost the same thing. Literature was the books that a literate person read. Now we keep the words apart and give them specialized meanings; literacy for social usefulness, literature for certain selected texts that, by tradition or personal taste, are considered to be well-written and that are to be read, somehow, differently. I want to bring the two words together again so that literature does not depend for its definition on private opinions of its worth but is simply the writing that people do, while literacy is about reading and writing texts of all kinds and the entitlement of all. (Meek, 1991, p. 28)

Twenty years ago an interim report entitled *Children's Reading Interests* was published (Whitehead *et al.*, 1975). Interestingly, its production coincided with that of the Bullock Report, *A Language For Life* (HMSO, 1975) commissioned by central government in an effort to discover the current condition of literacy in schools. Whitehead's work involved a survey of some 8000 children aged between 10 and 15, and about 10 per cent of the schools in the sample took part in follow-up interviews. In its conclusion, the report makes the following points:

While most children between the ages of 10 and 15 regularly read a number of comics and many read some books, there is a sizeable minority of both sexes who do not read any books in their leisure time. This minority, which increases with age and reaches at 14+ the disturbingly high proportion of 32 per cent of girls and 40 per cent of boys, naturally includes some who are weak in their level of reading attainment, but it also includes many more whose reading skills would enable them to read interesting books if they chose to do so. The group contains a high proportion of children from manual working-class families where books play little part in the life of the home. Schools should be alerted to their responsibility to identify these children and to seek out, provide and recommend the books that will induce them to take up the satisfactions available to them from book reading. Experience shows that there are very few children, if any indeed, who cannot be 'hooked' on books if the right ones are put in their way. (Whitehead *et al.*, 1975, p. 47)

In 1995, the optimism of that final sentence would no longer be universally voiced. Politicians, industrialists and the media, amongst others, have in the intervening period continued to pronounce upon what schools and teachers need to do to 'put right' the imagined wrongs of our educational system. During the period of the present government an emphasis upon the need to go 'back to basics' in our society, in terms of attitudes and values, has been a prominent feature of political dogma. Within this context, and the period of Thatcherism which created it, the development of a National Curriculum largely imposed from the centre has been in educational terms an important feature of government policy. The recent period has also witnessed the restriction of teachers' contractual and negotiating rights, the imposition of a national assessment system in the face of much professional resistance, the creation of a new system of institutional inspections directed from a reorganized Office for Standards in Education and the concomitant diminution in role and power of the previously independent Her Majesty's Inspectorate.

Such typical developments have been combined with a series of legal and financial restraints upon the powers and responsibilities of local education authorities, enabled through the 1988 Education Act and subsequent Parliamentary developments. The institution of local management of schools, devolving considerable powers to headteachers and school governors, and the institution and planned expansion of the numbers of grant-maintained schools, directly and advantageously financed from central government, have further weakened the power of local authority officers and restricted the range and operation of their services. In effect, the attempt has been to create an entrepreneurial, client-driven, business approach to state education, in which context loosely applied terms such as 'standards', 'value for money', 'law and order', 'corporal punishment' and 'accountability' have again been widely scattered through the popular press and cynically exploited for a variety of overtly political ends. The recent 'James Bulger' trial was perceived by many people as having apocalyptic significance nationally, both in terms of the issues it raised about the nature and condition of 'childhood' in British society and, more broadly, in terms of the wider moral issues and public debate stimulated by the trial.

As a result, it has become familiar to engage with the question 'What kind of society have we become?' This is linked with other such questions. 'What do we expect of and from children?' 'What are the roles of the public services, of parents and the broader community in the socialization and education of the young and their development as responsible citizens in the next generation?' 'What are our schools doing about it?' Such questions are never new. They do, however, in the context of the current social and political climate, and particularly in view of the radical alterations to the state educational structure, have a new sense of urgency about them. If it is some-times true that we are led by a government 'that knows the cost of everything and the value of nothing', then that government reflects its people. It becomes uncomfortably difficult to apportion blame elsewhere.

Parents, children and teachers have important voices in determining the kind of society we are. As we anticipate the next millenium, it is perhaps timely to look back as well as to look forward. What Raymond Williams called 'the extending irrationalities of our time' demand that those involved in education, as well as those now training and those who will in future do so, consider 'where we are' and help to plan where we might profitably go.

This book attempts to provide some sense of an historical context to the issues raised, by examining developments relating to the introduction and implementation of the National Curriculum and some of the associated ques-tions posed for those in education. In a period of change, innovation and development, the book also attempts to look forward, in both the short and medium term.

The structure is intended to help enable teachers to relate historical and developmental issues in the teaching of English to suggestions for current and future practice. While, in the short term, we seek to provide helpful strategies for teachers in schools facing the task of implementing the English orders to be introduced from September 1995, we believe that such strategies must be seen as part of a new rationale for English and need to be related, where relevant, to school policies and common agreed practice.

Section 1 'Contextual Issues' contains, therefore, a chapter on the place of literature in schools which attempts to provide a general yet brief review of the role of 'literature' in the curriculum over recent years. This is followed by a piece by Mick Saunders and Chris Hall, which clearly and cogently analyzes recent political events in the determination of educational policy, exposing the educational irrationalities of the present government's handling of a wide range of issues affecting the National Curriculum and its chrono-logical drift. The third chapter, continuing this theme, expresses concern over more recent developments in English in 1995, and looks forward to consider some issues that need to be addressed in the longer term if the curriculum offer is not to remain limited in content and scope.

Section 2 'Classroom Issues' is a series of articles based around specific practical concerns with literacy and its development in both primary and secondary schools. An attempt is made to relate theory to contemporary good practice, and there is a deliberate emphasis here upon practical approaches teachers might choose to take in their work. The section begins with a de-scriptive analysis of some methods employed by Liz Slater to stimulate a fresh approach to reading in Key Stage 1 by developing the reader's response to text through the use of related games. This chapter offers a fascinating account of the way in which practical activity can be fruitfully linked to wider theory and good primary practice.

This chapter is followed by an examination, with examples, of the ways in which the choice of particular texts at Key Stage 2 can and does influence how children perceive the reading process, and again offers some suggestions for using and developing the issues the texts raise.

Jenny Marum then examines some central issues teachers at Key Stages 3 and 4 need to face and address, describing her concept of the reader's 'reading journey', and linking this to the use of group reading. She goes on to consider some ways in which teachers might address the requirement in the revised English orders that they teach prescribed nineteenth-century texts, suggesting helpful strategies for doing so, while also dealing with related issues of concern to teachers teaching this age range.

James Pattenden goes on to provide a detailed analysis, from his perspective as a practising Head of English, of the important factors surrounding assessment issues in the secondary school, and offers thoughtful and practical advice for colleagues as to how they might in future organize their English departments to facilitate reliable procedures.

In the final chapter in this section, Neil Campbell addresses thematic issues embedded in the analysis of some prominent African-American texts now commonly in use at GCSE and 'A' levels, raising historical and social issues relating to views of 'education' manifest in the texts he discusses. Again, the emphasis here is on relating theory to good classroom practice, by suggesting ways in which teachers tackling texts at more 'demanding' levels, might construct and organize their approach.

The third and final section of the book 'Principles in Practice' anticipates likely developments in the future, and considers theoretical and practical issues which schools will need to review as part of their future organisation and teaching. Our understanding of 'literacy' in that future context, it is argued, will need redefinition. Our sense of the ways in which children learn will also help focus the nature of our teaching in new directions. This redefinition of policy will need to be accompanied by corresponding changes in practice which will have wider implications for in-service training and staff development in the post-National Curriculum era.

As an entity, therefore, the book seeks to examine the problematics and methodology of English teaching as we approach the new millenium and to suggest some positive options for development, considering the role of 'literacy' as it might in future be viewed, and the ways in which those involved in teaching might address what for all of us will continue to be important concerns in the 'schooling' process.

The role of children in their own learning is also reappraised. The book as a whole is produced, not from an impossibly idealistic vision of a new educational Utopia, but from a perceived and shared need to play a constructive part in shaping the type of education experienced by the children in our schools, in the years before and beyond 2000.

The contributors believe that, by drawing attention to issues we see as of increasing contemporary importance, we can help suggest some positive ways forward. As a result, we hope that parents, children and teachers might themselves look forward with greater confidence than has been possible in recent years to the educational prospect ahead of us all.

References

HMSO (1975) *A Language for Life*, London, HMSO.
MEEK, M. (1991) *On Being Literate*, London, Bodley Head.
WHITEHEAD, F. *et al.* (1975) *Children's Reading Interests*, Schools Council Working Paper 52, London, Evans/Methuen Educational.

Section 1

Contextual Issues

Chapter 1

Literature in Schools: A Brief Review

Ed Marum

... While the myths and symbolism of the societies depending on tradition-direction support the tradition by integrating the rebellious tendencies of the listener into a pattern of the culture, the word-in-print may disorient as well as orient its audience. This is evident in the cry for censorship which goes up as soon as literacy becomes widespread. And not only formal censorship. (Riesman, with Glazer and Denney, 1964)

Back to the Past

I shall begin by referring to a short series of statements regarding the requirements made of pupils studying English in school. In these examples, 7-year-olds are required to read 'a short passage from a book not confined to words of one syllable', to copy from print, using capital letters, and they are also expected to be able to identify nouns. Pupils at 12 years of age are required to read from Shakespeare or an alternative standard author, to compose a letter demonstrating competence in spelling and handwriting, and to be familiar with common prefixes in word formation. Such requirements as these will be familiar to many contemporary readers; those teaching English in state primary and secondary schools will be engaged in teaching precisely these skills, included at the relevant stages of the National Curriculum programmes for English, most recently amended in January 1995.

These statements, however, are taken not from the recently reviewed National Curriculum document, but from the Board of Education's English schedules for the year 1900. Almost a century, that is, after the introduction of such requirements for children in schools, it seems that the 'progressives' are again rediscovering what Shayer over twenty years ago called old-fashioned theory (Shayer, 1972). His comments have a curious irony in the context of contemporary 'schooling':

Such a programme as that given above more often than not represented the sum total of English work done by children in the elementary schools at the beginning of the century, though we must remember the nature and purpose of elementary schooling (not 'education') as it was conceived at the time and also the fact that the overriding consideration was still to combat sheer illiteracy. The diet remains incredibly dull for all that. (*ibid*., p. 6)

If such a diet was dull a hundred years ago, how much more so it must seem to children and teachers now. If the pragmatics of contemporary politics have sought to define a new 'illiteracy' and to construct a curriculum to cure it, this will prove a misconceived attempt which may well prove costly in more senses than we realize. Our notions of schooling, and of what children should and need to know, as we approach the third millenium, seem to recede into distant history in the vain attempt to keep the world that which our grandparents and parents knew. For political parties, in the short term, such policies can win votes.

But for the children in schools undergoing the daily drudgery of arbitrarily and mechanistically conceived programmes, education becomes, more even than it ever was before, a series of hurdles to be scaled, or to fall at, in the search for the social and financial respectability that ultimate success in the education system continues to promise. Such a system must be essentially based on the concept of 'losers', rather than on that of collaborative enterprise. If the British have in fact come to believe that there is no such thing as society, then we have constructed an appropriate curriculum. Contrary to what appears to be the majority expectation, this curriculum will, in the next five years, need to be replaced. It may seem curious to say so, coming so recently after a new Secretary of State for Education has promised no substantial educational change in that period of time[1], but I believe that parents, working with teachers and pupils, will achieve such a change. Before I go on to consider some of the implications of our current situation, I should like to review the main detail of how we got where we are.

When Rome Burns

Over twenty years ago, and two years before Prime Minister Callaghan's 'Ruskin Speech', Britton argued in *New Movements in the Study and Teaching of English* (Britton, 1973) that 'What is important is to recognize that a "map" of English activities is of no value without an accompanying key representing priorities'. He went on to say that 'if I try (as I must) to make a map representing "what goes on in English lessons", I need to begin by distinguishing sharply between using the mother tongue and studying it' (*ibid*.). Later confusions which arose in the continuing 'great debate' on English, in the 1980s, between the language competences of children and specific forms of knowledge about language, raised the same issues in a changing political context. While recognizing the reciprocal relationship between what English is as a subject and what its purposes are, Britton believes, in my view quite rightly, that the 'ultimate question is not what is English as a subject, but what is it aiming at?' (*ibid.*). To a large extent, over the last twenty years of British politics, it has been politically convenient in party-political terms to foreground the first issue and to relegate or ignore the importance of the second. Unfortunately, over this same period there has generally been a lack of organized response from the education sector to prevent this situation from developing as it has.

Hence we arrived at a situation, in 1989, where the general professional response to the Cox proposals for a National Curriculum in English was a sense of relief that things might have actually turned out worse than they seemed to have done, rather than a sense that we had in fact arrived at an unprecedented central control of the state curriculum, at the expense of professional integrity, and as a result of public manipulations of a weakened teaching profession, both by government and its officers and by the mass media. The factors at work in this process have been admirably summarized by Owens in an intelligent chapter of a perceptive volume:

> Debates about education never go short of participants, some of them worthy and informed. Unfortunately, those who have dominated the current debate always get their say and have the cultural power to be heard. Like shrapnel, their frantic, pernicious slogans have cut and wounded every which way. Among them: falling, or fallen, standards; lazy and incompetent teachers; all ideology, no education; all theory and no practice in teacher-training institutions; flabby, woolly curricula; too much do-good concern with equal opportunities, pandering to ethnic minorities while denying 'our' children the attention that is their cultural right; nothing can be worse than what went before. Sound bites of that kind, neat and sealed, viral and infectious, catch on fast. They strut like natty conclusions of sensible debate when in fact they are choked up as the first reactions of tangled guts, seized as the premises that debate might reasonably proceed from, resistant to the complexities of that which they have already misrepresented. (Owens, 1992, pp. 97–8)

The ostensible sense of relief which greeted the Cox proposals, and which was voiced by a large number of English teachers, was in part the response of a profession which had just managed to survive the process Owens describes, despite a large number of casualties. That things have actually got worse since 1989 shows the lack of organized resistance within the profession during a period of government 'consultations' on, and rewritings of, the Cox proposals, which has ended (perhaps temporarily) with the redrafting of the English orders in January 1995, and which has produced in consequence, and despite media protestations to the contrary, a more impoverished English curriculum than that Cox was able to negotiate with his public masters in the late 1980s. This revised version of English is discussed in the following chapters.

At this point, however, the background to recent developments, developments which I see as part of a long-term, orchestrated government policy to directly control and constrain state education, requires some consideration.

How We Got Here

Over the period in which English has been recognized as a distinctive subject in the school curriculum there has been a number of studies attempting to document the changing nature of the subject and the components which come together to give it a particular identity. (for example, Doyle, Shayer, etc.)[2]. Over the years, a number of different subject ideologies, or 'versions' of English, have developed. Goodson and Medway (1990)[3], for example, have made a useful contribution to work in this area. Here I shall briefly consider the implications of some of these 'versions' of English which have been advanced in the recent history of the subject.

Within these accounts, considerable attention has been paid to the role of literature in the subject. Ball, Kenny and Gardiner (1990), for example, trace the development of English from the nineteenth century to the 1980s, linking the development of the subject to the rise of the city and the expansion of the mass working class. They quote Gordon as being illustrative of a particular strain of thinking about English which can be traced from the nineteenth century to the present:

> England is sick and . . . English literature must save it. The churches (as I understand) having failed, and social remedies being slow, English literature now has a triple function; still, I suppose, to delight and instruct us, but also, and above all, to save our souls and heal the state. (Baldick, 1983, p. 156)

Ball *et al.* (1990) go on to argue that the 'cultural heritage' view of literature can be traced through a line linking Arnold, Sampson, Newbolt and Leavis, and can be described as one of the two main paradigms evident in thinking about English, that is 'English as literature'. The other paradigm, 'English as language', can be linked to writing and thinking of the 1960s and 1970s, which effected a shift of emphasis within the theory and teaching of the subject. They go on to cite Kenneth Baker, then Education Secretary, quoting a 1986 speech as representative of a subsequent shift back in thinking to the 'English as literature' paradigm. This speech is important in the context of subsequent developments in the 1980s and 1990s, firstly in that it gave rise to the Kingman Committee, and secondly in that it led to the establishment of the Cox Committee and the subsequent production of National Curriculum proposals for English. Baker said in the speech:

> . . . while there was widespread agreement about the purposes of English teaching, the importance of dealing with language in use,

spoken and written, and about the centrality of literature in English teaching, there was no agreement or consistency about what children of various abilities should be expected to achieve at various ages . . . I would like to see bench marks for progress in English which actually set out lists of the sort of books or authors which children should be able to read and understand at particular ages and levels of achievement. (pp. 4–9)

Despite my belief that Baker was wrong in his assertion that there was (or is) common agreement as to the 'purposes' of English, the years since Cox's proposals in 1989 have seen revisions of and amendments to the subject committee's draft proposals, including a series of public 'consultations' which have resulted in lists of suggested authors of the type Baker seems to have had in mind being included in the 'definitive' post-Dearing version of the revised English curriculum, published in January, 1995.

The political considerations implied behind Baker's sense of 'common agreement' have also been carried forward by others in the present government. Rosen (1994) provides a more recent example of such attitudes:

We know now, if we didn't know it before that what language is, how it works, how we learn it and what is the meaning of literacy are all sites of the sharpest contention. If ten or fifteen years ago we could engage in honest, open debate about dialect, about working-class language, we now have to contend with a Prime Minister who can stand up in a conference and mock cockney speakers with an insulting and travestied version of their language. (p. 9)

Other writers have in recent years also added to our understanding of the ways in which the historical development of 'English' and 'literature' may be understood. Hillocks (1971), for example, identifies two distinct traditions in the teaching of literature:

. . . a conservative approach that has its roots in the humanistic tradition of Western civilisation . . . and a progressive approach that has been traced to the philosophy of John Dewey . . . whereas the conservative avoids didacticism, the progressive attempts to use literature didactically to help individuals adjust to society . . . the conservative focusses attention on the work itself. The progressive . . . is concerned primarily with the emotional effect the work has on his (sic) students or with the extent to which the work can help solve extraliterary problems . . .

Hillocks is here talking of the way in which literature may be handled, through using different teaching methods, for sociopolitical purposes, but his point may I believe be fairly extended to encompass wider issues, in terms of the traditions and values implicit in practice and the way in which practice is itself defined in terms of theoretical 'stance'.

In this context I wish to make an obvious but relevant point that pupils' experience is mediated through a variety of cultures which impinge upon their lives in different ways; in school this is further mediated by the institutional culture which frames their 'schooled' experience; their experience is also mediated by the culture of a specific (English) teacher; by the cultures within which classroom activities take place, and by the broader sociopolitical culture in which the education system as a whole may be seen to operate. Despite Kenneth Baker's wish for some form of 'national' entitlement for pupils, the experience of 'schooling' thus becomes, for all in primary and secondary phases, a particularly rarified experience, subject to national, regional and local factors capable of considerable diversity of character and of interpretation. The sense in which a 'national' curriculum can, in practice, be claimed to exist is at best a very limited one.

Another writer who attempts to frame a broader cultural context in which to consider the place of literature is Hunter (1988). He provides an account of the birth of modern literary education — describing the emergence of English or literary pedagogy and the formation of modern criticism — in which he describes the ways in which the various forces within and outside the profession have come together to produce a 'movement' in critical ideology which can itself be seen as resulting from the wider sociopolitical context in which the education system exists. Other recent attempts have also been made to analyze the constituent factors underlying relative theoretical positions on English. Davies (1989), for example, takes issue with the Cox Committee's 'fifth' view of English — the 'cultural analysis' view — and traces this in terms of Leavisite influences on the subject. He argues the need for research into PGCE English programmes, believing that students should be offered a range of subject philosophies, interestingly suggesting that such a framework is now essential for aspiring secondary teachers.

In his well-publicised work, Doyle (1989) traces the history and development of English as a discipline, seen from a variety of important and formative theoretical perspectives, including those he feels are demonstrated in the Newbolt Report (in terms of its cultural, social and nationalist assumptions); by the English Association; and by the 'Review', etc. He goes on to consider succeeding generational perspectives on English, including the 'new Right' and English methodology, and discusses the so-called 'Cambridge crisis' of 1981 and the redefined emphasis on the 'canon' of English literature which in part developed from this and which was later to have such a deadening effect upon the revised National Curriculum English proposals.

More recently, Jones *et al.* (1992) review the then current state of curricular advance in an intelligently critical manner, which places them outside the broad consensus of those who, anticipating something even worse, were relieved by the findings of the Cox Committee. Events have moved on since that publication, but I take up some of the important issues it raises in a later chapter, in the light of the most recent revisions to the English orders and the further dilution of the original Cox proposals.

It is no accident, in the context of the continuing public debate on 'English', that recent government advisers on the curriculum have included representatives from higher education who have espoused a redefined emphasis upon the traditional literary 'canon'; their influence has been at work in seeking to transfer such values into the reformulated school curriculum legislated through Parliament, and has particularly been in evidence in the revisions to the original proposals made by the Cox Committee, resulting in the naming of suggested texts for study at Key Stages 3 and 4 of the secondary curriculum.

The fact that 'literature' has once again assumed centre-stage in the contemporary educational debate is not surprising, for the selection and range of literature studied necessarily reflects the contemporary social and cultural assumptions informing the scope and content of the curriculum. That is, as I have attempted to briefly indicate, the way in which literature is defined, read and evaluated is an indicator of more than the education system of which it forms part; it is an index of the condition of society at a given historical point. By examining how literature is defined, and by whom, by acknowledging the different readings of literature which are possible and the criteria that are employed in evaluating the nature of the literary experience offered, we can collectively learn more about the educational system at work but, equally importantly, we can also see where that system may be heading and begin to reappraise our own relationship to it. Accepting, for the moment, the commonly-held view of the 'centrality' of literature to English teaching, as it has been historically defined, there remain a number of salient issues regarding the identity of the subject to be discussed.

While views on what constitutes that elusive category of 'literature', as part of broader cultural experience, remain varied and context-bound, capable of a wide range of different readings by the various participants involved, it should not be forgotten that there are also other considerations to be borne in mind which are nowhere addressed in the National Curriculum. One of these considerations must surely be the perspectives of children on their own education.

Given the social context of contemporary schooling, it should come as no surprise that children should not automatically accept the 'standards' and 'definitions' of literacy they are often offered. Meek (1990) has characteristically made this clear:

> If writing really does change consciousness, as Ong suggests, then I believe we should know more about the nature of the changes. If the proposals of the Cox Committee (1989), that children should understand and respond to 'all kinds of writing', are to carry any weight, then we need to know what counts as evidence of this kind of attainment.

Unfortunately, the revised English orders of 1995 do nothing to clarify our understanding of this, emphasizing as they do a partial and tendentious view of the types of supposedly relevant 'testable' evidence the revised curriculum will reveal, evidence which at best reflects no more than a small part of what is involved in the process of English teaching as a child experiences it. Meek again draws our attention to an important, yet often disregarded, consideration in evaluating children's experience:

> If we agree that children's interactions with text, i.e., reading, still need sensitive exploration at all ages and stages, we must agree to look at the relation of reading to all other forms of language use: speaking, listening and writing. We may also have to include what we often ignore: children's refusal to be involved in what they are expected to read, their belief that what we like is not likeable, as well as the reading they do that we think does not count. School 'reading and responding' is by no means the whole of children's literacy, but their wider literacy gives school reading much of its contextual reference' (*ibid.*).

Aside from the fact that the National Curriculum, as currently expressed, fails to give an adequately coherent account of the relationship of reading to other language forms, it takes no account whatsoever of the equally important point that 'schooled' experience of literature is only a part of the child's general education; that ease of access to media other than the book (such as video, film, radio and television) is a central, continuing, formative and daily experience for the young long before they enter the nursery, and much more pervasive and determining in its social effects than is the narrow kind of 'solitary' reading experience all too often encouraged in schools.

After all, children make their interpretations of the world before they are of an age to go to school. Schools can certainly make a difference to the development of children's powers of critical analysis and discrimination, but I believe they can most usefully do so only by fully recognizing the extent of the multimedia communications experience which children bring with them when they arrive in the nursery; schools should not attempt to relegate that experience to some assumed realm of lesser importance. If they do so, I believe teachers run the risk of being considered culturally precious and partial in their own teaching about and experience of life. The 'marginalization' of school experience by a wide range of young people is, I believe, evidence of this truth. I return to this subject in a later chapter.

'English' Now

It remains true today that considerable differences exist amongst commentators as to the nature of 'English' and the characteristics attaching to definitions of the subject. As we have seen, there has been much writing around the issues. In the recent past the debate has continued, on occasions, as in previous ages, at the behest of governments. Thus the Bullock Report, *A Language for Life* (HMSO, 1975) attempted to set out parameters for the subject's future development. Many of its recommendations were never implemented. The report itself has been variously interpreted in terms of its salient findings. In the 1980s the government set up the Kingman enquiry into the teaching of English language, only to follow this by supporting a Language in the National Curriculum project (LINC), based on its work, but ending by prohibiting the publication of the project's suggested teaching materials, after considerable state expenditure had been incurred on their production. Again, Kenneth Baker set up the Cox Committee to enquire into what should be the basis of English in the newly-proposed National Curriculum legislation only to insist, against Cox's wishes, that the resulting report be printed back to front, starting with chapters 15 to 17, (the attainment targets and programmes of study) and relegating the explanatory chapters 1 to 14, 'which he thought unnecessary', to an appendix (Cox, 1991, p. 3).

Subsequent debate, further complicated by the arrivals and departures of recent Education secretaries in the same period, has tightened government control on the stated definition and scope of 'English', departing quite markedly, via a series of revisions, from the original Cox proposals. The subsequent Dearing enquiry, instituted by a government increasingly impatient with the protests of English teachers at aspects of the new arrangements, and embarrassed by a successful professional boycott of the new testing arrangements for English in 1993 and 1994, has again redrawn the contemporary 'map' of English, publishing its latest series of proposals in January, 1995. Some important issues regarding the government's 'consultation' procedures are considered by Mick Saunders and Chris Hall in their chapter 'Reading the English curriculum: An analysis of intention and effect'.

For the present, perhaps we should remind ourselves again of Britton's point that what matters about English is what it is aiming at. Considerable attention has been diverted from this issue, for the reasons I have outlined, and directed towards the issue of what should be the content of an English curriculum. By controlling the content, greater control can in turn be effected by central government upon those who are teaching that content, as well as upon those who are taught it. Content is of course important, but it is only one aspect of overall educational provision. Without a larger, more coherent sense than that expressed through National Curriculum proposals of what is meant by 'education', it is impossible to go very far in setting out theoretically a policy for good practice. There is now, I believe, a need to consider, as a matter of some urgency, how we wish to collectively address the character and purposes of education in our society and how we intend to match these definitions to our future needs. It is clear that the National Curriculum has lamentably failed to do this.

In essence, a 'national' curriculum which is not in fact national, which is also the product of a series of legislated impositions upon teachers and children, and which is based upon implicit distrust of the educational profession, a failure to understand contemporary 'childhood' and 'youth', and a fear of teachers of English in particular, rests upon no secure foundation. Because it has sought for politically expedient reasons to evade the important, central question 'What is the aim of English?', the government's National Curriculum in its present form lacks a clear philosophical base, and in the longer term will fail to convince both the education profession and the public at large of its practical as well as of its theoretical credibility.

In doing so, it will fall victim to the fate of successive government pronouncements upon education, predicated on outworn values and false assumptions. With the publication of the 1995 revised orders, that process has already begun. The next five years will continue to see the gradual erosion of the existing arrangements for English in the National Curriculum, a process which has marked the various redraftings and changes of direction which have already taken place since 1989. The unfortunate and outdated attempt made in the proposed curriculum to recreate what Shayer called a nineteenth century 'dull diet' cannot succeed in winning the hearts and minds of young people. By the year 2000 there will be a reluctant consensus that 'English' as the government have sought to define it, is an outmoded discipline and needs to be formally reconstituted anew. The final word here should be Britton's:

> There are teaching situations where, in my view, any ad hoc grammatical studies would be a form of Nero's fiddling. And we need above all to be clear about what we do when Rome is in flames. (Britton, 1973, p. 15)

Notes

1 Gillian Shephard, Secretary of State for Education, speaking about the release of the revised English orders in November 1994.
2 There are several very useful accounts of the development of English as a discipline. These include Doyle (1989), Goodson and Medway (1990), Shayer (1972) and Widdowson (1982).
3 This contains a valuable collection of articles on the politics of English in schooling.

References

BALDICK, G.C. (1983) *The Social Mission of English Studies*, Oxford, Blackwell.
BALL, S., KENNY, A. and GARDINER, D. (1990) 'Literacy, politics and the teaching of English', in GOODSON, I. and MEDWAY, P. (Eds) *Bringing English to Order*, London, Falmer Press.
BRITTON, J. (Ed) (1973) *New Movements in the Study and Teaching of English*, London, Temple-Smith.
COX, B. (1991) *Cox on Cox: An English Curriculum for the 1990s*, London, Hodder and Stoughton.

DAVIES, C. (1989) 'The conflicting subject philosophies of English', *British Journal of Educational Studies*, **37**, 4, November.

DOYLE, B. (1989) *English and Englishness*, London, Routledge.

GOODSON, I. and MEDWAY, P. (Eds) (1990) *Bringing English to Order*, London, Falmer Press.

HILLOCKS, G. (1971) *The Dynamics of English Instruction: Grades 7–12*, New York, Random House.

HMSO (1975) *A Language for Life* (The Bullock Report), London, HMSO.

HUNTER, I. (1988) *Culture and Government: The Emergence of Literary Education*, Basingstoke, Macmillan.

MEEK, M. (1990) 'Why response?' in HAYHOE, M. and PARKER, S. (Eds) *Reading and Response*, Milton Keynes, Open University Press.

OWENS, R. (1992) 'The multicultural politics of teaching English', in JONES, K. (Ed) *English and the National Curriculum: Cox's Revolution?*, London, Kogan Page in association with the University of London Institute of Education.

RIESMAN, D. with GLAZER, N. and DENNEY, R. (1964) *The Lonely Crowd: A Study of the Changing American Character*, New Haven, CT, Yale University Press.

ROSEN, H. (1994) 'The whole story', *NATE News*, summer.

SHAYER, D. (1972) *The Teaching of English in Schools 1900–1970*, London, Routledge and Kegan Paul.

WIDDOWSON, P. (Ed) (1982) *Rereading English*, London, Methuen.

Chapter 2

Reading the English Curriculum: An Analysis of Intention and Effect

Mick Saunders and Chris Hall

Every nation has the government it deserves. (De Maistre, J.)

Introduction

There is nothing new about wishing to define a literary curriculum. What people should read, who should have access to the skills of literacy and for what purposes, what values can and should be inculcated through literary study: these questions and others have exercised interested parties down the ages in literate societies. When these sets of questions are posed in relation to a state system of schooling and to a curriculum to be followed by all young people of school age, the interested parties become large in number. Teachers and pupils are most obviously affected by what goes on in the curriculum. Parents have an immediate concern too. Because of the commercial implications and opportunities of 'set' syllabuses and reading lists, publishers and examination boards have a direct involvement in curricular matters. And once the notion of a 'national' curriculum takes hold, politicians have direct interests too. They will wish, quite legitimately, to consider what kinds of skills and aptitudes should be provided for and encouraged in an educational system which prepares people, amongst other things, to make a contribution to the economy as wage earners and producers. They also have an interest, perhaps less legitimately, in setting out what knowledge and sets of attitudes should be importantly defined as 'national'.

In some subject areas there is less room for controversy than others. But in history, for instance, there are huge dangers in allowing political influences to define what counts as the nation's history, both in terms of content and of what skills and concepts should be brought to bear in 'doing' history in schools. Whose history, and whose interests are served by its dissemination, are awkward questions, necessarily contentious, and deeply educational. Not surprisingly, the definition of a 'national' history curriculum has proved controversial. Similarly with English. A person's language is inescapably bound up with questions of identity and value, both individual and social. Therefore, the attempt to lay down a disembodied notion of what might be 'standard' English, and to invite teachers to teach it to pupils as though any form of language could have meaning or be deemed 'correct' outside the circumstances of its use, was certain to lead to all kinds of difficulties. By the same token, to devise a set of categories of fiction, or to produce a list of approved titles, and to say this constitutes a 'national' literature, is actually a wrong-headed and ultimately futile exercise. It has nevertheless been insisted upon, and the curriculum has in this manner been overtly politicized in ways that have been surprising for many teachers. Conversely, teachers have resisted this interference in ways that have surprised many politicians.

Perhaps it should not have been all that surprising. But the nature of the prescriptions and the rhetoric accompanying their imposition run counter to the means by which the political management of state education has been taken forward during the course of this century, up to the Education Reform Act of 1988. It has also been borne in upon teachers that the 'reforms' are in themselves a denial, both of the developments in educational thinking and methodology which have taken place over time, and of the professional standing of those who have responsibility for, and experience of, the education of young people. A brief look at a previous attempt to define an English curriculum will give a flavour of the 'back to the future' aspect of current legislation.

Traditional Values?

In 1900 the Board of Education was publishing 'English Schedules' which gave the following indication of what was to be expected of students in senior classes in the Elementary School system.

Standard 7 (13 years)
Reading   To read a passage from Shakespeare or Milton, or from some other standard author, or from a history of England.
Writing   A theme or letter. Composition, spelling and handwriting to be considered.
'English'   Analysis of sentences. The most common prefixes and terminations generally.

To a modern reader this may seem a horribly limited and limiting diet. By 1904, however, there is a different spirit informing the Regulations. The introduction asserts the purpose of elementary schooling to be 'to form and strengthen the character and to develop the intelligence of children entrusted to it' and as part of this process the 'taste for good reading and thoughtful study' was central. The mechanical business of reading aloud (hitherto tested by the Board's inspectors) has a diminished emphasis from 1905 through to

1908 in favour of the encouragement of silent reading, and by 1908 the grammar component is optional and then only for the higher classes. The crucial development however is that from the 1904 Code onwards, schools under the administrative umbrella of the newly-formed local education authorities have freedom and choice in the curricular decisions they are called upon to make. Examples of appropriate choices for a literary curriculum were indeed offered, but under the new dispensation there is a clearly expressed wish to avoid coercion. There is an acknowledgment that curricula should be differentiated according to the abilities and interests of the pupils, that teachers should be engaged in determining as well as in delivering the curriculum, and that the future lay in opening up possibilities for choice and diversity (an irony given the current coinage of that slogan) rather than closing them down.

This information is taken from David Shayer's *The Teaching of English in Schools 1900–1970* (1972). The book traces the swings of fashion and thinking over the decades of the title. It is a fascinating history. Shayer points up the familiar pendulum effect between polarities of 'creativity' and 'prescription' through a survey of publications and what can be inferred from them about the methodological practices of teachers. Certainly the progress of English in the curriculum is not easily or straightforwardly described as a smooth transition from one view of the subject (or of learners) to another. Two things are remarkable in the account of governmental publications however. The first is that they do reflect aspects of thinking about English that were current and which established theory supported. The second is that, in curricular terms, nothing was ever offered beyond 'guidance'.

If we sought to bring the story more up to date, something similar could be said about *A Language for Life*, (the Bullock Report, 1975) which represented a distillation of the ideas of widely respected and influential practitioners and theorists. James Britton on writing, Andrew Wilkinson on oracy, Frank Whitehead on literature, Douglas Barnes on classroom interaction and teaching styles, and so on. This is not to say, of course, that such views would go unchallenged. David Holbrook's *English for Meaning* (1979) for example, disputed the whole basis on which the Bullock Report invited teachers to develop their work. Similarly for earlier reports which sought to make particular lines of thought 'official', there were always alternative views trenchantly expressed. But the point remains that, until the time of the 1988 Education Reform Act, the tenor and purpose of governmental publications was to give a platform for contemporary and informed opinion concerning good practice.

It is disturbing therefore to note how the tone and spirit of 1900 has returned to current rhetoric about what might constitute a satisfactory English curriculum, not as an expression of informed opinion, but in combative dismissal of it, and forwarding an agenda inspired by political rather than educational argument. There is an irony that, in a chapter of a publication looking towards the year 2000, one needs to draw attention to such reactionary and retrogressive tendencies.

The Influence of the Political Right

Echoes are there in the notion that the 'Englishness' of a National Curriculum is somehow importantly defined by a limited and given literary canon, and in the attention to language which emphasizes correctness over appropriateness and insists on the teaching and learning of rules. The most direct expression of these ideas (other than in the words of politicians, to which we will turn later) has come from the Centre for Policy Studies. The credentials of this small group to speak on questions of education are extremely flimsy, and the inadequacy of every publication has been exposed by what the group chooses to call the 'educational establishment'. Nevertheless its pronouncements have been used in order to forward particular sets of prejudices and a particular view of what state schooling should offer.

Sheila Lawlor's 1988 pamphlet, for example, on the assessment of English within the National Curriculum, takes us back unapologetically to the educational diet recommended for elementary school pupils at the turn of the last century. Fourteen-year-olds, she says, should

> also have read carefully at least one play by Shakespeare and a variety of poetry, including some written before this century; and know by heart several passages from the authorized version of the Bible; a speech or soliloquy by Shakespeare; several short poems (or extracts from longer poems) by Milton, Pope, Wordsworth, Keats and Tennyson.

Our particular interest is literary, but since notions concerning 'the canon' are not easily separable from broader questions of language and use, it is worth referring also to the Lawlor version of what counts as adequate evidence (again for 14-year-olds) of knowledge about language. They should be able to

> identify nouns, adjectives, verbs and adverbs in most contexts, and pronouns, conjunctions and prepositions in most simple contexts; and analyze a simple sentence in terms of subject, object and predicate.

What we have here is a provocative retreat to a version of English in school which bears no relation to the ways in which language works grammatically or socially in the outside world and in people's lives. There is a clear connection here with broader currents in contemporary politics. One way of making sense of the perversity of legislating for the first time for set 'heritage' texts for all pupils in state schools is to see these curricular imperatives in the context of political responses (however inadequate) to current social and economic difficulties.

This is not, of course, a uniquely British phenomenon. At times of economic depression, and in societies where there is a sense of declining influence in the world at large, there is often retrenchment and insularity when the national interest is articulated. Accompanying this is a tendency towards nostalgia: looking for answers to contemporary problems in the imagined stability and tested virtues of a more civilized and predictable past. Commenting on how such tendencies were discernible in the United States in the 1920s and 30s, W.M. French (1962) makes it clear that what goes on in schools cannot be insulated from such pervasive currents of feeling, particularly if there is political advantage to be gained from tapping it.

> If a society holds that the good life consists largely of a recapitulation of the past, a static curriculum centering around the classics of long-dead sages will be prescribed. (p. 219)

In such circumstances American school children were to be taken through the Hundred Best Books programme. What we have in the latest version of our own National Curriculum is an attempt to insist upon something similar — that somehow the virtues in literary pieces which have stood the test of time will have a morally and intellectually beneficial effect on those who are made to read them.

Certainly the recapitulation of the past is a constant theme for conservative politicians in the UK and it is applied with particular fervour to educational issues. This is where Sheila Lawlor chimes in so appropriately. She seems to give some justification for the even cruder line of rhetoric which goes something like 'We all know things are dreadfully wrong at the moment. Things used to be better. Therefore we should return to practices reminiscent of the past in order to improve things now'. This can be particularly powerful emotionally if one can play on a sense that young people are currently out of control (truanting, or criminal), or that that they are failing in school, or that schools are failing them. So John Major will get his ripple of applause for saying

> English exams should be about literature, not soap opera. And I promise you this: there'll be no GCSE in *Eldorado* — even supposing someone is still watching it.

John Patten's contribution to the same Party Conference (1992) went along similar lines.

> I am afraid that the interests of children are not served either by some of the examination boards. One recently defended the use of a hamburger advertisement in a public exam by claiming that it provided just as important 'food for thought' for children as our great literary heritage . . . They'd give us Chaucer with chips. Milton with mayonnaise. Mr. Chairman, I want Shakespeare in our classrooms, not Ronald McDonald.

There is no sense here that what constitutes a literary heritage is in fact arguable and shifting — that one of the purposes of literary study is to question, reorder and add to what might be included in a canon. The assumption is rather that there are certain indisputably great texts and schools should systematically deliver them to student readers so that they can all be in possession of 'the' literary heritage.

This is an unsustainable assumption and rhetorically dishonest. The notion that media texts are necessarily simple, for instance, and do not call for sophisticated reading, is mistaken. Similarly, it is wrong to assume that a particular pupil's reading of a 'great' text will have a more profound or civilizing influence than a reading of something else. The quality of a reading depends upon the reader and the understanding derived from the process of questioning and reflecting upon a text. The quality of a reading obviously cannot reside in the text itself.

This is what makes the moves towards prescribing the English curriculum more tightly in terms of 'heritage' and Standard English so regrettable. They fly in the face of what teachers have learned both about the reading process and about what to take into account in order to make pupils thoughtful about language. Choices of books (and other texts) and stipulations about methodology and assessment are not neutral matters which can be left to others to determine. These are responsibilities which depend upon teachers' expertise and professionalism. And that expertise and professionalism is dependent upon the teacher's conceptualization of intellectual and aesthetic development. Views of knowledge and the acknowledgment of the centrality of the learner in the relationships of the classroom are not disposable bits of 'theory' which teachers can be insulated from or choose (or be ordered) to ignore. The curriculum, for individual pupils, results from a playing out of personal, social and intellectual relationships within a context shaped by the teacher's view of what is to be learned and how. It cannot be a given, determined elsewhere and simply delivered in a more or less technically efficient way.

English teachers are concerned, as they have always been, to get people to attend to texts. It is a life-skill of indisputable importance. Attending themselves to what politicians have to say about their work, and to the text of the National Curriculum in its various and increasingly diminished versions, English teachers' own reading skills are brought fully into play. This case, surely, proves the point that sophisticated reading does not depend upon texts of high quality.

Shifting Sands: The Post 1988 English Curriculum

It is instructive to trace how, since 1988 and the Education Act of that year, the English curriculum came to the point of the Dearing review. The story is a catalogue of ideologically driven proposals, pseudo-consultation, and amendments hastily and thoughtlessly implemented. The themes have emerged clearly: a government impervious to arguments of educational principle; successive Secretaries of State (with John Patten as the prototype) inept in the implementation of (undesired) change. It is instructive also to note how those appointed to do the work of drawing up the curriculum and managing its implementation (presumably on account of a sense of fellow-feeling or perceived agreement with governmental objectives) have found themselves in the long term — and sometimes in the rather shorter term — at odds with the arbitrary crudeness of political interference with the shape and detail of reform.

The appointment of Brian Cox to chair the English National Curriculum working group was in itself provocative given his authorship of the reactionary Black Papers of the 70s. But his engagement with what an English curriculum for all pupils should seek to do and his consultations with those in a position to advise him led to proposals with structures and descriptions with which teachers could work. Of course there were doubts concerning an emphasis (which now seems mild) on standard English, the failure to celebrate bilingualism, or to incorporate in a properly inclusive way the elements of drama, IT and media studies within the English curriculum. And there were substantial questions around the descriptions of what might count as progress within attainment targets. But English teachers nevertheless found themselves able to sustain what Henrietta Dombey referred to (in her address to the 1993 NATE conference in Brighton) as 'a fairly rich, stimulating and varied life' for themselves and their pupils within that given curriculum.

The Cox curriculum was short-lived. Its redrafting was given over to David Pascall at the National Curriculum Council (the man who notably invited teachers to correct pupils' non-standard uses of language if overheard in the playground). This revision was itself never implemented, being overtaken by the wholesale review of the National Curriculum overseen by Ron Dearing, in the face of teacher opposition and a growing realization that, for a variety of reasons all of which had been predicted, the totality of the enterprise could simply not be made to work. There is now a growing body of evidence (from those who were given substantial roles to play in the original preparation of the curriculum) of governmental duplicity, ignorance and an insistence on dogma in the face of contrary evidence. Any reading of what we currently have on offer has to be affected by the knowledge of how it came to be produced, what was rejected on the way, and whose interests were served by the redraftings. For English teachers who have overwhelmingly taken the view that each revision has been for the worse, the testimony of Duncan Graham (who oversaw the whole exercise) of Ron Carter (whose Language in the National Curriculum materials were suppressed because they did not take an acceptable line on matters of grammar and standard English), of Brian Cox (whose *Cox on Cox* gives an account of the deeply illiberal tendency of the Department for Education) and of Paul Black (whose Task Group provided the framework for assessment in the original curriculum) provides supportive, if depressing, reading.

Given the fundamental relationship between what particular areas of learning are for and the measures employed to make judgments about proficiency and achievement, it is perhaps worth spending a little time considering what Paul Black has had to say about the government's involvement in matters of assessment. The arts curriculum (within which we can include English with its concern for creativity and the imagination) has always posed particular difficulties for those wishing to test outcomes. There were, therefore, considerable anxieties around what the Task Group for Assessment and Testing might propose in the field of assessment.

In his contribution to *Assessing the National Curriculum* (1993) Paul Black reproduces a passage from Kenneth Clarke's Westminster Lecture, given in June 1991.

> The British pedagogue's hostility to written examinations of any kind can be taken to ludicrous extremes. The British left believe that pencil and paper examinations impose stress on pupils and demotivate them. We have tolerated for twenty years an arrangement whereby there is no national testing or examination of any kind for most pupils until they face GCSE at the age of 16 . . . This remarkable national obsession lies behind the more vehement opposition to the recent introduction of 7-year-old testing. They were made a little too complicated and we have said we will simplify them . . . The complications themselves were largely designed in the first place in an attempt to pacify opponents who feared above all else 'paper and pencil' tests . . . This opposition to testing and examinations is largely based on a folk memory in the left about the old debate on the 11+ and grammar schools. (p. 62)

He then offers an analysis of these remarks which connects in clear ways with what we have said previously about the crudeness of Conservative rhetoric on educational themes. Not surprisingly, what Clarke refers to as 'complicated' or a 'complication' is seen by Black as a deliberate misrepresentation. It is a reference to the Standard Assessment Tasks which the TGAT report proposed, and which were subsequently developed, for assessment purposes. The 'tests' were 'designed as pieces of classroom activity rather like a good teaching activity' (*ibid.*). These original SATs were designed to provide circumstances in which rich and reliable evidence of what pupils could actually do would be forthcoming, produced in circumstances where there was a closeness of fit between the curriculum itself and the procedures for assessment. There was a deliberate avoidance of external tests of the 'paper and pencil' variety for very good reasons. External tests are bound to affect what teachers do to prepare pupils for them — particularly when the intention is to publish results. 'The aim therefore must be to make the test such that preparation and rehearsal is a good way of learning. So the assessments were designed to be models of good learning with assessment firmly built in' (pp. 62–3). Black

27

finds it offensive to have such thinking and its consequences dismissed as 'complicated' when 'principled' would be the appropriate term. Even more worrying to him are the dishonest elisions in Clarke's 'argument' whereby the British pedagogue becomes the British left and TGAT's 'complications' are ascribed to motives which did not in fact come into play in the design and implementation of the SAT initiatives.

> The results of such indiscriminate arguments will be a return to tests of poor validity, dangerous unreliability and with a heritage of damaging effects on pupils' learning. It is not clear why these traditional tests are so preferred — it appears that they bear the image of 'traditional values' in this field, that they might have the advantage that teachers who are not to be trusted are not involved in them, perhaps even that they must be good because the 'pedagogues' and/or the 'left-wing' don't like them. (p. 63)

English teachers will find much to confirm these remarks in their experience of what has happened since the abandoning of the pilot development of Standard Assessment Tasks by the CAT and ELMAG consortia. 'Tasks' have been redefined as 'tests'. Teacher assessment is to be subsidiary to externally set timed examinations. At Key Stage 3 pupils are to be examined on set texts (including Shakespeare) and an anthology (including an extract from *Rasselas*) in ways directly reminiscent of GCE. And at Key Stage 4, in the face of almost universal opposition, the 100 per cent coursework arrangements for GCSE have been discontinued, in spite of the evidence of its success as a form of properly moderated assessment which motivated students and teachers alike, and led to unprecedentedly high achievement.

The successful boycott of the Key Stage 3 English tests in 1993 had much to do with teachers' refusal to accept a form of assessment which was so violently at odds with their ideas of the purposes of learning in English and with the complexities of achievement in the subject. Although John Marenbon (a member of the Centre for Policy Studies), can assert in *English our English* that one competent reader's interpretation of a literary text will be much like another's, it is a view which is unacceptable to the majority of English teachers. This is because it is wrong. It is simply not true that individual readings of the same literary text are similar. The age of readers makes a difference, so does their sex. Past experience of reading (and of life) affects what might be brought to current readings. Another, equally strong, reason for rejecting the Marenbon view of reading is that it can, and has been, used to justify the validity of reductive tests of the Key Stage 3 kind. This is what Michael Rosen (1993) had to say about them:

> They pretend to offer a model of literature that is non-interpretive. In the name of being non-ideological they will ask supposedly neutral questions of fact and precision. But of course such questions *are* highly

interpretive. They treat literature as sequences of mini-conundrums
. . . (Shakespeare) plays are treated as if they are pages of poems, not
dramatic action. All this is highly interpretive, offering one model of
criticism that in order to be tested has to be taught. It strips literature
of open interpretation. (p. 18)

The response to the boycott of tests has typically and deliberately missed these
points of principle and treated the problem in a reductive and opportunist
way. External markers for the tests meet the objections about teachers' work-
loads, but external markers are also part of the depersonalizing of the process
which, in the crudest form of argument, is seen as a guarantee of 'rigour'.
Paul Black's fears were clearly fully justified.

Revision and Review: The Dearing Report in Context

The response to the broader question of curriculum overload has been the
Dearing review. And what vision of English (and of reading in particular) is
offered there? Whether or not these proposals turn out to be the final version
of the English curriculum it is of course impossible to say. They are, however, the latest, and the issues raised in reading them (that is to say offering
an interpretation from our personal points of view, taking into account the
context we have sketched, and acknowledging the necessary partiality of our
analysis) are likely, we hope, to remain pertinent.

Let us begin with the positive. Whatever the reason (and it may have
been simply a pragmatic retreat from specifics and detail) the move away
from separate statements of attainment to generalized level descriptions is
welcome. As the NATE guidance for teachers' completion of the English
Response Form indicated, the level descriptions imply a greater reliance on
and acknowledgment of teachers' professional judgment, and they are a 'manageable basis for making end of Key Stage judgments'.

This is an interesting way of putting it. Manageability should not be
confused with meaningfulness. Level 10 reading, for instance, is described as
follows:

Pupils sustain and develop interpretations of texts, supporting their
views by references to them. They analyse argument and opinion,
identifying implications and recognising inconsistencies. They respond
cogently to a range of texts, making appropriate connections between
them.

What this reveals is the unhelpfulness of conceiving of reading development
in terms of an individual's incremental display of identifiable skills increasing
in number and sophistication. Teachers (and parents) will be able to point to
children achieving level 10 (in terms of this description) at Key Stages 1 and

2. What is crucial, and crucially missing from the level descriptions, is a consideration of the nature of the texts being read, the circumstances accompanying their reading, and the skill with which opportunities for discussion, evaluation and interpretation are provided and fostered. Reading is an interactive process: not a context-free application of a discrete set of skills. So very substantial difficulties remain with these descriptions. Nevertheless, they are an improvement on what was there before — the fragmentary statements of attainment — and they provide spaces into which teachers can move, to question, justify particular interpretations, and make adaptations.

Other aspects of the revision are less welcome. In reviewing some of these it is possible to trace the effects of the right-wing rhetoric referred to earlier. The point could be made by looking at any of the three programmes of study, but for the purposes of this chapter the focus will be on reading. It is interesting, if depressing, to trace the changes in tone in the various versions of National Curriculum English. The chapter on literature in *English for Ages 5–16* (June 1989) begins with these words:

> To foster in pupils a love of literature, to encourage their awareness
> of its unique relationship to human experience and to promote in
> them a sense of excitement in the power and potential of language can
> be one of the greatest joys of the English teacher. (7.1)

The Programme of Study in *English in the National Curriculum* (March 1990) is introduced as follows:

> Reading activities should build on the oral language and experiences
> which pupils bring from home. Teaching should cover a range of rich
> and stimulating texts, both fiction and non-fiction, and should ensure
> that pupils regularly hear stories, told or read aloud, and hear and
> share poetry read by the teacher and each other. (p. 29)

The Pascall revision (*English for ages 5–16*, April 1993) has this first sentence:

> This programme of study focuses on the acquisition of basic reading
> skills, more advanced reading skills, the development of sensitive and
> critical reading of literature and the retrieving, handling and under-
> standing of information. (p. 27)

The Dearing review (Draft Proposals, May 1994) introduces reading in this way:

> This programme of study is concerned with the development of pupils'
> reading. Pupils should be taught to
> • read accurately and fluently;
> • understand and respond to literature of increasing complexity,

drawn from the English literary heritage and from other cultures
and traditions;
* analyze and evaluate a wide range of texts. (p. 8)

The key words tell their own story: from love, human experience and excite-
ment, through richness and stimulation, to basic and advanced reading skills,
and finally to accuracy, understanding, response, analysis and evaluation. It is
not that anyone would wish to argue that there is something wrong with
seeking accuracy and understanding, and encouraging (and planning to promote) the capacity to analyze and evaluate. Of course these will be amongst
the aims of any teacher of reading at all the key stages and beyond. But the
human and humane touch is filtered out of the terminology. Associated with
that is an emphasis on what is to be done by teachers to children that is
reminiscent of the Lawlor/Marenbon view of the curriculum and the 'discipline' of teaching.

The impression of something more hard-nosed and transmissional is reinforced in the detail of the programmes. In Cox's *Proposals* and in the subsequent curriculum characteristic phrases within the programmes of study are
'pupils should be guided' . . . 'the reading materials should include' . . . 'pupils
should be helped to' . . . 'teachers should encourage' . . . (pp. 30–1). The implication of this kind of statement is that teachers are to be regarded as
facilitators, whose professionalism and expertise is bound up in and demonstrated by the appropriate circumstances for learning created in their classrooms. The Dearing terminology has a different ring. The teacher delivers
rather than creates. There is a confident spelling out of the 'key skills'.

Pupils should be taught to read with fluency, accuracy and understanding. They should be taught the alphabet, phonic skills, the basic
conventions of books and print, and effective techniques for reading,
understanding and responding. (p. 8)

There is little sense here of the crucial nature of what children bring with
them to texts which affects motivation and interpretation. Or the crucial skill
of successful teachers in making judgments about appropriate material and
methodology. Teaching to read is seen as a matter of being quite clear about
technical matters. So 'the areas to be taught are as follows — phonic knowledge, graphic knowledge, word recognition, grammatical knowledge and
contextual understanding' (p. 9). There is a no-nonsense siding with 'traditional' approaches here, and even an endorsement of (unspecified) reading
schemes (p. 10).

Within the Review, in the name of rationalizing and making manageable
a total curriculum which, particularly with the proliferation of statements of
attainment, had overburdened both teachers and pupils, English is reduced in
ways which diminish the nature of the enterprise and teachers' professionalism. Areas which are deeply (and properly) contentious are presented in a

manner which denies complexity or legitimate alternative views. The methods by which reading should be taught is one example. Another would be the insistence on attention to standard English. The word order in the strand titled *Standard English and Language Study* in the proposed amendments is indicative of the stance taken. Standard English is purposely foregrounded in this crude way, rather than being presented as an essential but partial aspect of language study. This is related to the arguments we have touched on previously with regard to the politicizing of the curriculum. Standard English, together with the Literary Heritage, has acted as a kind of totem in the political discourse around education, and the programmes of study in the Dearing proposals are bent to accommodate those prejudices.

Within the Reading Attainment Target at Key Stage 1 pupils 'should be taught to use their knowledge gained from reading to develop their understanding of the structure, vocabulary and grammar of standard English' (p. 10). This is a skewed notion of what reading should be used for. Teachers and pupils should focus, surely, in the texts they read, on what questions and issues are genuinely raised by them. Concerns of language, broadly conceived, will be inescapable. But the notion that the Dearing definition of standard English could or should be to the fore in the attention people are asked to give to what they read is highly questionable. At Key Stages 3 and 4 we are told that students should 'consider features of the vocabulary and grammar of standard English which are found in different types of text, for example, technical terms in reports, rhetorical devices in speeches' (p. 16). All this sounds very focused and direct, but it masks a real looseness of thinking. Technical terms are not necessarily or essentially embedded in texts of standard English, and rhetorical devices will be found in speeches of whatever dialect. What will be of interest (potentially) is the vocabulary and the rhetoric rather than whether or not it might fall into the 'standard' category.

In attempting an analysis of the Dearing Review a number of difficulties emerge which are, in a sense, exemplified by the NATE notes, (referred to earlier), which were offered as a possible guide to issues that might be raised by English teachers in response to the invitation to 'consult'. As with the original Cox report (or before that Kingman) there is a sense that it could have been worse. We have already mentioned the welcome move to level descriptions. Also, within the review there are elements of 'good practice' which one feels it would be wise to applaud rather then deny in a wholesale rebuttal of the entire exercise. For instance, this paragraph on 'range' has points to recommend it:

4.1 During these Key Stages (3 and 4) pupils should be given opportunities to read a wide variety of literature and non-literary texts. They should respond to the substance and style of texts, on occasions through detailed study. They should also be encouraged to read independently and solely for enjoyment. The texts read should be progressively more demanding and introduce pupils to the literary heritage. Some texts should be studied, but the main emphasis should be the encouragement of wider reading by independent, responsive and enthusiastic readers. Pupils should learn to discriminate in what they choose to read. (p. 16)

Wide variety, independence, enjoyment, enthusiasm — all this hits an acceptable note for the majority of English teachers, and is reminiscent of the Cox terminology of which we earlier approved. But there are also things to deplore side by side with the positives. 'The literary heritage' makes its appearance again as though what it means is settled and understood. The failure to unpack what is meant by 'study' and 'discriminate' is also worrying. The text exemplifies what is known to have gone on in the workings of the advisory group — that particular stances have been debated and agreed regarding choice, implied pedagogy and details of wording, only to be denied or altered at the stage of final draft. So the political buzz-words mentioned before, concerning correctness, grammar, study, set books and so on, come through in ways easy to identify but disturbingly at odds with some other sentiments and positions taken in the document. It reminds us that what Dearing represents is not a coherent view of what English should or might be in the curriculum, but rather another stage in the continuing clash between versions of what literacy might be for in a modern society and what values should underpin the relationships between teacher and taught.

For that reason it may have been myopic and ultimately fruitless to take too seriously the invitation to respond to the detail of Dearing, because involvement in the minutiae takes attention away from the broader and more important picture of cultural and political currents within which the Dearing review is set. The pace of politically driven change has been such that it takes an effort of will to pause, and to be reminded that at each stage of the journey from Kingman to Cox to the National Curriculum orders to the Pascall revision to the Dearing review there have been responses which have articulated a willingness to work with, and develop, what was currently in place. There is a certain irony in returning to 'The case for not revising the English Order' made by Pat Barrett in *Language and Learning*, (October 1992) or the document from NATE (1993) which began 'The National Association for the Teaching of English urges the withdrawal of the curriculum proposals recently published by the National Curriculum Council'. Things move on. And, at each stage, the 'things-could-be-worse' reaction is understandable.

For instance, Dearing has avoided the worst scenario with regard to the literary curriculum. At Key Stages 1 and 2 the literature is to be 'wide-ranging'. The categories to be covered, though narrower at KS 2 than for KS 1, are not as restrictive as might have been feared. (The classic poetry section, with *Sea Fever*, *The Wreck of the Hesperus*, *The Jumblies* and the *Pied Piper of Hamelin*, gives an interesting insight, however, into what some members of the committee felt was appropriate in 'heritage' terms.) Texts are offered as examples rather than being 'set'. At Key Stages 3 and 4 it could be said that (with one Shakespeare play, one choice of fiction from the pre-twentieth century and twentieth century categories, two pre-twentieth, and three twentieth century poems from the 'approved' lists) the prescription is minimal. But given the apparently inexorable movement to a narrower and narrower curriculum, such a response would be mistaken. Again, it is worth returning to comments made about previous, and less prescriptive versions.

> The argument of this chapter (Ken Jones' contribution to *English and the National Curriculum: Cox's Revolution*) is not that 'Cox' builds its curriculum on pure Black Paper foundations. The comments of NATE are to a considerable extent accurate: the report *does* validate many aspects of current 'good practice' in English teaching. At the same time, however, it maintains a resolute blankness towards the cultures of school-students and the communities in which they live. (Bedford Way Series, 1992, p. 9)

Although, in terms of prescription, Dearing gives a bleaker picture than Cox, it would be perfectly reasonable to argue that 'good practice' can be reflected in teaching which focuses on set texts. As a matter of fact, skimming through recent editions of *English in Education* reveals the extent to which (post-1988) there has been an enthusiastic sharing of experience regarding the teaching of texts which fall unambiguously into 'the' (Dearing approved) literary heritage. Admittedly, articles such as 'The politics of Shakespeare' (McAvoy, 1991) pursue arguments and describe procedures which call into question 'traditional values and interpretations' (p. 76). Equally, Robert Jeffcoate's 'Dickens in the junior school' (1992), gives an account of work which is some distance from the kind of literary critical attention which those most vocal in justifying the literary heritage as an obligatory feature of National Curriculum English would seem to favour. The programme he describes depended heavily on a simplified text of *Great Expectations*, the David Lean film version, and drama activities (hot-seating, choral reading, mime, tableaux), familiar to many teachers who know and employ the approaches made popular through the Shakespeare in Schools Project. The general point to be made, however, from these and other pieces is that there is no problem for some teachers in teaching Shakespeare, or Dickens, or the Brontes, or any other 'heritage' author in ways which agree with currently approved pedagogical practice or which raise the questions about 'reading' which are encouraged by contemporary approaches to texts.

Restricting Growth in the English Curriculum

The difficulties arise from what an insistence on a limited number of authors across the board does to how teachers are able to perceive their work. This relates both to the choices open to them in matching texts to particular pupils and particular purposes, and to the relationship they are able to have with classes they are preparing for 'tests' over which they have no control. In an earlier section we referred to the nostalgia which seemed to drive so much educational policy: an apparent need to get back to the imagined clarity of purpose which the 11+ or the GCE gave to teachers and pupils in those fondly remembered times. What was actually in place then was a system which institutionalized false relationships, so teachers could do work which interested them and their classes until such time as preparation for the exam became insistent and they had to abandon principle for a diet of coaching and exam practice. Both those being taught and those teaching them were demonstrably imposed upon. This shift from control to controlled is not a trivial matter. Not only does it demonstrate to all concerned that teachers and pupils have little voice or influence over curricular concerns and none at all when it comes to assessment. It announces also a view of schooling which is at odds with what is known about the circumstances which promote genuine learning and allow for it to be demonstrated.

The work of Gordon Wells shows clearly the language development of children, across a range of class and backgrounds, in the auspicious circumstances of home (see, for example, *The Meaning Makers*, 1987). The challenge for schools in the face of such evidence is not to devise systems of instruction to remedy linguistic deficit (or to iron out and correct what is non-standard) but to find ways of making classrooms environments which encourage supported discussion, reflection and risk taking in language, and where cultural diversity is not problematic. We might remind ourselves of Michael Halliday's assertion that 'children know what language is because they know what language does' and have our primary focus on language as a tool for learning and self expression (Halliday, 1975, pp. 169–73). Or, to bring matters even more directly into the area of teaching and learning, and to questions of methodology, we should consider again what Douglas Barnes (1976) has had to say about 'school knowledge' (that which is learned superficially in order to get through the business of schooling) and 'action knowledge' (that learning which is fundamental to us in that it affects the way we think, the way we perceive the world and our means of making sense of it) (pp. 81–2). This, in turn, is connected with how teachers conceptualize the relationship between themselves and their pupils: those who (wrongly) see knowledge as 'content' to be 'transmitted' and those who (rightly) see the only sensible way of conceiving knowledge as involving the knower. The teacher therefore is inevitably child-centred and in an interpretive rather than a transmitting relationship: not out of a sentimental feeling that children should be left to mature at their own pace without interference, but through a clear understanding of the circumstances which optimize children's cognitive, emotional and moral development. It is clear in which direction the National Curriculum English proposals are travelling with the emphasis on *what* is to be *delivered* and how this is to be *tested*, and also clear how this is at odds with attitudes and evidence which respect what people can do with their language, their capacity to make sense of their world, and their ability to discriminate and be critical.

As Michael Rosen indicates in the piece cited earlier, there is a view of childhood implied in the language of the National Curriculum and the procedures recommended in it which is deeply depressing.

> The National Curriculum documents . . . are remarkable for their total ignoring of the question of what is a child, what is an adolescent. Only such crass ignorance could have come up with . . . attainment targets, levels and key stages. However, this is not to say that these documents have *no* model of childhood implied within them. The attainment target system sees children purely as objects not subjects. A process called education is enacted on children. When they have received slugs of education they move on to the next. It's a model derived from Fords. (Rosen, 1993, p. 19)

What the Dearing proposals fail to do therefore is to set a framework sufficiently *inclusive* to encourage principled relationships between teacher and taught to flourish. It belittles the achievement of those teachers who find ways of teaching Shakespeare or Dickens in motivating and illuminating ways if the written examination does not and cannot acknowledge what has been done. In looking at the lists of approved authors the unavoidable arbitrariness is obvious. It is clear that if lists of approved authors exist the capacity for teachers to make other choices and justify them is diminished. It is not just that one might look at the lists from a feminist or a multicultural perspective and despair at what is ruled out. Neither is it at the level of detail where one might say where is Natalie Babbit or Bernard MacLaverty? (We could all come up with our own list of surprising omissions.) It is the way in which such prescriptions will be destructive of the enthusiasm with which teachers in primary schools and in secondary English departments read new material, try it out, revise what they do, and have, as a part of their essential professional responsibilities, a voice in determining what the developing literary curriculum should be. Where is the space, and where is the invitation, in this curricular framework, to bring together thoughtfulness about language and literature (of all kinds) and the worlds which pupils inhabit?

In this respect, the marginalizing of media studies within the proposed slimmer curriculum is significant. This is the area in which children's tastes are most obviously appealed to, formed and expressed, where their access to information and entertainment is freest and clearest, and where they are 'expert' and an acknowledged audience in ways very different from the world of 'schooling'. Again, the opposition to the notion that popular choices (particularly those made by young people) can be sophisticated or discriminating gets its baldest expression in political statements.

> (A good English curriculum) can provide pupils from whatever background with a key to an extensive range of literature which challenges

the imagination far beyond anything offered by television, films or video. (John Patten, *The Guardian*, 16 April 1993)

A moment's thought exposes the crudeness of this assertion, and Cary Bazalgette convincingly dismantles it in her article 'From cultural cleansing to a common curriculum' (1993). In it she opposes the idea of the curriculum as a set of objects of cultural status to be studied. She proposes an alternative notion of a curriculum which would introduce to its students conceptual tools for the analysis, discussion and potential understanding of a very wide variety of cultural products. A list of set texts, as we have already noted, will always be arbitrary, contentious and limiting, and it will always be an imposition, however willingly accepted or attractively mediated.

> Consensus can never be won around a canonical list or a hierarchy of skills. But it can be achieved — through debate — if the goal is to identify the powerful concepts that help us make sense of our whole culture, past, present and future. (p. 14)

Her argument is that questions such as 'how real is this text meant to be?' or 'why does this text not use a natural chronology?' are fascinating ones to bring to bear on any text, and are powerful because they relate to the crucial concept of representation. That concept (or those of audience, narrative, popularity and value) is as applicable to *Silas Marner* as to *Neighbours* and therefore includes rather than excludes. It does not obviate the difficult business of choice (not every potential text can be read, viewed or listened to) but it invites people to be party to those decisions, and to attend to what is important or motivating to them (or what can be made to be). It is perhaps worth emphasizing that Tennyson, Eliot, Dickens and Shakespeare are not omitted or sidelined by a curriculum conceptually rather than textually grounded. But it does mean that a much broader definition of culture can come into play, which can acknowledge and make available for attention, analysis and discussion the circumstances of and the influences on people's lives.

Such a definition immediately broadens rather than narrows the potential educational opportunities. If one moves from a position of 'inducting into the literary heritage' into a set of purposes involving an examination of 'ways of reading', then powerful and enabling consequences follow. Gemma Moss gives a particular example of this in 'Rewriting reading' (1992, pp. 183–93). Her concern in the article is to draw attention to how it may be useful for teachers to interest themselves, not so much with 'personal response' in reading, but more with how readings are shaped by social and cultural practices. 'This would enable contrasts to be made between different forms of reading and different groups of readers' (p. 188). Such an approach to reading allows attention to be given to comics and magazines, for example, not to dismiss them as sub-standard literary products, but to examine them in terms of production and reception, and how their reading differs from other kinds of reading with different purposes. It also allows for an opening up (a reading?) of the sociology of the kinds of attention given to texts, and of other behaviours in and out of the classroom. Gemma Moss' clear intention is to give students conceptual tools to consider, understand and perhaps challenge the ways in which people are socially positioned, including the ways assumptions are made about them as readers, writers and speakers. The lesson she describes makes it clear that how people 'read' one another is a fundamentally important concern, in classrooms as elsewhere, and merits close attention. It is an attitude to teaching which seeks to stretch and engage students morally and intellectually, and though capable of being caricatured, is light years away from the *Daily Mail* mythology of left wing teachers colluding with children to underachieve.

Conclusions

It is time to bring this particular reading of the National Curriculum to a close. The chapter began by drawing attention to the irony of a curriculum for the twenty-first century having distinct connections with what was in place a century ago. The desire to insist on a static and conservative 'tradition' was linked with political responses to economic decline and social uncertainty. The various versions of the National Curriculum have been discussed and the narrowing tendency pointed to. The relationship between the curriculum and assessment has been examined together with competing views of how teaching and learning should be conceptualized and supported. We have considered how a text-based curriculum misses much out, and in arguing for a concept-based approach to reading we have used examples informed by media and cultural studies.

It would be easy to be depressed by the terminology and omissions of the current curriculum. It represents a low point in the history of political interference. It is important, though frustrating, to keep track of the detail of current proposals and legislation, and equally important to place them in the context of similar agendas for the health service, social work and public services generally, with their (past?) association with local government. The inappropriate notions of the market-place, competition, accountability and value for money lie behind the curriculum documents and the workings of the committees which played a part in their formulation and revision. This partially accounts for their incoherence and meanness of spirit.

It is, however, possible to retain some optimism. We have already had one experience of successfully resisting reductive forms of testing. Perhaps that success will be repeated. There is plenty of evidence from current practice to show that texts, of whatever kind, can be taught in ways which validate and exemplify a variety of illuminating and empowering approaches to reading. It is equally clear that a heritage curriculum simply cannot do the job for (or to) pupils which the political right envisages. Martin Kettle is here writing

about 'high culture' in music, but his remarks apply just as tellingly to literature. He draws attention to the declining audiences in British concert halls at
a time when the Classic FM radio station is enjoying great success.

> If this paradox was put to John Major or to John Patten then their
> answer would probably be a course of back to basics. Not give them
> muck, like Nellie Melba, but give them Beethoven and Tchaikovsky
> and all will be well once more. The trouble is that this has been
> shown to be a doomed path . . . In this case tradition leads inexorably
> if gradually to extinction . . . Just as newspapers do not have one
> readership but many, and just as political parties do not only have one
> base of support but several, so concert halls do not have one audience
> but a whole series which must be nurtured and encouraged in differ-
> ent ways. This is not an age of overarching homogeneous culture,
> but of diverse and partial cultures, and the art of the future is in
> knitting them together rather than pretending that there is a single
> right answer which will work for all time. (*The Guardian*, 16 July
> 1994)

Because school teachers, more immediately than directors of concert halls, are
concerned to nurture and encourage the 'audiences' entrusted to them, they
cannot do other than be alert to cultural variety and acknowledge and respect
it. The current curriculum fails to address that real, various and developing
world. Teachers will find a way of working with it, and subverting it where
necessary, as they always have. But it is unreal. It will therefore, eventually,
have to go.

References

BARNES, D. (1976) *From Communication to Curriculum*, London, Penguin Books.

BARRETT, P. (1992) 'The case for not revising the English order', *Language and Learning*, October.

BAZALGETTE, C. (1993) 'From cultural cleansing to a common curriculum', *The English
and Media Magazine*, summer.

BLACK, P. (1993) 'The shifting National Curriculum', in O'HEAR P. and WHITE, J.
(Eds) *Assessing the National Curriculum*, London, Paul Chapman Publishing.

CARTER, R. (1990) *Knowledge About Language and the Curriculum — The LINC Reader*,
London, Hodder and Stoughton.

COX, B. (1991) *Cox on Cox: An English Curriculum for the 1990s*, London, Hodder and
Stoughton.

FRENCH, W.M. (1962) *American Secondary Education*, New York, Odyssey Press.

GRAHAM, D. (1993) *A Lesson For Us All: The Making of the National Curriculum*, London, Routledge.

HALLIDAY, M. (1975) 'Relevant models of language', in WILKINSON, A. (Ed) *Language
and Education*, Oxford University Press.

HMSO (1975) *A Language for Life* (The Bullock Report), London, HMSO.

HMSO (1988) *Report of the Committee of Enquiry into the Teaching of English Language* (The Kingman Report), London, HMSO.

HOLBROOK, D. (1979) *English for Meaning*, Windsor, NFER.

JEFFCOATE, R. (1992) 'Dickens in the junior school', *English in Education*, spring.

JONES, K. (1992) *English and the National Curriculum: Cox's Revolution*, London, Kogan Page.

LAWLOR, S. (1988) *Assessing English*, London, Centre for Policy Studies.

McAVOY, S. (1991) 'The politics of Shakespeare', *English in Education*, autumn.

MARENBON, J. (1990) *English Our English*, London, Centre for Policy Studies.

MOSS, G. (1992) 'Rewriting reading', in KIMBERLEY, K., MEEK, M. and MILLER, J. (Eds) *New Readings: Contributions to an Understanding of Literacy*, London, A&C Black.

NCC (1989) *English for Ages 5–16* (The Cox Report), London, NCC.

NCC (1989) *English for Ages 5–16* (the revised David Pascall proposals), London, NCC.

NCC (1990) *English in the National Curriculum*, London, NCC.

ROSEN, M. (1993) 'More heritages in England . . .', *NATE News*, summer.

SCAA (1994) *English for Ages 5–16* (The Dearing Review), London, SCAA.

SHAYER, D. (1972) *The Teaching of English in Schools 1900–1970*, London, Routledge and Kegan Paul.

WELLS, G. (1987) *The Meaning Makers*, London, Hodder and Stoughton.

Chapter 3

Childhood and Schooling in the 1990s

Ed Marum

You can never plan the future by the past. (Burke, Letter to a Member of the National Assembly)

The 'Revised' English Curriculum, 1995

In a previous chapter I briefly outlined some of the relevant historical developments affecting the rather confused picture of 'English' that we have come to inherit today. Mick Saunders and Chris Hall have gone on to examine in more detail the nature of developments in English over recent years, highlighting pedagogical and practical issues which have not been addressed by central government. In this chapter I wish to examine some of the thinking which seems to be exemplified in the most recent 'revision' of the English proposals in the National Curriculum, and to indicate some of the ways in which these recent developments fail to relate to the nature of contemporary British society.

I hope I have already clearly indicated my concern that the curriculum in English which is being advanced through the revised National Curriculum proposals is lacking in coherence as well as in roundness. It is grounded, on the one hand, on a political imperative which is built on mistrust of English teachers and their ideologies, however defined, and on the other in a gravely mistaken view that one can, by tampering with the academic curriculum and controlling those in state schools who are charged with 'delivering' it, somehow ensure a return to the social attitudes and values of a previous golden-age world-order. The latter has been variously characterized as being 'Victorian' or 'Empire' in its cultural and social stance and is expressed through such loose and unhelpful formulations as the 'need to go back to basics', or the need to 'instil proper social values in tomorrow's citizens', and other such misconceived formulations, similar in kind and tone to those previously referred to by Owens. While I believe that Cox genuinely attempted, in framing the original submissions on English, to be both balanced and moderate in the position taken, whilst also having regard to the need to be genuinely inclusive of a range of views on the subject, later developments have clearly shown, as I outlined in the opening chapter, that such moderation was not welcomed at government level. Mick Saunders and Chris Hall have pointed out the series of blunders, miscalculations and mishandlings of curricular issues which has characterized the style and manner of the present government, both before and after the Cox submission.

There can be little doubt that these issues have not been closed, for the implementation of the revised orders begins incrementally to be phased in from September 1995 for Key Stages 1 to 3. Arrangements for Key Stage 4 will be phased in for the following year. The possible reactions of teachers and their associations to the revised proposals are far from predictable despite recent events. At the time of writing, for example, a major professional teaching association, which has been unhappy with the revised arrangements for testing currently being suggested, has agreed to postpone action on tests in 1995. There remains grounds for concern regarding the new arrangements. I should now like to address what I see as some important considerations for the future teaching of English, looking firstly at the substance of the 'revision' which has taken place.

The new proposals have been greeted in the media as representing an attempt at compromise over issues that have bedevilled the debate on English.[1] There are, however, few signs that the actual orders display any such sense of compromise. I hope to demonstrate this in the following short analysis.

Broad, Balanced, Coherent?

In the opening section of the document, entitled 'General Requirements for English: Key Stages 1–4', which comprises four brief sections, the place of standard English is emphasized in three of these sections; the fourth concerns arrangements for Wales (SCAA, 1994a). In each of the four programmes of study for the key stages which follow this opening section, there are at each key stage three headings used under which guidance is given. These headings are range (this might well have been entitled 'aims'); key skills (these might well be described as 'objectives'); and standard English and language study. The last category includes comments which emphasize ways in which understanding and knowledge about standard English can be established through specific study. The final section of the document sets out the revised attainment targets for speaking and listening, reading and writing respectively. Each element now has eight level descriptors, followed by a descriptor for 'exceptional performance' in that element.

In the event, we are left with what seems to me to be a rather unbalanced, functional and 'transmissional' view of English. While the vocabulary used has in some instances been 'softened' or diluted to appease previous objectors to earlier proposals, there seems to be little change in *essential content or emphasis* from earlier versions. I shall examine some of the proposals for reading, for illustrative purposes, in more detail. The guidance produced for Key Stage 1 is particularly telling. We need to remember that pupils in this age range generally come to school with both a knowledge of and love for picture books, fostered at home and in nurseries. Their proposed induction into the joys of the reading process are set out in the revised orders in a manner which will clearly do little to foster that interest and love and may well militate against it. Let me try to summarize the guidance provided here to teachers.

The 'key skills' which are identified at this stage of reading are listed in four sections (a), (b), (c) and (d). Whilst it is true that the entire Key Stage 1 guidance of reading does mention the word 'enjoyment' once, it goes on to say (under Key Skills — section (a)) that pupils should be taught the alphabet; 'be made aware of the sounds of spoken language in order to develop phonological awareness' (and for no *other* reason!); that they should 'also be taught to use various approaches to word identification and recognition' and to 'use their understanding of grammatical structure and the meaning of the text as a whole to make sense of print'.

What a partial, limited and narrow-minded view of the early reading process is demonstrated here! But this is not all. The document goes on under (b) to say that 'within a balanced and coherent programme, pupils 'should be taught to use the knowledge, understanding and skills' relating to (i) phonic knowledge; (ii) graphic knowledge; (iii) word recognition; (iv) grammatical knowledge and (v) contextual understanding.

What is *not* emphasized in any of this is what *else* needs to be done to create a balanced and coherent reading programme. This suggested content here will clearly not do that job! Section (c) goes on to list specific activities pupils should be given in reading, while section (d) says, very briefly, that 'pupils should be taught to use reference materials for different purposes' and should be taught 'structural devices for organising information, for example, *contents, headings, captions*' (italics in original).

By what stretch of the imagination can the totality of the above be regarded as a credible or satisfactory possible grounding for the long and complex process of developing well-motivated, enthusiastic and fluent readers who will carry forward their love of reading into adulthood? It seems clear that a close analysis of what is being suggested here raises considerable doubts as to the breadth, balance and coherence of the reading programme being advocated. And this is before we go on to see that at Key Stage 2 pupils are now expected to study 'challenging literature' which should include 'classic poetry'. What rationale or developmental process underpins such a transition from Key Stage 1 to Key Stage 2? This, unfortunately, is typical of the document and is nowhere made clear.

Similar concerns arise from a consideration of reading in Key Stages 3 and 4. The literary 'canon' remains prescriptive: 'pupils should be introduced to major works of literature from the English literary heritage in previous centuries'. Note the recurrence of that telling phrase, 'English literary heritage'. Two plays by Shakespeare are to be read; at least one of these should be read in Key Stage 3. There is, moreover, extraordinarily little emphasis on the desirability of engaging with writers from non-English cultures, other than the Welsh. This latter stipulation applies of course only to schools in Wales! The only, and very general, injunction made is that pupils 'should read texts from other cultures and traditions that represent their distinctive voices and forms'. Interestingly, there is no specific requirement in this context; no exemplary writers or writings are provided. However, the 'exemplary' dramatists are listed: they are all male; there is also an emphasis upon the necessity of reading 'poems of high quality by four major poets whose works were published before 1900'. Pupils are, further, to be 'given opportunities to . . . appreciate the characteristics that distinguish literature of high quality' and 'appreciate the significance of texts whose language and ideas have been influential'. In the latter category, three examples of texts are provided. These are (again in italics) '*Greek myths, the authorised version of the Bible, Arthurian legends*'. The provision of such exemplary details reinforces 'western', 'classic', and 'Christian' literary perspectives which at least by implication excludes other forms and literary traditions.

Looking Forwards?

To summarize, I hope I have sketched out in the above comments that, at various levels, there are worrying features present in the revised document in terms of the attitudes and values underpinning it. In many respects it is a hybrid and rather confused 'version of English' which seeks to take us back to a world and cultural view grounded in a narrow interpretation of reading and literary development. And which will do little to prepare young people for the rapidly changing, multicultural, pluralistic society in which they live and grow. Meek (1990) has summarized some relevant concerns well:

> My belief is that, until most, indeed all, children in school have access to, and are empowered by, critical literacy, including the understanding that reading and writing are more than simply useful, then we are failing to educate the next generation properly. (p. 10)

She goes on to say what it seems to me now clearly needs to be said yet again in the light of these revised orders:

> One thing is certain: we shall make no difference to the education of a single child by complaining that literacy isn't what it used to be. Indeed it is not, and therein lies our need to acknowledge the complexity of our subject and to face the fact that most of what we have to discover about literacy is embedded in the social practices for which we use it and in the ways which, if we are not careful, we may use it to divide rather than to unite us. (*ibid.*, p. 11)

There are related important considerations I should like to raise here in passing. By implication, as well as by omission, the report fails to acknowledge the cultural and racial richness of our society in the way in which its guidance has been framed. For example one concern, which I feel will be shared by a large number of teachers, arises from the lack of reference in the orders to the importance of reading a range of texts from non-British perspectives. While it is true that there is a cursory suggestion in the 'General Requirements' section to the effect that the literature read should include that 'from other cultures and traditions', and while there is another statement that 'Where appropriate, pupils should be encouraged to make use of their understanding and skills in other languages when learning English', one has to look at the section on reading at Key Stages 3 and 4 to find *any* other comment on the subject.

Here it is suggested that pupils 'should read texts from other cultures and traditions that represent their distinctive voices and forms, and offer varied perspectives and subject matter'. This is merely a brief elaboration of the earlier general statement, and needs to be considered against the central and weighty requirements for specifically British reading I have already outlined. Even supposing an individual teacher was personally keen to use a range of fiction, poetry, etc., from other cultures, how much scope will she have to do so in practice, given the time-consuming and quite specific demands being made upon her to deal with a range of British literature? The additional pressures upon the teacher to prepare pupils for new forms of tests and examinations to be taken at the end of these key stages leaves even less scope for time to be spent on other literary material; in effect, therefore, the teaching of non-British literature is clearly marginalized by these orders.

Similarly, there are grounds for concern at the lack of reference in the orders to texts other than those in book form. Previous criticism of the earlier proposals was in part grounded on their failure to reflect the need for a broader range of media studies in schools than was being suggested. Once again, the revision seems to have changed little. While there are passing references made, for example at Key Stage 2, to the need to teach pupils 'how to find information in books and computer-based sources . . .', these have a very minor place in the overall programmes suggested. At Key Stages 3 and 4 we are informed that pupils 'should be introduced to a wide range of media, for example *magazines, newspapers, radio, television, film*'. And that they should 'analyze and evaluate such material, which should be of high quality and represent a range of forms and purposes . . .', but the question to be asked is surely what kind of rational curriculum can be constructed for schools which does not specifically state a *need* for primary schools to educate children to read the media? In what sense can such a curriculum be thought of as developmental across key stages? Again, if the material to be studied in secondary schools 'should be of high quality', how will pupils be helped to address and deal with the informational and persuasive techniques of advertising, daily tabloid newspapers, computer games and soap operas, which is part of their daily childhood and adolescent experience? Are schools to assume that such contemporary and universal communication systems are outside of their educational remit? Again we come back to the central question: 'What evidence is there that some coherent thinking has informed these orders, and how relevant are they to the daily lives of our population as we approach the third millenium?' The clear facts of literacy set out by Meek are nowhere addressed in this document; it is evasive in its formulations and seeks to distract us from the reality that —

> Literacy has two beginnings: one, in the world, the other, in each person who learns to read and write. So literacy has two kinds of history: one, in the change and development over time of what *counts* as literacy; the other in the life histories of individuals who learn to read and write, and who depend on these skills as features of their lives in literate societies. (*ibid.*, p. 13)

Ironically, Jones' comments on the English proposals, made *before* they were amended in the Dearing review, still remain true after the latter's publication:

> This insistence, wrapped up in the language of 'heritage', on the centrality of particular kinds of literature is accompanied by an almost complete lack of interest in the teaching of non-verbal literacies . . . it is difficult to avoid the thought that, in a document on the future of English, the marginal status given to non-print texts represents a remarkable and worrying indifference to modernity. (Jones, 1994)

The broader implications for study of non-book media are clearly not convincingly addressed in the Dearing review. The limitations of perspective evident in the 'Reading' section have again been anticipated, on this occasion by Bazalgette:

> . . . the less confident or inexperienced teacher looking for direct references to justify and support media eduction will find them (the proposals) excessively cautious: requirements for paying attention to the use of language in radio and television (never cinema, never video), which insist that pupils must listen but not, apparently, watch; read a newspaper but not, apparently, study the photographs. (Bazalgette, 1993, p. 8)

The relevant section of the amended orders is improved in its emphasis, but in general I believe still vindicates Bazalgette's criticisms. It now reads:

> Pupils should be introduced to a wide range of media, for example, *magazines, newspapers, radio, television, film.* They should be given opportunities to analyse and evaluate such material, which should be of high quality and represent a range of forms and purposes, and different structural and presentational devices. (*ibid.*, p. 20)

However, it seems to me that this brief comment on the media education of 11–16-year-olds remains a token one; it fails to acknowledge the importance of non-book media in our society and the particular importance of such media to the everyday experiences and cultural understandings of young people. Had the orders incorporated Bazalgette's suggested 'modest amendment' to the effect that 'pupils should be encouraged to discuss and reflect upon the ways in which images can inflect or enhance the meaning of words', they would certainly have had more clarity and strength. The fact that the orders avoid such issues is I believe a reflection of their failure to come to grips with contemporary issues of significance in literary education, of their marginalization of the 'non-book' experience, and of the narrow-mindedness and cultural bias of the general position which gave rise to their articulation.

If further evidence were needed of the obsolescence of the proposals, it is equally depressing to read the SCAA report, *The Review of the National Curriculum: A Report on the 1994 Consultation* (1994b). We are told this particular 'consultation' involved ten 'English-specific sessions' as 'part of the national launch conferences in May'; seven workshop conferences for teachers held in June; additional meetings between professional officers for English with teachers and advisers; and 'consultation meetings' with a range of associations. In addition, there were 6681 responses to the consultation questionnaire and written comments were received from 'individuals, schools and others'. In view of this, it seems rather surprising that the resulting report contains less than eight lines on media, less than four lines on drama and less than five lines on information technology. Within this coverage, there are statements such as 'about a third of respondents felt that the proposals contained too little reference to media'; 'respondents felt that there was too little reference to drama' and 'nearly a third of respondents overall thought there was insufficient emphasis on information technology, with this view strengthening in the later stages'. If the mandatory lists of authors at Key Stages 3 and 4 were 'thought to be too prescriptive by over half of respondents', then why does such a prescriptive list still feature after 'revision'? What, one might reasonably ask, looking at the post-Dearing proposals as they have emerged, have been the tangible outcomes of the series of 'consultations' entered into and how can it be that the views expressed in such consultations are not reflected in some significant changes to the latest series of proposals? If the document implies, as I believe is clear, a disregard of consultees' views, what is its credible status as a guide to contemporary thinking about the teaching of English? In my view it has no entitlement to be regarded as a balanced or descriptive account of modern thinking about the nature and direction of teaching in the subject.

The revised orders for English in the National Curriculum represent the latest phase of an awkward, misconceived and politically-bungled attempt to achieve 'compromise' against the social and political contextual background of Britain in the 1990s, at a time when the government is defensive on broad political fronts and understandably feels vulnerable to both internal and external criticisms. As a basis for policy, the orders are defunct; as an expression of a coherent view of 'literacy' they are lamentable; as a blueprint for the future, they are worthless. In so far as they give expression to any 'version' of English that might be so-called, they are backward-looking, regressive and extraordinarily partial in character. They fail to provide clear guidance for those involved in teaching English; they offer no vision for the future to those who are training to become English teachers and, above all, they fail to address the interests and needs of our young people. Consider, for example, the kind of educational 'philosophy' embedded in the revised performance level descriptions (see appendix). Despite the assertion made by Gillian Shephard that there will be no need to review the proposals for the next five years, their removal and replacement must now be only a matter of time; we need to plan forwards to what will advance our understanding of 'English' in the curriculum and to consider its organization and delivery in tomorrow's curriculum.

An Indifference To Modernity

As a result of the complex developments which have taken place since 1989, when the Cox Committee first submitted its proposals, England is now left with a curriculum for English which has signally failed to seize on the opportunities to review and plan for future educational and social needs. The opportunity afforded to redefine 'English' for the future has not been taken. It is scarcely surprising that this should be so, given the provenance of the review, but the fact itself leaves us with the conviction of a lack of educational purpose and direction behind government planning. The rather mechanistic and narrow diet which has been 'prescribed' for state schools limits the educational and literary opportunities of the next generation in what I regard as a disturbing way. It seeks to reformulate an English 'package' which is already obsolete; it relegates the theory and applications of information technology, media studies, and a wide range of language genres to seeming insignificance, while simultaneously resurrecting the 'learning as book' model of education first made possible by Caxton. It fails to acknowledge, let alone reflect or plan forwards from, the multiracial and multicultural linguistic and literary character which determines and will continue to determine Britain's identity and future. Such a curriculum lacks balance, common sense and vision; it is a curriculum devised for 'a nation of shopkeepers' at a time when many shops — local, high street and city centre — have already closed down; many others seem destined to follow.

Given our current starting point, the second section of this book makes an attempt to suggest ways in which teachers might, despite the present proposals, positively plan and work with pupils to enrich the curriculum the latter will experience, which is to be introduced with effect from September 1995, in all state schools. In the third and final section, I outline possible longer-term developments in the subject and consider ways in which educational planning might in future be related to defining new literacies and to establishing a reformulated curriculum to take us beyond the year 2000 with confidence.

Note

1 See, for example, Blackburne, L. (1994) 'Controversy comes to a full stop', Times Educational Supplement, Curriculum Guide, 11 November, p. iii.

References

BAZALGETTE, C. (1993) 'From cultural cleansing to a common curriculum', *The English and Media Magazine*, summer.

DES (1995) *English in the National Curriculum: Revised Orders*, London, HMSO, January.

JONES, K. (1994) in *English and Media Studies Magazine*, **30**, Summer.

MEEK, M. (1990) *On Being Literate*, London, Bodley Head.

SCAA (1994) *The Review of the National Curriculum: A Report on the 1994 Consultation*, London, SCAA.

National Curriculum Revised Orders for English, January, 1995

GENERAL REQUIREMENTS FOR ENGLISH: KEY STAGES 1–4

■ **1.** English should develop pupils' abilities to communicate effectively in speech and writing and to listen with understanding. It should also enable them to be enthusiastic, responsive and knowledgeable readers.

a To develop effective speaking and listening, pupils should be taught to:

- use the vocabulary and grammar of standard English;
- formulate, clarify and express their ideas;
- adapt their speech to a widening range of circumstances and demands;
- listen, understand and respond appropriately to others.

b To develop as effective readers, pupils should be taught to:

- read accurately, fluently and with understanding;
- understand and respond to the texts they read;
- read, analyse and evaluate a wide range of texts, including literature from the English literary heritage and from other cultures and traditions.

c To develop as effective writers, pupils should be taught to use:

- compositional skills — developing ideas and communicating meaning to a reader, using a wide-ranging vocabulary and an effective style, organising and structuring sentences grammatically and whole texts coherently;
- presentational skills — accurate punctuation, correct spelling and legible handwriting;
- a widening variety of forms for different purposes.

■ **2.** In order to participate confidently in public, cultural and working life, pupils need to be able to speak, write and read standard English fluently and accurately. All pupils are therefore entitled to the full range of opportunities necessary to enable them to develop competence in standard English. The richness of dialects and other languages can make an important contribution to pupils' knowledge and understanding of standard English. Where appropriate, pupils should be encouraged to make use of their understanding and skills in other languages when learning English.

3. In Wales, the linguistic and cultural knowledge of Welsh-speaking pupils should be recognised and used when developing their competence in English. Teaching should ensure that such pupils are given access to the full scope of the programmes of study. Provision at Key Stage 2 for pupils in Wales who have not followed the Key Stage 1 Programme of Study for English is given on page 32.

4. Pupils should be given opportunities to develop their understanding and use of standard English and to recognise that:

- standard English is distinguished from other forms of English by its vocabulary, and by rules and conventions of grammar, spelling and punctuation;
- the grammatical features that distinguish standard English include how pronouns, adverbs and adjectives should be used and how negatives, questions and verb tenses should be formed; such features are present in both the spoken and written forms, except where non-standard forms are used for effect or technical reasons;
- differences between the spoken and written forms relate to the spontaneity of speech and to its function in conversation, whereas writing is more permanent, often carefully crafted, and less dependent on immediate responses;
- spoken standard English is not the same as Received Pronunciation and can be expressed in a variety of accents.

ATTAINMENT TARGETS

LEVEL DESCRIPTIONS

The following level descriptions describe the types and range of performance that pupils working at a particular level should characteristically demonstrate. In deciding on a pupil's level of attainment at the end of a key stage, teachers should judge which description best fits the pupil's performance. Each description should be considered in conjunction with the descriptions for adjacent levels.

By the end of Key Stage 1, the performance of the great majority of pupils should be within the range of Levels 1 to 3, by the end of Key Stage 2 it should be within the range 2 to 5 and by the end of Key Stage 3 within the range 3 to 7. Level 8 is available for very able pupils and, to help teachers differentiate exceptional performance at Key Stage 3, a description above Level 8 is provided. The scale does not apply at Key Stage 4.

Section 2

Classroom Issues

Chapter 4

Playing the Book: A Response to Literature at Key Stage 1 (5–7)

Liz Slater

A classic is something that everybody wants to have read and nobody wants to read. (Twain, M.)

Introduction

The detailed focus of this chapter is on one particular response to literature which I have explored, both as a classroom teacher and as an advisory teacher — that of book-based games. However, this needs to be set in the context of the wide-ranging nature of children's response which is both characteristic and to be encouraged at KS1.

What is the Nature of Children's Response to Literature?

An Underpinning Context for Response

'Are we allowed to look at the book too?' Alan, Steven and Ian had peeled themselves off my year 2 line after assembly, and stood in front of me. I had just led a whole school assembly with the Spanish Armada as the theme and shown posters and books from the National Maritime Museum Armada Exhibition. I had read aloud brief sections from the first pages of *The Spanish Armada* (Martin and Parker, 1988) then, to my shame, had offered the book to any juniors who cared to come and ask for it. Surprised, I agreed. Back in the classroom, Alan, a fluent reader, confident with lengthy prose, started to read a paragraph of this 296 page book at random. 'That's no good', he said. 'I can't understand it.' 'Let's look at the index', said Steven, who received learning support help. They gave up on that, too, as they had no clear idea of what they wanted from the index and it was small print and ran into six pages. They then turned to the contents page and had a giggle over 'The great bog of Europe'. Finally they found the pictures I had used in assembly from the mass of picture plates in the book; Alan and Ian read the picture captions, and Steven listened and commented.

What exactly is happening here?

First, the children were responding to their need to know more, and to find for themselves the things they had just heard. The tiny sections of narrative — not intended for children, but intertwined with glossy posters and my own retelling, at a time when the subject was topical (summer, 1988), had caught their imagination. Their enquiry was not teacher-directed — in fact, almost discouraged! — and was also entirely authentic.

Second, they were responding in just the same way as they would to children's literature that interested them, but here, I think, with an added fascination also because it was not fiction. The book begins with creating an atmosphere of suspense and anticipation, although the outcome is known:

> Shortly after dawn, the watchers on the cliff saw the first Spanish ships: fleeting shapes glimpsed far offshore through banks of mists and squally showers. The tar-soaked brushwood of the beacon burst urgently into flame, and within minutes a replying pin-prick of light to the east confirmed that the alarm was passing along the chain to Plymouth and the waiting English fleet . . .

Thirdly, they considered that the book was for them, and questioned my own assumption that it was not. They were behaving as confident readers, expecting something from the text, despite varying reading abilities, and using and adjusting strategies to get what they wanted. Their guiding criterion was the purpose — readability did not figure, even when it became obvious that the unmediated text was fairly impenetrable for them.

Another incident is from the previous year and involves one of the same children. We approached the teaching and learning of reading through the apprenticeship style of teacher-pupil reading relationship (Waterland, 1985) and the use of Big Books. The broad range of texts we used is best described as 'complex human texts' (Whitehead, 1987). He had no core reading scheme, but a wide range of fiction, including stories from scheme material, which was discretely colour coded according to the Cliff Moon system (Moon, 1993), alongside a comprehensive assessment and monitoring procedure; teachers used the colour coding if they found it helpful.

> Ian, already a competent reader at year 1, was looking for something to read. He passed Karen, who was not progressing as rapidly as her peers in reading as far as de-coding skills went, but nevertheless was deeply absorbed in her current favourite, *Not Now Bernard* (McKee, 1980). She knew it by heart. Ian spotted what she was reading and said, 'Oh, I've been looking for that. Hurry up, Karen. I want to read it again when you've finished.'

This is a straightforward response to literature — enjoyments being re-discovered and anticipated. What is significant is that I think that Karen's own view of herself as a reader was enhanced by Ian's attitude: he wanted the same text and obviously didn't regard it as beneath him, although both of them were very aware that she needed a lot of help with her reading. He also spoke in exactly the same way as he might have done to the most fluent reader in the class, thereby implicitly recognizing that she was able to enjoy *Not Now Bernard* just as much as he did. My experience in an earlier classroom situation, where we used only reading schemes in a graded progression, was that children like Karen were already seeing themselves as non-readers, losing heart and motivation. Karen, however, was an enthusiastic 'reader'; none of us pretended that she didn't need help, but the range of 'complex human texts' enjoyed by all ensured that this pleasure in reading was also accessible to her. Because she was not discouraged, she was motivated to persevere. Although Karen would not and could not have been a successful KS1 SAT statistic, this perseverance led to success later, at Y3.

These and other incidents led me to reflect further on my own practice at the time. I realized that for me, as a classroom teacher, most of all I wanted the children I taught not only to read, but to *expect* to read, to *want* to read and to *continue* to read. Selection of literature is obviously significant in this, but it is the opportunities provided for a range of response which makes literature and response not only accessible to all, but part of readers' development from before the time when they can read the words off the page.

It seems to me that there are two intertwined embedded concepts which are rather like common denominators to written language and are the contexts for authentic response. First, in the very broadest sense, writers write for their own or someone else's *use*, and second, readers read to *discover*. The communicative intent by the composing writer is fulfilled by being 'used' — responded to in some way — by readers, whether known or unknown, intended or unintended. This 'use' may be explicit, as in the use of information texts, or the development of activities related to fiction. It may be implicit and subsumed in the involuntary response to a range of written language, read or listened to. Expecting to read begins with this — young children being able to see themselves as prospective readers, because they have an implicit understanding of the purpose of written language — that someone has written something to be 'discovered'. Their first and involuntary response to text is therefore essentially one of enquiry. Pre-school children who start to ask '*What does that say?*' (replacing the similar labelling question, '*What's that?*' about objects) about the print around us are beginning to be aware that those arbitrary symbols carry specific meaning. Reading is about finding out — whether this is *rediscovery* of familiar texts, endings, sections, facts, and enjoyment and satisfaction, or *discovery* of new facts, debates, situations, characters, plots, structures and organization — and new sources of enjoyment and satisfaction. Where the main criterion for children choosing texts is constantly readability level, with little reference to the purpose, then some readers may never learn about the 'use' and 'discovery' bed-rock for written language, and may only see books as a means to learning to read and progressing up the ladder of reading difficulty. If this is their main concept about reading, then they may also have learned what we never intended them to learn — that when they can read, they don't have to any more.

This is where opportunities to respond to texts — whatever they are — fiction, non-fiction or non-literary — are so important in the classroom, as response depends on the 'use' and 'discovery' attributes. Children look *through* the language to get at and respond to the meaning. When children like Alan, Steven and Ian are so deeply motivated by the activity that the level of reading is not a consideration, the act of reading words off the page becomes a means to an end which they may feel has little to do with learning to read, but, which, in fact, I believe has a great deal to do with learning to read. In the same way, both Ian and Karen were motivated by the enjoyable experience of one text to seek to re-read it, although their reading abilities were very different; Ian did not consider the text 'too easy'. I think that children behaving as confident readers — at whatever stage of reading — expect texts *they want to read* to work for them in some way and if they can't yet read them, will seek help if they want to be specific about the content and know that they can't yet read any or some of the words on the page. In this sense, the 'use' and 'discovery' attributes disregard the familiar information/fiction boundaries, although of course different reading skills may be needed for using information texts and fiction. Helen Arnold explores this more fully (1992).

Looking *through* language does not preclude looking *at* language, but my experience is that a concentrated look *at* language is usually better done at a different time — in groups, or whole class, especially with Big Books, in the context of well-known text — and within combined spelling/handwriting approaches — which there is no space to enlarge upon here.

Teacher-framed Contexts for Response

Games which are based on familiar books are a focused context for reading development which is dependent not only on the sorts of response to literature just described, but also on the variety of experiences that teachers offer in relation to stories in the classroom. Three categories of teacher-framed contexts are described below, with their relevance to the book-based games.

The Importance of Listening to Stories, Read or Told by the Teacher

First, the teacher can generate quite different types of response: 'the teacher's mediation and her metatextual commentary during story reading conveys important social, cultural and cognitive messages to the children . . . Story reading is a major part of young children's early literacy experiences. It is mainly through story reading at home and at school that young children learn about literacy processes. The teacher's understanding of these processes and the manner in which they are introduced to children can either support or restrict children's learning' (Kirby, 1993).

Henrietta Dombey (1988) describes one teacher's practice in these terms: 'Her telling is essentially an interactive matter. The children are not merely recipients of the telling, but partners in the telling, even though they cannot yet read and have not seen the book before . . . Her story-time is surrounded by formality, created out of her shaping intentions. But inside this formality the only rule that governs is the rule of relevance and this is conceived as something more complex and powerful than the recitation of facts and also communicated clearly and repeatedly to the children.' The children are active and creative in their own learning, having a voice of their own. This is also so when children are playing the games.

Kirby (1992), comparing different practices in reading stories, comments, 'This important notion of developing a "reciprocal process" between the teacher, the text and learners in terms of the reading process is a crucial one. It is possible for teachers to reduce the sharing of literature with children to a series of oral comprehension tests and questions, that is making literature act like a reading scheme.'

Secondly, the nature of texts matters. One important criterion is whether they lend themselves to being read aloud — or sung, as in the case of nursery rhymes. These have a particularly special place. Not only do they, with other rhymes, provide the opportunity to explore onset and rime (Goswami and Bryant, 1990), but 'by dragging a child into a topsy turvy world we help his intellect work, because the child becomes interested in creating such a topsy turvy world for himself in order to become more effectively the master of the laws governing the real world' (Vygotsky, 1971, in Britton, 1992).

Listening to stories is the way that young children get a sense of story structure and become familiar with the language which is characteristic of stories — 'we are helping them to develop an ear for the language in a way that no text book can' (Perera, 1987). Myra Barrs quotes Anne Thomas' study on the place of intonation — the tune — in early reading, and points out that it is likely that the '"texts that teach" will be *tuneable* texts, with tunes and structures that support the reader' (Barrs, 1992). It is also an opportunity for the standard form of the language used for writing story to be heard — to fall on the ear. These language structures are 'borrowed and rehearsed on the ear' (Taylor, 1990). As children begin to read with each other and for themselves, the 'tunes' are built on and reinforced. These are all features which are evident in the shared reading characteristic of the playing of book-based games.

Thirdly, the stories need to be heard again and again. The 'core book' approach builds on the concept of supporting children's reading development through hearing and rehearing a collection of favourites and having access to them; some may also be 'Big Books', where there is the opportunity to work with a group on particular language features in the context of a well-known text. The games offer this kind of repetition.

Finally, there is evidence that young children's oral story-telling is influenced by the stories that they have had read to them (Fox, 1993); the influence of stories heard and read on young emergent writers and readers may also be evident in their own writing. 'Sooner or later they become part of the child's productive capability as they become assimilated into their framework for novel utterances in speech and/or writing' (Taylor, 1990).

Figures 4.1, 4.2 and 4.3 show a selection of examples of story writing from KS1. Children's writing often reflects the range of their reading, or at least, the reading which is given status by the adults who are supporting them. The range and quality of texts made available to young children therefore has an important influence on their development as literacy users.

Story Writing from KS1

Figures 4.1, 4.2 and 4.3: These examples of children's writing demonstrate the way that their writing is influenced by the stories that they have read.

Figure 4.1: shows pages from Charlotte's book (Y1) written for her sister. She has used her knowledge of the format of one of the Heinemann Sunrise series — *I am* — (Cuttings, 1989) and adapted it to create this book. She is also applying all her current phonic knowledge to her spellings; she knows about the soft sound that *g* can have and uses it to represent the *j* sound that *dr* in *draw* can sound like: her own accent probably influences the spelling of *build* and *dance*.

Figure 4.2: At Year 1, Ian's listing of prepositional phrases has strong similarities with *Rosie's Walk* (Hutchins, 1968); his final line is comparable with Rosie getting home in time for tea. There may also be echoes of the traditional *We're going on a bear hunt* (Rosen, 1989) with the references to mud and grass.

Figure 4.3: Kostas (Y2) writes a long seven-page story about pirates — this is one page. He uses subordinate adverbial clauses to open the sentence (such as '*When he had freed us, we grabd a sowrd and went abuve*') instead of 'and then', and this is from the story-telling language of stories he is familiar with. He uses story-telling phrases like, '*In no time at all . . .*' The most astonishing construction, however, is, '*Nely a year we saild untill we saw an ilanind!*' — there are strong resonances here from *Where the Wild Things Are* (Sendak, 1963).

Figure 4.4: Illustrations for *Mrs. Lather's Laundry* game by Y1 and 2 children

Figure 4.5: Rosie the hen activity —
(a)   as first used;
(b)   as used later — with adaptations for the fox as well, the permutations are endless.

Figure 4.6: An example of a scaffolding diagram to accompany Extract 5. The complex reading interchange is very evident this way.

Transcription for Figure: 4.2

Long Neck and Pterodactyl
Once a Pbshcps (?), Long neck, was floating in the river.
He was bored . . . he wanted to visit his friend the Pterodactyl.
He got out of the river.
He went through the grass,
past the volcano,
through the mud,
through the desert,
into a cave.
He saw his friend.
They had something to eat.
He stayed til 9 o'clock
and then he went home
to sleep in the river.
The end

The Individual Reading Session

When Liz Waterland (1985) suggested that the phrase 'read with me' should replace 'read to me', such a small change in language signalled the possibility of an interactive sharing of the text rather than an arrangement which is only a monitoring and performance-measuring activity. The likelihood of properly interactive reciprocal processes occurring became greater, I think, through that enabling phrase. The activity of reading aloud to the teacher can be very odd — in real life, we only read aloud to someone else in very formal situations, or to less experienced readers who need to know what something says or want to be read to, or in story reading situations, or when we have a 'listen to this' kind of need to share something that we have just read. If we can look for ways in which this activity can become more purposeful, and in which we, as experienced readers, can model the response of listeners interested in not only what is being read but also in the children's response to the books that they are reading to us, then we are being more helpful to the children reading with us. Aidan Chambers (1993) has explored this in detail. The playing of the game offers this purposeful opportunity to read to/with someone-else: the listeners are interested in what is being read and in the reader response, although that is prescribed by the situation.

Teacher-directed Response to Text

There is a widespread practice, particularly at KS1, to develop activities from texts — either (a) within the context of a subject area or a cross-curricular topic or theme; or (b) with the main focus being the book. There are publications with ideas linked with literature to use and develop (see appendix). However, there are possible problems: there is the danger of over-response (Baldry and Smith, 1991; Smith, 1992), as the texts should also be read for

my sister
can Play

my sister
can Play
gam5

my sister
can Biwd

my sister
can gump

my sister

myglster
cankis

mysister
cunsip

mysister
cadldrns

Figure 4.1: Charlotte's book

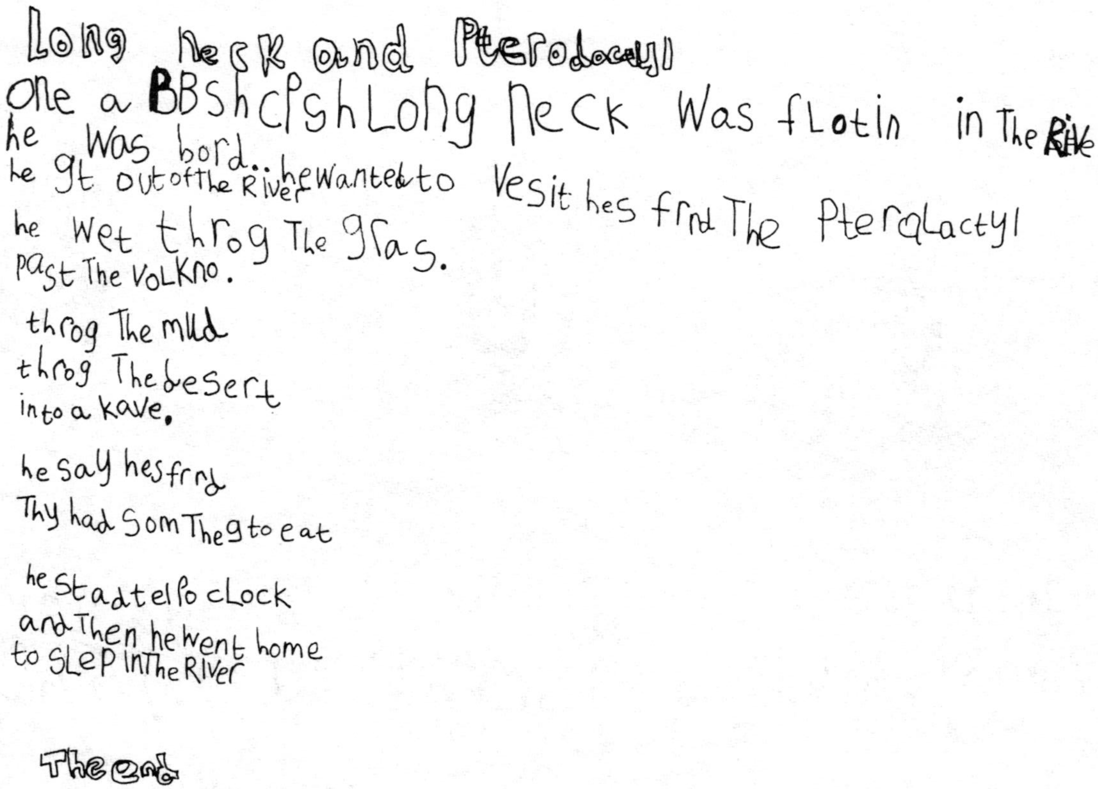

Long neck and Pterodactyl
One a BBshcpshLong neck was flotin in The Rive
he was bord... he wanted to vesit hes frnd The Pterdactyl
he gt out of the River

he wet throg the gras.
past The volkno.

throg The mud
throg The Desert
into a kave.

he saY hesfrnd
Thy had SomTheg to eat

he startet lo cLock
and Then he went home
to sLeP in The River

The End

Figure 4.2: Ian's list

is. when he had freed us we
grabd a Sowrd and went abuve.
when they saw us they pulled
there sowrds and ran towrads
us. my team was winein. in no
time atall we had the piruouts
tide up. when we had thron them
over bord we chanengd the
flag. ndy a yaer we salld
antill we saw an ilanind! we
kwikle loade the life boat.
Some Sales were left on bord
to keep an ely on thigs. when

Figure 4.3: Kostas' story

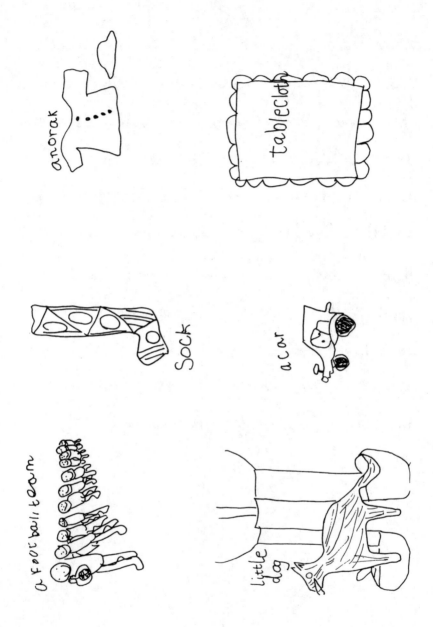

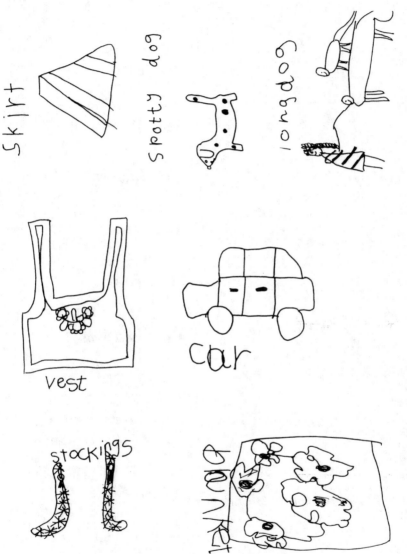

Figure 4.4: Mrs Lather's Laundry Game

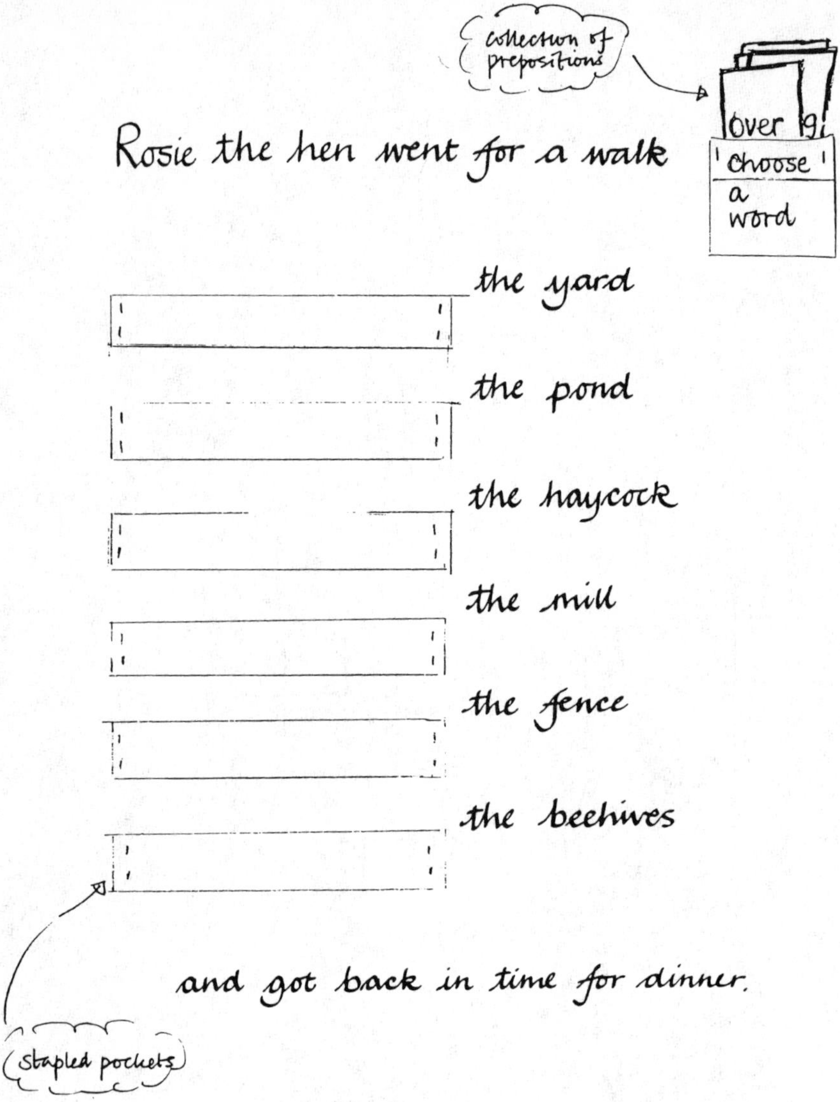

collection of prepositions

Rosie the hen went for a walk

over

choose a word

the yard

the pond

the haycock

the mill

the fence

the beehives

and got back in time for dinner.

(stapled pockets)

Figure 4.5(a): Rosie the hen activity — as first used

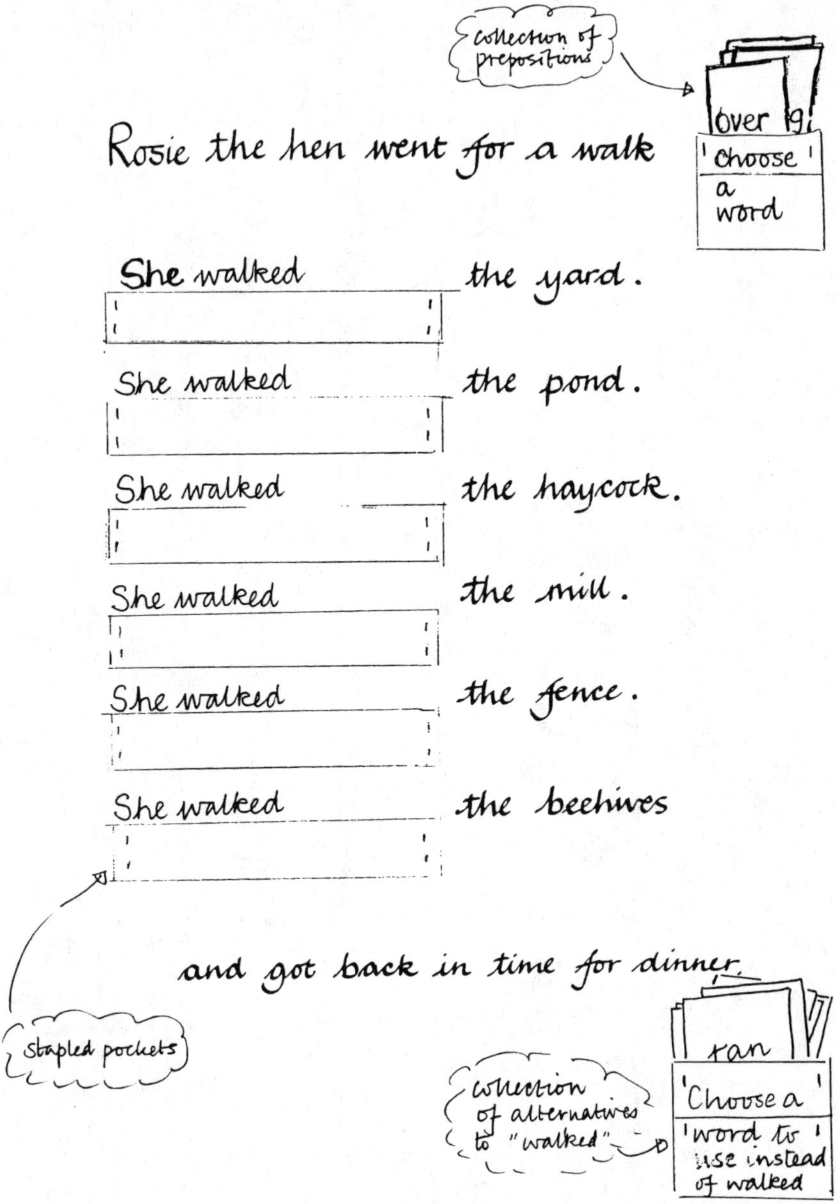

collection of prepositions

over
choose a word

Rosie the hen went for a walk

She walked _____ the yard.

She walked _____ the pond.

She walked _____ the haycock.

She walked _____ the mill.

She walked _____ the fence.

She walked _____ the beehives

and got back in time for dinner.

stapled pockets

collection of alternatives to "walked"

ran
Choose a word to use instead of walked

Figure 4.5(b): Rosie the hen activity: as used later

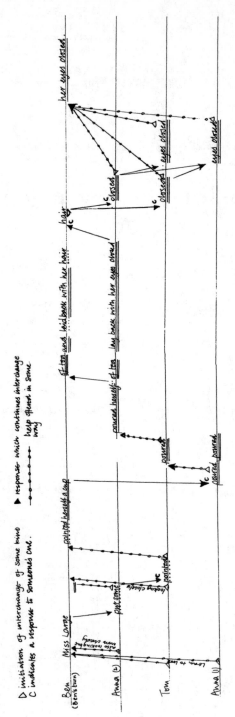

Figure 4.6: Scaffolding diagram for Extract 5, showing the complexity of the series of interchanges that occur

themselves and be able to stand on their own; they do not need to have a systematic application of activities. Secondly, there is the nature of the response. Aidan Chambers (1993) warns that 'the "Tell Me" approach is *not* a mechanical textbook programme. It is not intended that readers of any age should be given lists of questions . . . it is not meant to be slavishly followed'. Philippa Pearce (1992) deplores the tendency of some publishers to develop activities on texts which have grown out of the old style comprehension. Both the overworking of titles and inappropriate work, far from enhancing children's response, can destroy the authentic response that we would wish to encourage. So while some publications remain useful as a resource, as teachers, we need to be discriminating — when the purpose, the audience and the situation for the intended activity inform our selections and decisions at any time in the classroom, then we are more likely to get it right! There is a difference, too, between working on a text — whether it is on its language, or on its content, or on the ideas conveyed — and using a text as a springboard into a range of activities. Broadly, both kinds of activities involve response, but the first kind usually involves looking into and using the text, and the second kind, moving on from a stimulus.

Responses to Literature at KS1 in the English Proposals (May 1994)

References to response to texts, some specifically literature, occur throughout the proposals in all the English attainment targets. Response to literature is referred to in part of the PoS (Programmes of Study) for speaking and listening (SCAA, 1994, sections 4.1, 4.3 and 4.4). The range of vocabulary referred to in section 3 of the speaking and listening and the skills in sections 2 and 3 of the writing attainment target are really best done within some literature context, not as isolated skills. The proposed reading PoS have many references to response to literature, directly or indirectly (sections 1.1, 2.2, 3, 4.1, 4.3 and 4.4). These are detailed in appendix 1. The playing of book-based games meets many of the requirements (see pp. 126–30).

The proposals identify three main aspects of reading: development of the ability to read print, developing understanding, developing response to text. These three aspects demonstrate the recursive nature of learning. Unfortunately, listing the three aspects in the above order implies that response to text comes after skill of reading print and after understanding, whereas the process is more complex than that. Section 1.2 on page 8 is quite unambiguous — the proposals state that children with limited experience and understanding of literacy must start with what are referred to as 'initial stages of reading' i.e., the alphabet, and awareness of sounds and patterns of sounds in preparation for phonic work. Alongside this, children should have an 'extensive introduction to books and stories in order to help them develop an understanding of the nature and purpose of reading' (1.2, p. 8).

It is this statement about response to text that should be listed first, of course, as an all-encompassing context both for understanding and also for ability to read print, but then is constantly developing as understanding and the ability to read print develop. Making sure that there are opportunities for pre-readers to respond to text means that they are introduced to the nature and purpose of reading before they can read words off the page; they can best do this in an environment of written language which is used, referred to and enjoyed. *This* is the context for developing understanding and developing skills; the spiralling, recursive development continues with each aspect developing from and into the others. The reference to 'sounds and patterns of sounds as a preparation for phonic work' needs to be more precise to take account of the work of Goswami and Bryant (1990).

The new proposals do not mention the new literacies — media (televisual, with young children) or IT literacy. It is important that we recognize the non-literary forms of literacy with which many children come to school. Children need to become critical and responsive readers of these texts, too. We easily underestimate the effects on children when the school literacy bears little relation to the home literacy. Heath (1983) explores the differences in approaches to literacy in different communities and how this relates to the school approach to literacy. Barnes (1988) draws attention to this gap between the symbolic universes of school and the life-world structures outside school. Lake (1991) focuses briefly on possible strategies for raising the self-esteem of low achievers in reading — through teacher steering rather than directing of activities, particularly in the area of teacher-pupil talk.

It could be said the only life-world structures occurring in the proposals for reading in English are in the literature — response to literature becomes highly significant, then, for children from homes with little or no book experience but for whom there will be situations within books that they can identify with, as long as there are texts available which are 'complex human texts'. The selection of literature in the Proposals covers a wide range of genres (SCAA, 1994, pp. 10–11), including 'poems and stories with familiar settings and those based on imaginary or fantasy worlds'.

Book-Based Games as Supports for Literacy

What Kind of Games?

For a number of reasons, reading games which have traditionally been offered to children in school tended to concentrate on grapho-phonemic elements and word recognition for practice and diagnosis, to remedy decoding difficulties. But I feel that the problem is that such games often became a parody of what they are supposed to be modelled on. The intention was to help children to learn while enjoying a game. Statements such as, 'children will respond usually without inhibitions and are readily observed at their most natural' and that 'games allow class and teacher to share in some fun and to develop a corporate "oneness"', (McNicholas and McEntee, 1973) were laudable, but many of these games repeated the early patterns of decontextualized learning, with word, letter or sound recognition. To win, you had to be the best reader in the group of players in recognizing these. The context of need and opportunity that I believe is necessary for successful collaboration is not catered for in those games in which, in order to complete the game turn or move, players have to read correctly on their own, and be checked; therefore peer collaboration is not really seen as appropriate to those games — they have more in common with a test. I suggest that children playing those games who are completing reading tasks successfully are behaving as those games require, but children who are not, are breaking the unwritten expectations and code imposed by the games; and therefore there is a characteristic deeply embedded strand working against collaboration, almost an implicit taboo, underpinning the working of such games, which feeds a competitive, non-collaborative attitude in the players of those games. There is advice about competitiveness: 'In schools it would seem prudent to avoid making games too fiercely competitive . . . Most teachers . . . would try to let all children feel successful even if the rules have to be bent a little' (*ibid.*, p. 5). This statement seems to put in question the validity of the game — certainly any vestige of 'life-world structures' is totally subsumed by the 'symbolic universe'.

This is where the adult help given to children as suggested in these circumstances can be so unsatisfactory — without it, the game may be frustrating, but with it, players may feel that they have not completed something on their own and be left with a sense of unfulfilment or even confusion about the reading or the playing of the game. Competition needs to be related to the game, rather than the reading skills of the players, if the game has winners or losers. It seems to me that there must be a *purpose* in reading for the games to be successful and that purpose must be related to the game. The arbitrariness must be in the throw of the dice or the turn of the card, and not in the reading task, which must be as authentic as possible.

Examples of Book-Based Games

I first started to look at games based on books in my vertically grouped KS1 classroom. I wanted to add to children's favourite books interesting support material which children could use independently and to create opportunities for them to practise their reading in a focused, but enjoyable and purposeful way. At the time, I saw it as simply developing another 'holding' activity.

The children who played the first game that I developed, based on *Mrs. Lather's Laundry* (Ahlberg, 1981), surprised me with their commitment, involvement and enthusiasm. Players had cards with drawings of items of washing on them; the aim was to get rid of them all in Mrs. Lather's wash tub, but they could only put an item in the tub if the notice in the window allowed them to. Players couldn't get rid of socks, for instance, if the notice said, 'We wash anything except socks'. The notices were all from the embedded texts in the book.

I found that the game did more than I imagined — after being shown, all the children, including 'non-readers', played it on their own — the original text was picked up and read by more children, and an interest grew in the other books in the 'Happy Families' series. Above all, the children did not seem to disagree over the game, but appeared to be helping each other a great deal. Much later, with other classes, the game was made by the players: we wrote down all the washing items and added some more of our own and the children drew and labelled them. This meant that we needed a discussion on singulars and plurals, as much of the list was in the plural form (hankies, sheets, etc.) and only one item was needed on each card. The children also used the 'look, cover, write, check' approach, saying the word at each stage, by coming up to the list and going back to their work before writing it down. Some of their drawings are in figure 4.4 — the originals were brightly coloured.

Other games based on other books — *Rosie's Walk* (Hutchins, 1968), and *Don't Forget the Bacon* (Hutchins, 1976) — worked well. *Rosie's Walk* started as an activity for the children in my class who received learning support. I simply wrote out the text, omitting the prepositions. These, I put in a little pocket; the intention was that the children would put them in the correct places, with reference to the book, if necessary (figure 4.5). In fact, the children knew more about response to text than I did. They quickly subverted the activity and Rosie was walking *through the pond* and *under the haycock*, accompanied by much laughter, and as it was pinned to the wall, the activity was used and enjoyed by all the class. It had become an authentic 'rewriting' activity, which the children owned, as they had devised it. Children arranged and rearranged words and then found their friends to enjoy the joke. Later, I developed this rewriting further with other classes. We turned the phrases into sentences, looking at full stops and capitals, repeating the word 'walked', and then substituting other travelling verbs — Rosie ran round the pond, jogged past the mill, etc. When the children then also varied the prepositions and illustrated the new sentences, they made a collection of further adventures — some a little surreal — for Rosie.

Don't Forget the Bacon was a simple board game, where players used shopping lists (written and drawn) from the book — both correct and muddled and proceeded round the board with throws of the die, collecting items for their list.

At the time that the children first used these games with me, I tended to think that it was of greatest value when I could be present to hear and see what was happening. This view changed dramatically when I was able to video, transcribe and analyse the reading interchanges of a number of groups of KS1 children playing another game. This game was based on *Five Minutes' Peace* (Murphy, 1986).

The text has a structure, with a problem set at the start, a series of events to solve the problem, and a resolution. Mrs. Large, the mother elephant, who wants five minutes' peace away from the breakfast chaos, sets herself a tray of breakfast and retreats to the bath with it, where, unfortunately, her children interrupt her and she finds just a few minutes' peace in the kitchen again. The game is in three parts, based on the story. Each of the three parts of the game, while reflecting the text, involves different reading tasks. In the first part (where players set their trays with items from the breakfast table to take up to the bath, like Mrs. Large, the mother elephant), the game requires them to read an instruction which includes known or familiar or, at least, heard text — words and phrases from the story. For example, 'She took a tray from the cupboard' is used as '*Take a tray from the cupboard*'; the items on the tray are listed early in the story. The second part of the game involves new text in the context of the story and expands the part where Mrs. Large goes up the stairs by incorporating incidents which could have happened, for example, '*You stop to read the newspaper. Go back one step.*' The final part, lasting a timed five minutes (to see if the player can stay in the bath that long), reenacts Mrs. Large's constantly interrupted bath, and players read longer chunks from the text such as '*Lester played "Twinkle twinkle little star" three and a half times*', replicating the interruptions that occur; only one card instructs the players to get out of the bath. The players take cards to read according to the throw of the die; these cards tell them what they have to do.

At first, I looked primarily at the features of the book and the game, and the sort of KAL (knowledge about language) the players demonstrated. The importance of the role of collaborative reading help in the game then became apparent. Intrigued by the way this collaboration operated, particularly between peers, I then looked at the nature of the scaffolding in more detail.

Ideas about collaboration and scaffolding and the work of Vygotsky (1978) and Bruner (1983) are now increasingly familiar to teachers, thanks partly to the work of three national projects on writing, oracy, and knowledge about language. Edwards and Mercer (1987), in particular, have applied the concepts to teacher-pupil talk, but there is very little applied to the idea of peer-scaffolding in the classroom, and even less on peer-scaffolding in the context of reading together. Des-Fountain and Howe (1992) point out that 'there has been a surprising lack of close attention to, and evidence of, the complex ways in which talk between children supports learning'. In the context of the games there was very little off-task talk and the talk that occurred was to do with problem solving in the sense of sharing, questioning, supporting each other's reading acts.

The Centrality of Collaboration to all Learning and Development

Collaboration is deeply significant to human development. Where we ignore its importance in teaching and learning situations within the school context we disadvantage children. The way that young children's knowledge is socially constructed is significant in the context of the game. Edwards and Mercer (1987) have built on the work of Vygotsky and Bruner, describing the sharing of experience in the context of common knowledge — 'context *is* the common knowledge of the speakers invoked by discourse. . . . Continuity is a characteristic of context, being context as it develops through time in the process of joint talk and action. It exists as shared memory and intention, the conceptions and assumptions that participants hold, of what they have done and said, of its significance, of what the interaction is all about and where it is going' (p. 161). The context of the game provides an opportunity to build new knowledge through talk and reading together in the familiar contexts of the story and the game-playing. This development of new knowledge in the context of given knowledge has implications for any classroom learning situation — ideally, 'teachers and children establish what they both know and understand and then move on into new realms of understanding' (*ibid.*). The game provides opportunities for players to continually establish and reestablish knowledge and move on. It enables 'pupils to learn for themselves what has been planned for them in advance' (*ibid.*, p. 130).

Why Do these Book-Based Games Work?

What I noted through systematic observation of the game based on *Five Minutes' Peace* and informal observation of other games is, I believe, generally applicable to a wide range of book-based games.

(i) The game offers a social context in which to experience purposeful reading

Experience enables the learner to construct knowledge. Piaget put 'action and self-directed learning at the heart of learning and development' (Wood, 1988, p. 4). The game provides a very practical and purposeful activity which encourages the development of independent thinking — *but* in the context of support being available if required — from the game, from other players, or, with the younger children, from an adult.

The Vygotsky-Bruner concept that the use and function of language precedes its effective analysis (Bruner, 1983, p. 8) or that unconscious knowing precedes conscious control (Vygotsky, 1934, p. 90) is demonstrated in the game-playing. The function and use of language is carried through playing the game; the purpose provides each player with the motivation for reading. The game provides an example of *opportunities to* **use** *language* — reading written language — *as a means to an end*. The players do not even have to be able to read to win — they can, and do, ask each other for help, but all the time, they need to know what is written in order to find out what to do. The 'use' and 'discovery' attributes of language come into play. Piaget did not take account of language development in a social context, and yet experiences that young learners use to construct their knowledge are interactions with others.

(ii) The game depends on 'exposure' to literature

The children were familiar with texts, the way that story language works and story structure, not only from this book, but from other quality picture story books — the 'complex human texts' which were frequently read aloud in class were chosen by children to read to themselves, with friends, or to share with parents.

(iii) The game invites 'immersion' in literature

through the game itself and the opportunities for role play that it creates. It is not just about exposure to books, and supporting reading through 'osmosis', essential though this kind of classroom reading environment is to the development of secure and confident reading; it requires the players to reenact the story and to work at interpretation in order to progress through the game.

(iv) The game creates a referential framework of familiar contexts

which set the parameters for purposeful literacy acts. Real language is finely tuned to respond to audience, purpose and situation, consciously or unconsciously. Bruner explores context in relation to early talk (1983, pp. 128ff) — this is also applicable to the game; there are several contexts nesting within each other.

(a) playing a game;
(b) the situation (in this case, a familiar one of a messy breakfast time and an exasperated adult!);
(c) a well-loved book;
(d) a small social group.

The first two are the overarching contexts — that of the players' own experience of the familiar situation described in the book, *'Five Minutes' Peace'*, and similarly, their common knowledge of the procedures of most board games — through which players bring their knowledge to the group. These combine with the third to provide an imaginary role-play context (not always explicit, but there, underpinning the purpose of the game) for the physical and emotional context of the social grouping around a board game. Central to the operation of the game is Edwards' and Mercer's concept of common knowledge developing from the socially shared experience of joint activity and discourse, and becoming itself the shared experience for the development of further common knowledge (1987). This is the way the game is intended to work.

There was some evidence of different types of explicit role play while playing: (a) the sort one would expect, through a more or less natural assumption of role of the character — *'I'll be in the bath in a minute'*; (b) an extension of this identification by adding things that could have happened on the stairs — *'I dropped my toast'* — although the objects handled by the players for their trays were not used for this part of the game and that incident is not in the game; (c) mimicry, especially from the younger children — playing the recorder with Lester, for example.

The role-play, implicit and explicit, represents a certain kind of absorbed and identifying response to the text through the game, remaking the meaning. It is also the enabling context for significant interactions between readers, in the social grouping around the game, both with and without an adult participating. These interactions are rich with examples of scaffolding because of the cooperation involved. There is a similarity in the game with Barnes' categories of exploratory talk — 'working on understanding' — and presentational talk — 'final draft' (1992, p. 126) where children hypothesize together over the reading and repeat the finally agreed statement or instruction.

There were also examples of explicit knowledge of the world that they brought to this activity through commenting on it; '*A cupboard should not look like a wardrobe!*' (a comment on the appearance of the paper-engineered cupboard); '*It's not fair on Mrs. Large!*' (a comment when I was reading the part where Laura Large claims that her mother is not being fair to her). They also demonstrated knowledge of board games and die structure and turn-taking through their comments as they played.

(v) Playing the game builds on the players' knowledge of a popular picture book

The players are already familiar with the text in a number of ways:

(a) the story;
(b) the story structure;
(c) the story language.

The game refers to this past experience and offers new information in the context of the reexperience of the familiar text. This reflects Edwards' and Mercer's concept of common knowledge developing from the socially shared experience of joint activity and discourse, and becoming itself the shared experience for the development of further common knowledge (1987). This is the way the game is intended to work.

(vi) The game provides a well-organized structure in place of instruction

It is the teacher who has established the parameters of the activity based on the game which in turn has its own parameters derived from the book on which it is based; the expectation is that the children will discover what they are intended to discover.

Bruner (1983) writes about the external structures within which spoken language develops: 'how the *linguistic community* arranges *speech* encounters so that the young aspirant *speaker* can get a hold on how to make *his own communicative intentions clear and how to penetrate the intentions of others*' (p. 10). This statement could equally well apply to the children reading in the game, by just changing key words and phrases — the process he describes remains the same: 'how the **teacher-prepared framework of the game** arranges **reading** encounters so that the young aspirant **reader** can get a hold on how to make **her or his own interpretation of the text**' (*ibid.*). The reading of the short text invites interaction between the author's intentions and the player's interpretation and action; this is one level where the player is 'penetrating the intentions of others', occasionally it happens explicitly.

(vii) The game is an authentic activity
Freire (1985, p. 48) wrote of 'authentic dialogue' acting on the context of reality through critical analysis; the game activity is authentically purposeful for the players.

(a) The players *need* to read to find out what to do next
The communicative intent, or intentionality, that underlies Bruner's description of scaffolding in the context of the mother-toddler teaching/learning interaction is applicable to the game. What is such a powerful force for learning to talk, is that the communicative intent is there for both parties — a real need to communicate. In school literacies this is frequently weak in teacher-set tasks; where literacy is developed — or not — through 'symbolic universes' rather than 'life-world structures'. In real language 'intentionality' is present whether the language user is producing or receiving text (Harste, Woodward and Burke, 1984, p. 191, in Hall, 1987, p. 61). Without intentionality by the players in the game, there would be no effective scaffolding.

There is another aspect of authenticity — successful collaboration is developed in the context of need and opportunity — and here the need might be seen to have arisen out of a failure to read successfully, but successful reading by the turn-taker is not necessary for the game, so collaboration is appropriate; anyone can help the player to read the card to find out what to do.

(b) The random, limited repetition is meaningful and purposeful, because it needs to be read in the context of the game
An example of the success of this repetition is in the following extracts from one R and Y1 group. They are playing the last part of the game. It is Thomas' turn. He picks up the card which says, *Lester played 'twinkle, twinkle, little star' three and a half times.*

Extract 1
Thomas: (picks up card, shows it to me)
ES: (takes it, holding it for Thomas to see)
Thomas: *Laura p----*
ES: 'Do you remember the little boy's name in the story?'
Ben: (pointing to 'little') 'That says "*little*".'
Thomas, Kristelle and Kristina: *Lester*

ES: *Lester played*
ES, Kristina and Kristelle: *Twinkle*
ES, Kristina and Thomas: *twinkle*
ES, Kristina, Thomas and Ben: *little star*
ES, Kristina and Ben: *three and a half*
ES, Kristelle, Kristina and Ben: *times*

Extract 2

Seven turns later, the same card is picked up again by Thomas.
Thomas: *Laura*
Ben (echoing Thomas): *Laura*
Thomas: (doubtful and decides to check, showing me the card): *Lester*
or *Laura. . . .* that says *Lester* or *Laura?*
ES: *Lester*
Ben (having been given, as it were, a prompt cue, continues)
(Thomas' turn): *played Twin . . . kle*
Thomas joins in with **Ben**: *Twinkle, twinkle little star*
Ben (continues): *three and a half times*
Thomas ('correcting' Ben): *four*
Kristelle (delighted to find a word that she knows fits here, responding
to the 'tune'): *times!*
ES: *three and a half times*
Thomas (accepting this): *three and a half times*
ES (explaining): It's Laura who reads four and a half pages, isn't it?

Extract 3

The same card turns up at the very next go. It's Ben's turn.
Ben (probably recognizing the word 'little' again): *little*
Thomas (wanting to help, still getting muddled, but knows it's not
'little'): No, *Laura*
Ben (leaning away from Thomas, wanting to read it on his own): No
Thomas (remembering and responding to Ben's 'No'): *Lester played*
Ben (now holding the card so that Thomas can't see and studying it):
Lester played, 'Twinkle, twinkle, little star', three and a half times (repeating
and confirming the number after the conversation during the last turn):
three and a half times

Extract 4

The card is turned up again, this time, by Kristina, who looks at it briefly
and then hands it to me.
ES (taking card and handing it back to Kristina): Oh, that's the one
we've just had. Can you remember what it said?
Ben: I know. *Lester played . . .*
Kristina (looking carefully at each word as she read): *Lester played 'Twinkle, twinkle, little star' three and a half times.* I can read most of these. I can
read them!

(c) Players are naturally and purposefully engaged in response — to the requirements of the game and to each other.

(d) The game is 'real'

The players' purpose is not to read, but to play. The reading is integral and the means of playing. But because no-one's reading ability affected their position in the game even the younger group were not deterred by their own expressed opinion at the start of the game that they couldn't read. In fact, when the children added their own cueing system of associating die numbers with items for the tray, my questions, such as, '*What did it say?*' and '*Do you think you had better check?*' were plainly regarded as unnecessary — after all, the purpose of the game was not about reading, as far as the players were concerned. I was usually indulged as I was the teacher — in fact they tended to treat me as if I wasn't remembering. This can easily be altered so that there is a need to read, but it raises interesting insights into the players' perception of the purposes of the game.

(viii) The game provides motivation for children to remain on task

They are working within known and shared contexts and therefore can so easily bring their own experience to the task. There is a desire to read, a willingness to hypothesize, and therefore, a readiness to learn. The way that this works is evident in the above extracts. With the Y2 group, who are not looking to an adult for help, the supportive interaction can become quite complex (see extract 5, on p. 116).

(ix) The game provides time for children to learn at their own pace

Differentiation by task and outcome is built into the game, as children learn what they are ready to learn through the interaction with the book, the game and each other. The input from the 'text' of the game can be matched to needs, because (a) it is varied, (b) each reading turn lasts for very short periods, sometimes a few seconds, (c) it is repeated, randomly, and (d) anyone can join in to help the player whose turn it is to read, without affecting the outcome of the game. This, of course means that there is equality of opportunity as far as completing the game or winning is concerned — the players are on an equal footing — winning the game is arbitrary and does not depend on reading ability. Equality of opportunity is also provided in the way that the children can respond at the level and pace that they need to; there is support for less fluent readers in the purposefully repeated text and the peer and group scaffolding. Different stages of learning coexist — cognitive awareness, mastery and automaticity — according to the child, the situation in the group, and the part of the game. There was plenty of evidence of metalinguistic awareness from the younger players, as one would expect — '*What does that say?*' and '*What's that?*', but also an awareness of the writer's intentions in the game instructions — '*What do I do if I haven't got a tray and it says "Collect a milk jug for your tray?"*'.

The younger players' knowledge of story and the language used was called on and rehearsed more explicitly than by the older players. Children frequently joined in with the cards being read, completing statements in chorus.

In addition, there is an occurrence of the 'echo-reading' noted by Anne Thomas (in Barrs, 1992, p. 20) as significant in early reading, where some readers, particularly the less fluent, are 'shadow reading' fractionally behind my voice. This is often part of the chorusing. Chorusing also serves the function of scaffolding the 'echo-readers'. Some years earlier, Morgan (1976) suggested 'that simultaneous reading aloud by tutor and child' would 'help to maximize skill performance by providing a model and a means of reinforcement for the child' (in Beard, 1987); he called it 'paired reading' and developed it for 'retarded readers'.

Players' use of syntactic and semantic cues for reading was also evident, particularly with the older children in the part of the game with new text, or the last part with longer text, as in this example, with a group of four Y2 children — Anna, Ben, Tom and another Anna:

Extract 5

Ben picks up a card, which says, '*Mrs Large poured herself a cup of tea and lay back with her eyes closed*'. The aim of this part of the game is to stay in the bath for five minutes. One card says, '*They all get in. You get out*'.
Tom, and **Anna (1)** lean towards him to look.
Ben (with **Anna (2)** looking over his shoulder): *Miss Large*
Anna (2): *put some . . .*
Tom (looking at the card): *pointed*
Ben: *pointed herself a cup. . . .*
Anna (1): *poured*
Tom and Anna (1) together: *poured*
Anna (1): *poured herself . . .*
Ben, carrying on from where he was, and **Anna (2)** joining in: *of tea*
Ben: } *and laid back with her hair*
Anna (2): } *lay back with her eyes closed*
Ben: *hair*
Tom and Anna (2): *closed*
Tom and Anna (1): *eyes closed*
Ben: *her eyes closed*

This whole exchange was rapid and lasted less than half a minute. A 'scaffolding' diagram gives a clearer idea of the complexity, and who is talking at the same time (figure 4.6). The players are engrossed, helping each other to read the cards which are in arbitrary order. Anna (2) offers *put some*, using some phonemic and syntactic cueing; Tom has a go with *pointed*, also using syntactic and grapho-phonemic cueing. What is missing so far is any semantic sense, although Anna (2) might have been going to say something about tea in a cup. All these miscues help Anna (1) make sense of the word and she offers the word *poured*. Ben then reads *hair* for *her*, and eventually accepts the group's correction. There is a range of cueing going on here, with the constant supporting check of the group.

With younger children, some grapho-phonemic prompts were evident and also word recognition was occasionally voiced as in the extracts 1–4.

(x) There are opportunities for spontaneous contributions which are integral to the game and to 'scaffolding' by peers

Typically, while children are playing the game, meanings can be tried out and responded to; the group works together over interpretation; tentativeness is supported; assertiveness is usually accommodated. Ideas about language inter-action developed by Vygotsky and Bruner are important here. Vygotsky's important concept of the 'zone of proximal development' is applicable to the whole games activity. It 'is the distance between the actual developmental level as determined by independent problem solving and the level of potential development as determined through problem solving with adult guidance or in collaboration with more capable peers' (Vygotsky, 1978, p. 86). 'A child is enabled to advance by being under the tutelage of an adult or a more com-petent peer . . . until such time as the child is able to master his own action through his own consciousness and control. . . . Up to that point the tutor . . . performs the critical function of scaffolding the learning task to make it possible for the child to internalise external knowledge and convert it into a tool for conscious control' (Bruner, 1985, p. 89). The game is intended to work like this, with opportunities for players to receive and give help, and to read independently or with support. The metaphor of 'scaffolding' was origi-nally used by Bruner to describe the way in which young children learnt to talk with adult help and was developed in relation to Vygotsky's idea of 'a zone of proximal development'. In principle it is now being applied to learner-teacher interaction in the context of classroom talk. It can also be applied, I believe, to the pupil-pupil interaction in the game, with particular reference to reading. Maybin *et al.* (1992) define scaffolding as 'help given in the pursuit of a specific learning activity, one which has finite goals' and then go on to define that help as occurring (a) where there is 'evidence of a teacher wishing to enable a child to develop a particular skill, grasp a particular concept or achieve a particular level of understanding'; (b) where there is 'evidence that the "mentor" had tuned in to the learner's present state of ability or under-standing' and possibly, (c) where there is 'evidence of a learner success-fully accomplishing the task with the teacher's help' and conceivably, (d) where there is 'some evidence of a learner having achieved some greater level of independent competence as a result of the scaffolding experience' (p. 188).

I see the game and context as providing the format for 'teacher-learner' cooperation in passing on an aspect of literacy. The game represents adult-child interaction; the adult is me in the younger groups; but the adult is also represented by the provision of a prepared framework that is interactive, and by other players in their role as supporters; this is especially evident when children are playing entirely on their own. The game and context are the 'format' or 'scaffold'. Hall (1987) likens this to a 'safety net' (p. 14) within which safe context the child can hypothesize, take risks, and build confidence and knowledge to move on.

In the game, the children tend to spontaneously initiate interchange in response to their own and each other's reading needs. This may take place in different ways, which are only very briefly summarized here:

(a) when the player whose turn it is '**hands back**' the reading task to another (teacher or peer), becoming a **scaffoldee** to the **scaffolder**. Help is given by the scaffolder as the normal response to this;

(b) where the opportunity is offered by the scaffolder to the scaffoldee to start or continue the task — either to develop or complete it — an example of '**handover**' — Bruner's term (Edwards and Mercer, 1986). This happened more frequently with the less fluent readers and particularly with the younger groups, where I continually offer or hand over responsibility to the group to 'read it together' with me. There was never a negative response to this; at the very least players listened; they frequently joined in with the increasingly familiar text, often completing it in chorus and showed increasing interest in matching memorized text with seen text;

(c) where help is offered or given, unasked, by peers. **Uninvited help**, or **takeover** is a frequent occurrence and significant, I believe, in the working of the game. Uninvited help may be unwanted, or ignored or disagreed with but generally it is accepted, particularly as it is usually intended to be helpful to the process of the game (see extracts). Therefore, where such takeover occurs, it is not really any different in outcome or, really, in principle, from a fluent reader reading to a less fluent reader in a paired reading situation or one reader in a group reading situation — the text is still read, looked at and listened to.

(d) where the initiation is implicitly derived from the activity, not expressed by a player, but still evoking a response. The reading of the text in the game provides the challenge of indirect handover which is frequently taken up in response by other players as they join in in chorus. This meets the criteria for scaffolding suggested by Maybin *et al.* (1992, p. 188) — that the development of a specific need is being targeted (by the teacher provision of the game); that the structure tunes in with the learners' needs (through the social context of the activity); I also think that there are enough instances of not only successful accomplishment with help, but also moves to greater independence. This is particularly illustrated by the extracts from the younger group as they repeatedly practise a recurring card. Some of these instances involve corrections of a miscue, invoked by the collaborative rereading of the text.

(xi) The game provides opportunities for problem solving through talk — either about reading, or game organization. The group has to (a) make sense of new information (b) negotiate with each other (c) interpret and develop others' ideas.

What are the Implications of Book-based Games in the Classroom?

The games are an example of collaborative response to text within defined parameters. There is no doubt that collaboration is a strong feature in these games — involving either or both teacher-pupil talk and pupil-pupil talk, supporting a complex initiation and response structure of interactive collaborative reading, and accommodating uninvited help. The teacher-prepared framework of the game and the way it is played has a scaffolding function for the players, so that they are, according to degree of fluency, able to play without an adult, thus scaffolding themselves. The categories of 'handback', 'take-up' and 'takeover' may be useful additions to Bruner's scaffolding term of 'handover', in any close look at collaborative work.

The main implications for the teacher are:

(i) consideration of time-organization in the classroom. Such an activity, when played independently, acts exactly like a 'holding' activity allowing the teacher to 'buy' time for effective teacher intervention where needed. And yet it is not merely an engrossing holding activity. It moves the players on in their implicit knowledge of reading, and sometimes this is made explicit. Where the children need help any fluent reader can 'supervise' as the parameters are very clear and it is hard for the activity to go wrong — again this 'buys' time. The time spent in making such games can be seen as an investment. The criteria are (a) a story with a strong structure or plot, (b) some form of repetition, which may be syntactic or in the story structure, using the language in the text, (c) to try to keep the game so that it replicates all or part of the story. But, useful though this activity is, this is the least of it; there are implications about the opportunities for learning that we offer.

(ii) It may be important to explore and acknowledge other sorts of activity in the classroom which would benefit from opportunities for more collaborative work. For example, there are similarities between work around the word processor and the game, in the way that commitment and motivation are generated, although in detail this may vary according to whether the activity is creative (as in composing) or recreative (as the game is, and various class computer games).

However, there are deeper, embedded features shared, in addition to the talk and reading behaviour, which may be characteristic of successful collaborative work: (a) that the authenticity of the activity is based on a 'need to discover'; (b) that this takes place in the context of a problem-solving activity; and (c) that that activity is facilitated by some sort of 'tool' — for example, the game or the microcomputer — which can be touched and handled and changed as part of the actualization of hypotheses, but which itself imposes some practical organization to use — and (d) which 'is visible to all and owned by none' (Scrimshaw, 1992). Lastly, (e) there is an acceptance of group responsibility that has been noted in pupil-pupil computer work (Fisher, 1992), and this is also evident in the game with Y2 children from informal observations of independent playing.

(iii) There is a role in supporting reading through preparing frameworks for independent, collaborative reading; in modelling reading when involved in a game, (by reading slowly but with expression, pointing to words, and reading in order to respond). We also have to learn when not to expect 'the reading lesson' ground rules to operate in purposeful contexts, and therefore not expect to check reading for reading's sake. There must be a different opportunity for that.

(iv) In thinking about the place of book-based games in the classroom, it helps to remember that the activity is broadly equivalent to *shared/paired reading* when children are playing on their own; with an adult or older pupil present, there are similarities to a *group reading* situation. The reading activity that takes place is much more like the range of collaborative, independent and supported reading that operates during paired or shared reading, or, group reading. The now familiar idea of *'paired reading'*, with its simultaneous reading interrupted by a knock on the table to indicate that the child wants to be independent, has echoes in the way the reading works in the game, particularly with the younger groups; but the description of a modified version of this, *'shared reading'* could be describing the game just as well — 'where "partner" and child read aloud together but the "partner" pays no attention to the child's mistakes and continues reading even if the child can manage only a few words of the text'. Significantly the word 'partner' was chosen as the authors (Greening and Spenceley, 1984, in Beard, 1987) suggested 'that any person, adult or skilled child reader, who is able to use the method appropriately, can provide suitable support in reading' — and this is precisely how the game works but perhaps in an even more unconscious, informal, natural way, reflecting the Bruner-Vygotsky hypothesis of unconscious knowing before conscious control. *Group reading* works in a similar way to shared reading, but with an adult reading a book, usually a 'Big Book', with a group of children, and often using the opportunity for teaching and learning certain reading strategies.

(v) This activity, with the necessary book sharing that precedes it, meets many of the requirements of the proposed Programmes of Study for English. It might be helpful to note that in the PoS for Speaking and Listening, pupils will be responding 'appropriately and effectively to what they have heard' (2.2); that their 'understanding of English will be enhanced through their reading' (3.1); and that they are being given opportunities to talk in the following contexts — 'imaginative play . . . reading aloud . . . explaining choices . . .' (4.1). In the PoS for Reading, they are 'being given an extensive introduction to books and stories' (1.2); 'taught to use their knowledge of book conventions and story structure, and their background knowledge and understanding of the content of a book in order to confirm the sense of what they read' (2.1); they are being 'given opportunities to talk about characters, events and language in books . . . say what might happen next in a story . . . re-tell stories' — particularly in one sense (2.2); they are being helped to consider 'beginnings and endings in stories' (3.); teachers are meeting the 'needs of individual children' through offering opportunities to try out various reading supports and approaches, such as practising cueing systems, or shared reading, and pupils are being 'given an extensive experience of literature' (4.1); pupils are 'reading on their own, with others and to the teacher' (4.3); the books that they read and play games about have: 'interesting subject matter and setting which may be related to pupils' own experiences or extend beyond the knowledge of the everyday . . . a clarity of expression and use of language which benefits from reading aloud and rereading; language with recognizable repetitive patterns, rhyme and rhythm; straightforward characterisation and plot' (4.4).

Implications for the Pupils

These can be summarized as follows:

(i) **Children enjoyed the games.** Pupils often wanted to play the game again — immediately! and were always eager to get out the games in the classroom, and R and Y1 children would often persevere through all three parts of the *Five Minutes' Peace* game, which was really too long for them all in one go.

(ii) There is opportunity for the development of **knowledge about language** which is used, shared and learned.

(iii) There is a level of **involvement** that means there is a committed questioning of their peers in checking suggested ideas.

(iv) Children developed increased **confidence with reading**.

(v) Children had increased **familiarity with the language of the book**.

(vi) Children had a purpose in **returning to the book** — this involved intensive reading, or skimming and scanning to find particular sections.

  (vii)   Some players expressed an **awareness of being 'able to read'** or to read more.

 (viii)   Children developed familiarity and **interest in the series and/or the author**.

   (ix)   Players demonstrated **confidence in explaining** how to play to others.

    (x)   There was increased **independence and responsibility**.

Conclusion

Certainly my original aim of supporting readers in increasingly independent reading development was met by these games. But an even greater implication is that if the supports used and given by the children to each other, with or without an adult present, are as effective and efficient as they appear to be, then the role of children in supporting each other's learning needs to be recognized and accommodated in our classroom teaching.

These games do not stand on their own, however. They work not only because of the collaborative peer-scaffolding, but because of the context of literature within which they are developed. They are only one way of encouraging children to respond to literature, and within certain well-defined parameters. It is fitting, therefore, that the children, once released from the confines of the simulated reenactment of the story through the game activity, spill over with their new jointly acquired knowledge, understanding and enthusiasm into exploring texts again — rediscovering the same one, or finding another by the same author, or simply testing out their recently practised skills on fresh books and partners.

References

AHLBERG, A. (1981) *Mrs Lather's Laundry*, London, Penguin Group.

ARNOLD, H. (1992) ' "Do the blackbirds sing all day?" literature and information texts', in STYLES, M., BEARNE, E. and WATSON, V. (Eds) *After Alice: Exploring Children's Literature*, London, Cassell.

BALDRY, P. and SMITH, F. (1991) *Looking at the Language of Fiction*, Huntingdon, EastLINC EdPrint.

BARNES, D. (1988) 'Knowledge in action', in MURPHY, P. and MOON, B. (Eds) *Developments in Learning and Assessment*, Milton Keynes, Open University Press.

BARNES, D. (1992) 'The role of talk in learning', in NORMAN, K. (Ed) *Thinking Voices*, Sevenoaks, Hodder and Stoughton.

BARRS, M. (1992) 'The tune on the page', in KIMBERLEY, K., MEEK, M. and MILLER, J. (Eds) *New Readings: Contributions to an Understanding of Literacy*, London, A&C Black.

BEARD, R. (1987) *Developing Reading, 3–13*, Sevenoaks, Hodder & Stoughton.

BRITTON, J. (1992) 'The anatomy of human experience: The role of inner speech', in KIMBERLEY, K., MEEK, M. and MILLER, J. (Eds) *New Readings: Contributions to an Understanding of Literacy*, London, A&C Black.

BRUNER, J. (1983) *Child's Talk (Learning to Use Language)*, New York, W.W. Norton and Company.

BRUNER, J. (1985) 'Vygotsky: A historical and perceptual perspective', in MERCER, N. (Ed) *Language and Literacy Volume One*, Milton Keynes, Open University Press.

CHAMBERS, A. (1993) *Tell Me: Children Reading and Talk*, Stroud, Thimble Press.

CUTTINGS, G. (1989) *I Am* (Sunrise Series), Oxford, Heinemann Educational.

DAHL, R. (1980) *The Twits*, Harmondsworth, Penguin Books Ltd.

DANIELS, J. (1992) 'Stories we tell ourselves: Stories we tell others', in STYLES, M., BEARNE, E. and WATSON, V. (Eds) *After Alice: Exploring Children's Literature*, London, Cassell.

DES-FOUNTAIN, J. and HOWE, A. (1992) 'Pupils working together on understanding', in NORMAN, K. (Ed) *Thinking Voices*, Sevenoaks, Hodder and Stoughton.

DOMBEY, H. (1988) 'Partners in the telling', in MEEK, M. and MILLS, C. (Eds) *Language and Literacy in the Primary School*, Lewes, Falmer Press.

EDWARDS, D. and MERCER, N. (1986) 'Context and continuity: Classroom discourse and the development of shared knowledge', in DURKIN, K. (Ed) *Language Development in the School Years*, London, Croom Helm.

EDWARDS, D. and MERCER, N. (1987) *Common Knowledge: The Development of Understanding in the Classroom*, London, Routledge.

FISHER, E. (1993) 'Distinctive features of pupil–pupil classroom talk and their relationship to learning: How discursive exploration might be encouraged', London, *Language in Education*, **7**, 4, pp. 239–57.

FOX, C. (1993) *At the Very Edge of the Forest: The Influence of Literature on the Story Telling of Children*, London, Cassell.

FREIRE, P. (1985) 'The politics of education', in MURPHY, P. and MOON, B. (Eds) *Developments in Learning and Assessment*, Milton Keynes, Open University Press.

GOSWAMI, U. and BRYANT, P. (1990) *Phonological Skills and Learning to Read*, Hove, Lawrence Erlbaum Associates Ltd.

HALL, N. (1987) *The Emergence of Literacy*, Sevenoaks, Edward Arnold.

HEATH, S.B. (1983) *Ways with Words: Language, Life and Work in Communities and Classrooms*, Cambridge, Cambridge University Press.

HUTCHINS, P. (1968) *Rosie's Walk*, London, Puffin Books.

HUTCHINS, P. (1976) *Don't Forget the Bacon!*, London, Puffin Books.

KIRBY, P. (1992) 'Story reading at home and school: Its influence on children's early literacy growth', *Reading*, UKRA, **26**, 2, Oxford, Blackwell.

KIRBY, P. (1993) 'Story reading and literacy learning: A study of two early childhood classrooms', *Reading*, UKRA, **27**, 3, Oxford, Blackwell.

LAKE, M. (1991) 'Social background and academic performance — evidence from Buckinghamshire', in PUMFREY, P. (Ed) *Reading Standards, Issues and Evidence*, Leicester, DECP Symposium.

McKEE, D. (1980) *Not Now Bernard*, London, Andersen Press.

McNICHOLLS, J. and McENTEE, J. (1973) *Games to Develop Reading Skills*, Norwich, National Association for Remedial Education (Now Stafford).

MARTIN, C. and PARKER, G. (1988) *The Spanish Armada*, London, Guild Publishing (by arrangement with Hamish Hamilton).

MAYBIN, J., MERCER, N. and STIERER, B. (1992) 'Scaffolding learning in the class-room', in NORMAN, K. (Ed) *Thinking Voices*, Sevenoaks, Hodder and Stoughton.

MOON, C. (1993, 24th edn) *Individualized Reading: A Teacher-guide to Readability Levels at Key Stages 1 & 2*, Reading, Language Information Centre.

MURPHY, J. (1986) *Five Minutes' Peace*, London, Walker Books Ltd.

PEARCE, P. (1992) 'The writer, the children and box B', in KIMBERLEY, K., MEEK, M. and MILLER, J. (Eds) *New Readings: Contributions to an Understanding of Literacy*, London, A&C Black.

PEARCE, P. (1992) 'The making of stories for children', in STYLES, M., BEARNE, E. and WATSON, V. (Eds) *After Alice: Exploring Children's Literature*, London, Cassell.

PERERA, K. (1987) *Understanding Language*, Sheffield, NATE Publications.

ROSEN, M. (1989) *We're Going on a Bear Hunt*, London, Walker Books Ltd.

SENDAK, M. (1963) *Where The Wild Things Are*, Harmondsworth, Penguin Group.

SCHOOLS CURRICULUM AND ASSESSMENT AUTHORITY (SCAA) (1994) *English in the National Curriculum: Draft Proposals*, London, SCAA.

SCRIMSHAW, P. (1992) *'Word processing, collaboration and exploratory talk: Some preliminary results from the spoken language and new technology product'*, paper presented to the 1992 ECEC Conference, Melbourne, Australia.

SMITH, F. (1992) *Looking at Language Varieties*, Huntingdon, EastLINC, EdPrint.

SOLOMAN, J. (1983) 'Learning about energy: How pupils think in two domains', *European Journal of Science Education*, **5**, 1, pp. 49–59.

TAYLOR, M. (1990) 'Books in the classroom and knowledge about language', in CARTER, R. (Ed) *Knowledge About Language and the Curriculum: The LINC Reader*, Sevenoaks, Hodder and Stoughton.

VYGOTSKY, L. (1934) *Thought and Language*, Moscow-Leningrad, Soc-econom. izd.

VYGOTSKY, L. (1978) *Mind in Society*, Cambridge, MA, Harvard University Press.

WATERLAND, E. (1985) *Read with Me*, Stroud, Thimble Press.

WHITEHEAD, M. (1987) 'Reading, caught or taught? Some issues involved in changed approaches to the teaching of reading', in MURPHY, P. and MOON, B. (Eds) *Developments in Learning and Assessment*, Milton Keynes, Open University Press.

WOOD, D. (1988) *How Children Think and Learn*, Oxford, Basil Blackwell.

Further Reading

ANDERSON. H. (1992) 'Dr. Xargle's guide to earthlet knowledge about language' in BAIN, R., FITZGERALD, B. and TAYLOR, M. (Eds) *Looking into Language: Classroom Approaches to Knowledge About Language*, Sevenoaks, Hodder and Stoughton.

BADDELEY, P. and EDDERSHAW, C. (1994) *Not So Simple Picture Books: Developing Responses to Literature with 4–12-year-olds*, Stoke-on-Trent, Trentham Books.

BARRS, M. and THOMAS, A. (Eds) (1991) 'The role of the text' in CLPE, *The Reading Book*, London, CLPE.

BENNET, J. (1991, 4th edn) *Learning to Read with Picture Books*, Stroud, Thimble Press.

DAWES, L. (1992) 'Using books to develop children's knowledge about language' in BAIN, R., FITZGERALD, B. and TAYLOR, M. (Eds) *Looking into Language: Classroom Approaches to Knowledge About Language*, Sevenoaks, Hodder and Stoughton.

GRAHAM, J. (1990) *Pictures on the Page*, Sheffield, NATE.

KIMBERLEY, K., MEEK, M. and MILLER, J. (Eds) (1992) 'Part three: The deep play of literature', in KIMBERLEY, K., MEEK, M. and MILLER, J. *New Readings: Contributions to an Understanding of Literacy*, London, A&C Black.

MEEK, M. (1988) *How Texts Teach What Readers Learn*, Stroud, Thimble Press.

SLATER, L. (1992) 'Writing newspaper stories', in BAIN, R., FITZGERALD, B. and TAYLOR, M. (Eds) *Looking into Language: Classroom Approaches to Knowledge About Language*, Sevenoaks, Hodder and Stoughton.

Activities on Literature — Useful Publications

BALDRY, P. and SMITH, F. (1991) *Looking at the Language of Fiction*, Huntingdon, EastLINC EdPrint.

BENTLEY, D. and REID, D. (Eds) (1993) *Literacy Centres — Fiction, Red Box* (activities on texts for Y3 and Y4), Leamington Spa, Scholastic Publications.

CURRICULUM COUNCIL FOR WALES (CCW) (1991) *Literature-centred Approaches at Key Stages 1 and 2*, Cardiff, CCW.

SMITH, F. (1992) *Looking at Language Varieties*, Huntingdon, EastLINC, EdPrint.

WELSH JOINT EDUCATION COMMITTEE (1992a) *Knowledge About Language: The Very Quiet Cricket*, WJEC.

WELSH JOINT EDUCATION COMMITTEE (1992b) *Knowledge About Language: The Jolly Postman*, Cardiff, WJEC.

Selected References Relevant to Response to Texts Taken from the English Proposals for KS1 (May 1994, Subsequently *Revised* in January, 1995)

Reading (pages 8–11)

1.1 Pupils' developing **understanding** should be characterized by:
   • growing independence in choosing and reading books for themselves;
   • willingness to read new and unfamiliar material;
     Pupils' developing **response** to text should be characterized by:
   • choosing and reading books for pleasure;
   • the growing ability to express preferences about what they have read, giving reasons.

1.2 Pupils who begin school with limited experience and understanding of literacy should be given a planned and extensive introduction to the initial stages of reading. Pupils should be taught the alphabet and their awareness of sounds and patterns of sounds should be developed as a preparation for phonic work. They should also be given an extensive introduction to books and stories in order to help them develop understanding of the nature and purpose of reading. Those pupils who already are able to read with fluency, accuracy and understanding should follow only those parts of the programmes of study which are relevant to their needs . . .

2 Key Skills

2.1 Pupils should be taught to read with fluency, accuracy and understanding.
   They should be taught . . . effective techniques for reading, understanding and responding . . .
   The areas to be taught are as follows.
   Phonic knowledge . . .
   Graphic knowledge . . .
   Word recognition . . .

A significant marker of pupils' progress in reading at this Key Stage is the ability to read about thirty common usage words within simple, short narratives.

Grammatical knowledge . . .

Contextual understanding focuses on meaning derived from the text as a whole. Pupils should be taught to use their knowledge of book conventions and story structure, and their background knowledge and understanding of the content of a book in order to confirm the sense of what they read. They should keep the overall sense of a passage in mind as a checking device.

2.2 In understanding and responding to stories and poems, pupils should be given opportunities to:
  • talk about characters, events and language in books, beginning to use appropriate terminology;
  • say what might happen next in a story;
  • re-tell stories;
  • explain the content of a passage or a whole text;
  • choose books to read individually and with others;
  • review their reading with their teacher;
  • read and complete short texts;
  • re-read favourite stories and poems and learn them by heart;
  • hear stories and poems read aloud frequently and regularly, including some longer, more challenging material;
  • prepare, present and act out stories and poems they have read.

3 **Standard English and Language Study**
kinds of texts, *e.g. beginnings and endings in stories.* . . .

4 **Range**
  4.1 Teachers should draw on the various methods of teaching reading in a balanced and coherent way in order to meet the particular needs of individual children. Pupils should be given an extensive experience of children's literature.
  4.2 Parental support for children's reading is vital . . . Parents should be encouraged to read to and with their children as often as possible . . .
  4.3 Pupils should read on their own, with others and to the teacher from a range of good quality literature which includes nursery rhymes, poems, stories, folk tales, myths, legends, and picture books . . . Where reading schemes are consistent with the approach to reading in the National Curriculum they can be a valuable resource.
  4.4 The books and poems read and discussed should be used to stimulate pupils' imagination and enthusiasm. They should include some or all of these features:
    • interesting subject matter and setting which may be related to pupils' own experience or extend beyond the knowledge of the everyday;

- a clear viewpoint, with accessible themes and ideas;
- a clarity of expression and use of language which benefits from reading aloud and rereading;
- language with recognizable repetitive patterns, rhyme and rhythm;
- straightforward characterization and plot;
- the use of a variety of narrative techniques, presented in immediately accessible ways;
- illustrations which are visually stimulating and enhance the words of the text.

Level Descriptions for Attainment Target 2 (page 32)

Level 1
(Pupils) express their response to poems and stories by identifying aspects they like.

Level 2
Pupils' reading . . . shows understanding. They express opinions about major events or ideas in stories, poems and non-fiction.

Level 3
In responding to fiction and non-fiction they show understanding of the main points and express preferences.

Level 4
In responding to a range of texts, pupils show understanding of significant ideas, themes, events and characters, beginning to use inference and deduction. They refer to the text when explaining their views.

January 1995 Footnote: With reference to the comments on the implications of the English Proposals for responses to literature, the slimmed down version of the National Curriculum has one or two significant changes.

1. Although the phonic knowledge, graphic knowledge, word recognition, grammatical understanding and contextual understanding are still listed in that unfortunate order in Section 2(b) the preamble in the section 'Common Requirements' has a statement that 'The numbers and letters throughout the programmes of study are for referencing purposes only, and do not necessarily indicate a particular teaching sequence or hierarchy of knowledge, understanding and skills'. The reference to children with a limited experience and understanding of literacy needing to start with the 'initial stages of reading' (meaning alphabet, sounds and patterns) has thankfully, disappeared. Unfortunately, however, the Attainment Target for Level 1 still has only knowledge of letters and sound-symbol correspondence listed as the way to read words — and establish meaning! Semantics and syntax do not seem to

be considered as essential at Level 1. This is a serious omission and the addition of 'more than one strategy, such as phonic, graphic, syntactic and contextual' at Level 2 establishes a hierarchy which the proposals purport to disclaim — it is unfortunately the Levels and SATs which have had a regrettable but understandable influence on classroom practice in the past.

2. There is now a mention of IT 1(b), but not of media, unless one wants to interpret 'read information. . . . on screen' as a reference to televisual literacy!

The references to response to literature are thinner, but are there in the description of the nature of the materials that are to 'stimulate pupils' imagination and enthusiasm' 1(c), although the useful list of genres has gone. In 2c, there is a list of the kind of responses which should be encouraged. Response to literature is explicitly mentioned in section 1a in the programme of study for writing, and there are implicit references in the programme of study for speaking and listening (section 1(b), (c) and (d) and 3(a)).

Part 1 of Game

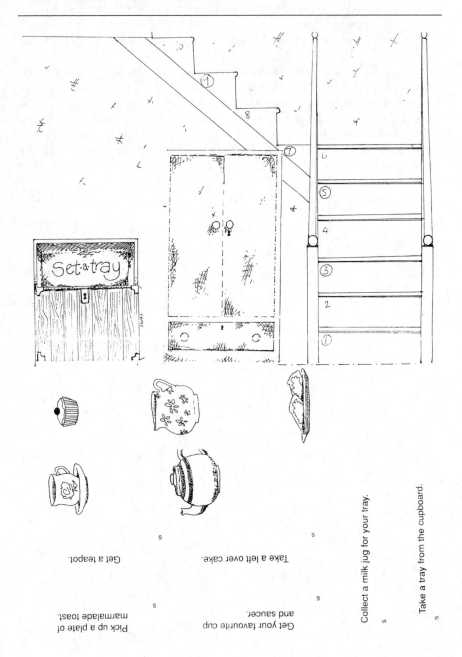

Get a teapot.

Take a left over cake.

Collect a milk jug for your tray.

Take a tray from the cupboard.

Pick up a plate of marmalade toast.

Get your favourite cup and saucer.

Part 2 of Game

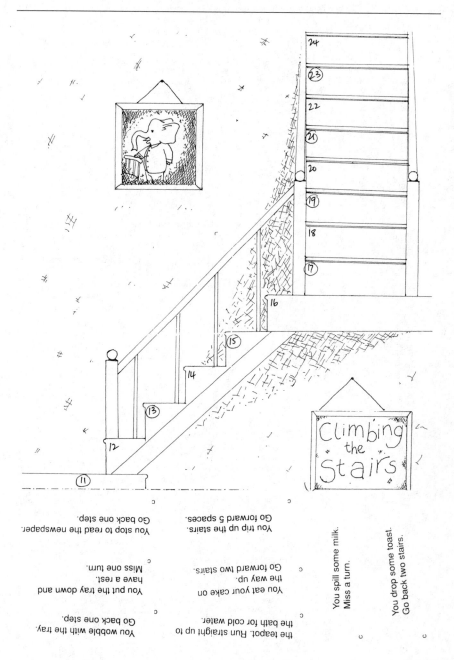

Go back one step.
You stop to read the newspaper.

Go forward 5 spaces.
You trip up the stairs.

Miss one turn.
have a rest.
You put the tray down and

Go forward two stairs.
You eat your cake on the way up.

You spill some milk.
Miss a turn.

You drop some toast.
Go back two stairs.

Go back one step.
You wobble with the tray.

the bath for cold water.
the teapot. Run straight up to

Part 3 of Game

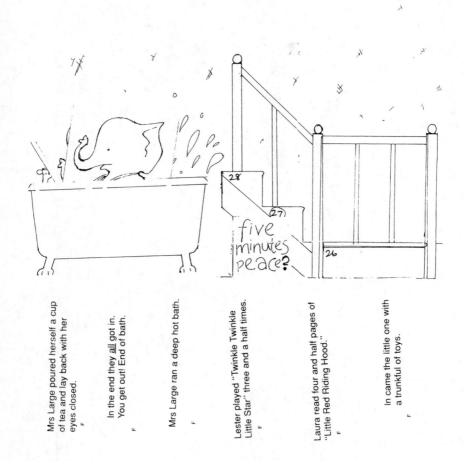

Mrs Large poured herself a cup of tea and lay back with her eyes closed.
F

In the end they all got in. You get out! End of bath.
F

Mrs Large ran a deep hot bath.
F

Lester played "Twinkle Twinkle Little Star" three and a half times.
F

Laura read four and half pages of "Little Red Riding Hood."
F

In came the little one with a trunkful of toys.
F

Chapter 5

Teaching Through Text: Developing Reading (7–11)

Ed Marum

> Few things are impossible in themselves; it is not so much the means
> we lack as the perseverance to make them succeed. (La Rochefoucauld)

The revised English orders for Key Stage 2 reading are, in some senses, one
of the more positive elements in the revised English document. They begin
with these sentences:

> Pupils should be encouraged to develop as enthusiastic, independent
> and reflective readers. They should be introduced to a wide range of
> literature, and have opportunities to read extensively for their own
> interest and pleasure, and for information. Pupils' reading should be
> developed through the use of progressively more challenging and
> demanding texts. (DFE, 1995)

What I should like to do in this chapter is to consider some of the texts
teachers might use across the 7–11 age range, and to suggest ways of dealing
with such texts in order to encourage positive response, and to maximize
flexibility and variety for teachers and pupils, enabling good practice to flourish.
I am not, however, going to comment on ways in which 'pupils should be
taught to expand their phonic and graphic knowledge', as I regard this as a
more limited 'mechanical' element of the overall reading process, and one
which is already widely practised and known. What I should like to concentrate on, because it seems to me to be of central importance in education, is
the ways in which teachers can share their enjoyment of books with pupils,
and in so doing enable pupils to become keen and regular readers of various
types of text. I shall begin with fiction, but will also wish to suggest that
other 'texts' than those in book form are necessary in order to develop an
appropriate sense of the widening range of readings that pupils can and do
make as they proceed through their primary school years.

A perhaps unexpected bonus of the revised English orders is that they
will continue to allow teachers to exercise control and professional judgment
over the most positive and powerful element of the education system — the

formal recognition of the power of story in learning. Through the selection and use of appropriate stories by teacher and pupils, conditions can be created for powerful and effective learning. Whatever disagreements there continue to be as to the definition of and values attaching to any literary 'canon', the fact remains that each classroom can and does create its own models, expectations and values, in this as in other matters, as part of the general school framework. Wide-ranging and imaginative fiction is a major tool; it both defines and develops our understanding of literacy in the contemporary context. It is also a prerequisite of continuing pupil enthusiasm for and commitment to the reading of a range of texts which help define the world we live in. This is one reason why, despite the revised orders' marginalization of cultures and traditions beyond the specific limitations of 'the English literary heritage', it remains extremely important that classrooms afford time and space to considering and using pluralistic, multicultural material to provide a broad and balanced literary offer.

The development of reading from 7 to 11 is a formative educational activity in the widest sense, opening horizons, broadening perspectives, stimulating childrens' imaginative powers, and making possible that which would otherwise not be so. The establishment and maintenance of quality reading experience is thus an increasingly important aim in a world of developing reading technologies; the 'power of the page' (Pinsent, 1993) becomes increasingly, not less, significant in our world. Good practice in this area will, as it always has, underpin the child's learning; offer real choice and variety of stimulus; acknowledge the need to share readings, but also emphasize the importance of individual taste, and employ a wide variety of strategies in doing so. In this section I wish to briefly consider some practical activities based around texts and to suggest ways in which the experiences of reading can be widened and effectively used by teachers and pupils.

Readings of The Jolly Postman

Since its appearance in 1986, *The Jolly Postman* (Ahlberg, 1986) has proved to be an extremely popular book with pupils and teachers. Part of its attraction lies in the multi-layered meanings of the text; it can also be read in different ways: as a postman's story; as a modern fairy tale; as a humorous mixture of everyday fact and imaginative fancy; as a narrative poem; as a mixed genre text; as a challenging picture book; as a story about the social importance attached to the taking of tea, etc. It therefore offers an unusually rich range of teaching and learning opportunities of various kinds. It would be impossible to document all these here; what I will attempt to do, however, is to provide a few suggestions as to ways in which readings of the book might be usefully made by teachers with children.

Before doing so, however, I need to say something of why quality books such as this help make readers. The narrative device used in the book is to have a postman delivering letters to a series of fairy-tale characters drawn from discrete fairy tales. The letters act as a connecting thread between the characters, but they also provide both fairy-tale characters and readers with the opportunity to move between stories, to interweave their texts into a complex, humorous narrative. This narrative partly depends for its remarkable success upon the reader's prior awareness of the 'traditional' fairy-tale genre; the reader's understanding of the intertextual process in which she is engaged is therefore enhanced by the prior knowledge she brings to the reading of the book. The postman, acting as the connecting device between the various fairy-tale characters, delivers letters from one character in story A to another character in story B, and so on. The postman, however, also acts as a link between the 'realistic' world the child-reader inhabits in her everyday life and the 'fantastic' imaginative world she inhabits in fairy tale. This movement across genres, across time and space, from the 'social realism' of the story's opening to the imaginative recreation of versions of fairy tales which the book is concerned to develop, is in some respects the particular province of children's literature. For example, books like *Where the Wild Things Are* (Sendak, 1967) and *Not Now, Bernard* (McKee, 1980) use the same basic device, crossing boundaries, entering new territories of the imagination available only through fantasy narratives, each in its particular way. But in *The Jolly Postman* the rich interweaving, at a variety of textual and pictorial levels, of combinations of stories, makes the book a particularly delightful and challenging creative reading experience. In another sense, of course, it is also the postman's story, in which he, as a central character, provides a gloss upon our understanding of fairy-tales. And because the text provides additional detail, in terms of the events surrounding the traditional story and the idiosyncratic quirks of stereotypical characters, such as 'the witch' and 'the giant' for example, we learn more about the stories and their characters than we had previously known. In essence, the book represents a modern retelling of some prototypical oral stories of the western story-telling tradition; in the telling of them it creates a new, humorous and exciting reading opportunity for those readers becoming fluent in the lifelong process of making readings.

Most importantly, because the book encourages the reader to make new connections between previously-known stories, surprising her into 'rereading' her previous understanding of fairy-stories, all the stories within the text are made new again. This process of 'making connections' which underpins the book represents an important lesson in reading which cannot be taught by any reading scheme. The realization that we bring our past with us, together with all the stories which made us who we are, to our reading of every new story we encounter is part of the 'reading journey' which determines our very identity.[1] Because our current reading experience is involved in a reciprocal relationship with our previous experience of reading, which both shapes and informs us, enabling a continuous series of new insights, revisions and understandings to our sense of what reading is, it becomes impossible to say that we ever 'understand' a book. Rather we need to say that our understandings are broadening as our reading experience is itself broadened. Because *The Jolly Postman*, like other good texts, challenges our understanding, it simultaneously reassures us of the value of continuing on our personal reading journey through life. Without that kind of challenge and reassurance, reading development simply cannot take place. To put this in another way, the reading journey which begins with versions of *Little Red Riding Hood*, and continues through *The Jolly Postman* to *The Stinky Cheese Man and Other Fairly Stupid Tales* (Scieszka, 1993) might eventually bring the mature reader to Angela Carter's *The Company of Wolves* (Carter, 1979).

Good picture books, like fairy-tales, make regular, enquiring adult readers. Books like *The Jolly Postman* can be read together in large or small groups, or in pairs, as well as by individuals. The picture of the witch's car, with its number-plate HAG 1, represents a kind of pictorial humour to which most readers will respond in the text. Developing readers, by attending to important detail, learn to know, in Margaret Meek's important phrase, 'what counts'. The book can also of course be linked to an interesting range of developmental activities of the kind that primary teachers are very familiar with. I should like to outline a few of these.

Aside from its intrinsic interest as a self-contained story, the book, like other quality texts, lends itself to a range of activities and subjects which are cross-disciplinary in character, and which also allow teachers to construct imaginative ideas for further exploration. Given the multiracial character of many primary schools, it should not be surprising to find children who are unfamiliar with traditional western fairy-tales. Some children will, however, know the texts from film or video versions; there has been a plethora of these over recent years, and the development of *Disneyworlds* has increased the general media advertising of them on television, for example. Video versions will as a result be well-known by a range of young children; in many senses, the video version has become the 'standard' version; children meeting written versions for the first time often comment on discrepancies between that version and the more familiar video interpretation. Some work in this area has been done, for example, taking a modern story such as *The Snowman* (Briggs, 1978) and comparing versions of the text. It is important to acknowledge that knowledge of video versions can be an interesting starting-point for work on fairy tales. Developing young children to become 'critical readers', aware of how information is handled and manipulated in texts, is acknowledged in the revised English orders as an important and worthwhile activity. This can be tackled in a wide variety of ways.

Because *The Jolly Postman* is an interweaving of characters from different stories in a new format, it opens up a range of activities for classroom work. These might begin, for example, with some reading and research of such stories as *Cinderella, Little Red Riding Hood, Goldilocks*, etc., where comparisons between written versions of the same story can be made and discussed.

Paired and group work can be easily organized along such lines and adapted to suit the abilities and interests of the children involved. Practical work can also be easily linked to such study; topics such as food, clothes, map-work, relationships, etc., can extend from a prior reading of *Red Riding Hood*; these can then be linked to other activities such as role play; puppet-making, developing the home-corner, etc., which take the activities beyond the 'book-bound' and make links which children can relate to and develop imaginatively at a variety of levels.

It seems a very obvious point to make here, but it perhaps needs to be repeated, that by handling texts in a way which allows young children to make imaginative leaps from the 'written' to the 'lived', their sense and understanding of story is reinforced; they begin to see what adults later realize more completely — that our lives are in fact composed of stories which interweave and make meanings at differing levels of our understanding. The initiation of children into the early stages of this process of understanding is an early but important part of their own reading journey. Neil Campbell develops this theme, within his chosen context, in chapter 8.

Figure 5.1 shows how the text can be employed as a springboard for a wider range of activities; this approach will be familiar to many primary teachers and needs little explanation. The study of characterization, highlighted in the revised English orders, can of course be directly addressed through establishing a specific focus in the story. In this example, the character of the giant can be used as a starting-point for analysis, discussion and a developed series of activities. Writing activities can be developed from issues raised in the story, and be designed to lead on to link with other activities. The sheet of possible activities (figure 5.2) can be adapted to suit particular needs, and can also be used as a linking device with other stories. The last activity, for example, asks the child to imagine herself replying as Mr. Wolf to the letter he has received in the story from a firm of solicitors. But the activity might also link with other textual versions of the story, and indeed with other books.

It might perhaps also be pointed out that the study of such quality texts as these can also be designed to lead away from written and oral communication forms to wider communications issues; hence the suggestion that the 'Post Office' range of activities could be instigated as an alternative method of proceeding from the known to the unknown. Quite obviously, letters, letter-writing and other forms of personal communication can be starting-points for a more developed and possibly longer-term study of communications, involving computers, broader information technology issues, etc. The suggestions made are, of course, examples and work can be variously structured and adapted to meet particular objectives. The main point I wish to emphasize here is that stories can be very profitably used as an excellent basis for thematic or topic work, linking closely with other core curricular areas, and additionally offering the possibility of other practical activities and outcomes. They are also of course, most importantly, the richest source for integrating

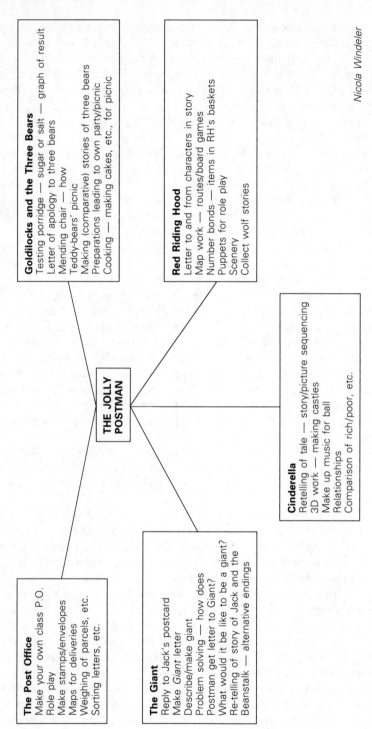

Goldilocks and the Three Bears
Testing porridge — sugar or salt — graph of result
Letter of apology to three bears
Mending chair — how
Teddy-bears' picnic
Making (comparative) stories of three bears
Preparations leading to own party/picnic
Cooking — making cakes, etc., for picnic

Red Riding Hood
Letter to and from characters in story
Map work — routes/board games
Number bonds — items in RH's baskets
Puppets for role play
Scenery
Collect wolf stories

THE JOLLY POSTMAN

The Post Office
Make your own class P.O.
Role play
Make stamps/envelopes
Maps for deliveries
Weighing of parcels, etc.
Sorting letters, etc.

The Giant
Reply to Jack's postcard
Make *Giant* letter
Describe/make giant
Problem solving — how does
Postman get letter to Giant?
What would it be like to be a giant?
Re-telling of story of Jack and the
Beanstalk — alternative endings

Cinderella
Retelling of tale — story/picture sequencing
3D work — making castles
Make up music for ball
Relationships
Comparison of rich/poor, etc.

Nicola Windeler

Figure 5.1

Decide who else you think Goldilocks might have invited to her party and draw a table seating plan.

Which products do you think the witch might like to buy? She only has enough money to buy three of them. Give reasons for the choices you make.

You have been asked by Sky Television to design an advertisement for one of these products. Complete the storyboard outline for the advertisement and suggest suitable actors for the characters in the script.

Write Giant Bigg's reply to Jack's postcard.

Write the story of Jack's first meeting with the other giant whose address he has taken.

Write Cinderella's reply to Mr. Piper's letter.

Cinderella also received a copy of a newspaper that morning. With your partner, write the front page of *The Fairytale Times* which covers the royal couple's honeymoon.

Design the birthday card you think Goldilocks might have received from the three bears.

Design a menu card for Goldilocks' birthday party.

Write the letter the jolly postman is reading at the end of his long day's work.

With your partner, write the radio playscript of the court proceedings against Mr. Wolf.

Write the recipe which Goldilocks' mum used for her birthday cake.

Write Mr. Wolf's reply to the solicitor's letter. He began it in this way:

> *Dear Messrs. Meeny, Miny and Mo,*
>
> *The official accounts of what happened on the occasions you refer to in your letter are all lies. I hate lies — especially lies about me. So let me tell you what really happened.*

Figure 5.2: The Jolly Postman: Some Possible Activities

theory with practice in a whole-school approach to literacy, encompassing speaking and listening, reading and writing in all their manifestations.

Children might go on from their study of *The Jolly Postman* to consider, later in Key Stage 2, narrative techniques in more demanding texts, such as Jon Scieszka's version of the traditional tale, *Little Red Running Shorts*, which employs a complex and subtle use of intertextuality, as the following extract shows (Scieszka, 1993):

'Okay, I've got things running smoothly now', said Jack the Narrator. And this next story is even better than the last three. See, it's about this girl who runs very fast and always wears red running shorts. That's where her name comes from, get it? So anyway, this girl is running to her granny's house when she meets a wolf. He tricks her into taking the long way while he takes the short cut. Now this is the good part because Red runs so fast that she beats the wolf

to granny's house. He knocks on the door. Red answers it. And guess
what she says? 'My, what slow feet you have,' And that's it. *The End.*
Is that great or what? So sit back, relax, and enjoy — 'Little Red
Running Shorts'.
'And now, like I already said — "Little Red Running Shorts".'
'You just told the whole story', says Little Red Running Shorts.
'We're not going to tell it again.'
'You can't say that', says Jack. 'You have to start with "Once upon
a time."'
'No way', says the wolf. 'You blew it.'

Texts such as this of course open up even more fascinating studies of the
interrelationship of language, literature and the media. I should like to outline
how teachers might tackle some relevant issues by looking briefly at Scieszka's
work as a good modern example of how texts can teach.[2]

Remaking the Old as New: The Narrative Techniques of Jon Scieszka

Over recent decades, readers of children's literature have become accustomed
to authors such as Sendak, McKee, Burningham and the Ahlbergs, who make
us think again about what happens with and to a story in the process of its
telling. This focus upon experimentation in narrative method, through picture as well as through text, is one of the characteristics of those books which
add a new dimension to the genre and which continually ask us to reassess our
understanding of what children's literature is and of how it works. Within the
past five years a new writer has emerged who makes an important claim to
wider recognition as an innovator in the genre and as a contributor to the
continuing debate about the future of children's books. Through his development of old themes and stories in a modern idiom, and through his reformu-
lation of story-telling devices, based upon broad and infectious humour, I
believe Jon Scieszka has made a central contribution to our knowledge of how
books work. In this section I hope to examine some of the techniques and
methods he employs and to draw attention to the processes at work in his
recent books.

The True Story of the Three Little Pigs appeared in the USA in 1989
(Scieszka, 1991). This was the first of Scieszka's books to gain wide attention
and in certain respects it is here that he begins to employ some of the narrative
methods he was to develop in later work. As with his later books, this story
is the retelling of a traditional tale from a new perspective. In this case the
story is told by the wolf in a highly personalized and informal style. He says
to his readers, 'You can call me Al', after having told us that we have not yet
heard the 'real story' because nobody has heard '*my* side of the story'. By
introducing this comment early on in the text the issue of perspective and

point of view is highlighted; the author is placing himself in that tradition of children's writers who are concerned to emphasize the relativity of truth in story by specifically drawing attention to the role of the narrator in formulating perspective for the reader. The 'reliability' of the narrator is here an issue, in the sense in which Booth (1961) drew attention to the centrality of this issue as part of general fictional technique in the 'adult' novel.

In other words, Scieszka begins his old story by asking us to think of it as a new one; in asking us to do this, he is also asking us to at least consider the wolf's version of events and to 'suspend our disbelief', at least temporarily, as we do so. By employing a supposedly — omniscient narrator to 'correct' the reader's previous 'misunderstanding' of the story-line, he is asking the young reader to enter the operational world of the experienced reader, to use judgment and discrimination in an analysis of 'truth' in fiction. The really experienced reader may understand the 'tongue in cheek' nature of this enterprise, but for the less experienced reader this role is a true learning experience, part of the process of becoming herself a more experienced reader. Like the other children's authors I have mentioned, Scieszka is helping the young reader to read in a new way and to extend her knowledge and understanding of the dialogue between author and audience that goes on in all demanding texts, and which forms part of the larger process the reader is engaged in as she comes to feel herself having a more confident sense of language and a growing appreciation of its realization in fiction.

Scieszka's use of idiomatic, conversational style is a characteristic feature of the engagement with audience his texts ensure, as when he has Al say:

But like I was saying,
the whole Big Bad Wolf thing is all wrong.
The real story is about a sneeze and a cup of sugar. (Scieszka, 1991)

By suggesting that the correct understanding of the story revolves around these latter two objects, the author invites the reader to reposition herself with regard to the narrative sequence, by examining the story detail from a new perspective and by having to 'seek out' significant detail in the light of this new information, rather than by the application of previous narrative experience and knowledge of earlier versions of the tale. Making that step 'from the known to the unknown' is of course at the heart of the reading process. Here, Scieszka's illustrator, Lane Smith, capitalizes upon the idea of the new learning experience involved for the reader by careful signing through visual text: the page with the important new information tells us *twice* to look out for two symbols. By simultaneously using the situation to symbolize a real 'lesson' for the reader, the page alerts her to the new story-twist which will follow (blackboard picture) (*ibid.*).

This device is in turn further reinforced on the following page by the use of capitalized headings, a collage of lettering and other symbolic elements which arise in the visual representation of story scenes during the book. Thus

But like I was saying,

the whole Big Bad Wolf thing is all wrong.

The real story is about a sneeze and a cup of sugar.

Way back in Once Upon a Time time,
I was making a birthday cake
for my dear old granny.
I had a terrible sneezing cold.
'I ran out of sugar.'

the reader is early taught that meaning is derived from the *interweaving* of picture and words, that our understanding of what story is being told to us is dependent upon our appreciation of the context clues on the page. This is not a new device: *Rosie's Walk* (Hutchins, 1968), for example, is another text which relies for its effects upon simultaneous multiple understandings in the reader. Here, however, the context clues are both more complex and diverse: the intertextual device is used in interesting ways, as with the inclusion of the framed picture of 'Granny' inside a whole-page picture, suggesting another possible variation upon another story I have already mentioned.[3] The connections to be made by the alert classroom teacher are I think quite clear, and open up wider opportunities for interesting classroom practice based upon a consideration of chronological and cultural variations of the 'story' base, allowing for more developed thematic treatment of the issues raised in the texts and the linking of these to broader curricular issues, along the lines I have already outlined.

Making the New from the Old: *Stig of the Dump*

As pupils progress through Key Stage 2 they will of course develop their abilities to work collaboratively, linking their personal and shared reading to an increasing range of skills pursued in pairs and groups, and extending from stories into other curricular areas of enquiry. Figure 5.3 shows how a more demanding text such as *Stig of the Dump* (King, 1963) can be studied and investigated in a similar way to texts met earlier in Key Stage 2.

Pupils who have been trained to work across traditional subject boundaries earlier in Key Stage 2 will have little difficulty in moving on to more demanding work with texts such as this. In this example, the editing of textual versions becomes an interesting exercise through the recasting of a written fictional form into a filmed version; the reworking of material into a television advertisement, for example, simultaneously allows for more considered and in-depth 'critical readings' to occur as children explore the texts together. The relationship between history and literature can thus be investigated; consideration of different genres will perhaps follow, and lead to a review of the use of different media for communications purposes. The use of workbooks based around texts also allows for more detailed study of language issues arising from the texts. Although such work books take some initial preparation, over a sequence of linked lessons they allow the teacher greater opportunity to monitor pupil activity more effectively and to provide specific help and support to pupils where it is needed. Some simple examples of sheets taken from such a workbook are provided here.

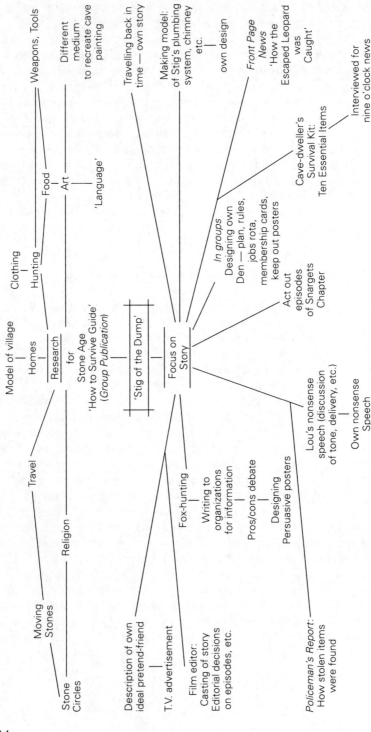

Figure 5.3: Investigating 'Stig of the Dump'

STIG OF THE DUMP

1 On page 12 there is a description of Stig's den. In your group, design a den:
   (a) Decide where would you make your den and explain why.
   (b) What would you build your den from? Explain how you would build it.
   (c) Write a list of rules for your den.
   (d) Draw a plan of your den, label every thing in it and explain what all the things are used for.
   (e) Decide on all the jobs which would need to be done, and draw up a rota of work for the members of your group.
   (f) Design a poster to keep non-members out.

2 Read pages 10(from*) to page 15 (end of third paragraph). Write a poem which describes Barney's and Stig's first meeting.

   9a On page 59 there is a description of a different kind — a fox hunt: There have been many arguments about whether this sport should be allowed to take place. In your group talk about fox hunting. Why do you think some people like to hunt foxes? Would you? Do you think it's necessary or just a sport? Why do groups of people try to stop the hunt? Is it a pastime/sport open to everyone?

   9b In your group make a list of the reasons why you think it should be allowed and a list of reasons why it should not.

   9c Design a poster in favour of fox hunting

                    or

       Design a poster condemning the hunting of foxes

Ed Marum

15 Write a policeman's report of how he found the stolen items.
Set it out like this

MARSH LANE POLICE STATION.

Police Constable: _____

Date: _____

Time: _____

Incident Investigated: Theft of valuables from three houses
                          in the district.

Name of witness: Barney.

Details of investigation: _____

16 Write a newspaper account of how the escaped leopard was caught. Make
sure you think of an exciting headline!

Such demanding work as can stem naturally from the fictional text relates closely to the revised requirements for English in the National Curriculum; while children are engaged with higher-order literacy skills, they are also breaking new ground in a practical as well as in a theoretical manner. They are, above all, extending their proficiency in and understanding of literacy in important and necessary ways that links school learning to life outside school. Despite its relative longevity, I believe *Stig* deals with interesting issues in a way which makes the issues fresh for the young child coming to the text for the first time. I have found it to be popular with both sexes and across wide age and social ranges, despite the early claim of Puffin Books that it 'will suit boys of 7 to 10 particularly, but will please adventurous girls as well' (frontispiece to *Stig of the Dump*).

John Rowe Townsend (1983) has summarized the story as follows:

> Here a small boy named Barney explores the dump at the
> bottom of the chalkpit near where he is staying, and finds
> there a cave-boy, from ages long past, who has made himself
> a house out of junk, with bottle-glass windows and a tin-can
> chimney, and has done all the marvellous things that small
> boys are sure they could do with what you find on rubbish-
> dumps, if only their mean old parents would let them. At the
> end it is left open whether Stig — the name Barney gives his
> cave-boy — 'really' exists, or whether he is a figment of a
> lonely child's imagination. The reader can take it either way.

Admitting its narrowly 'middle-class' language and ethos — the central young boy Barney's comments include 'Thank you for having
me', 'Jolly good idea', and 'I hope you liked the carrots' (all to a
'cave-boy') — the book has genuine appeal over generations; it has
retained a strong attraction in the face of changing styles and tastes in
popular children's literature. Like other quality books now out of
popularity it speaks directly to the individual reader learning the experience of childhood through story. More recently, the book has
made the successful translation to television. Consequently a lot of
primary children know about Stig.

  My experience with some teachers has led me to the view that
Stig may be read as a modern parable: it testifies to the powers of the
creative imagination in limiting circumstances. To make an unlikely
comparison, Barney follows the path taken by Don Quixote and
subsequently documented in the history of critical literature. From
the perspective of each, we see the paradox of life as reflected through
fiction. With Barney, the oral, rather than the written, tradition is
foremost. For the reader, as for the central fictional character, story
is essential in learning:

> The intuition of life that, beginning with Cervantes, crystal-
> lized in the novel is profoundly paradoxical: the novelist lu-
> cidly recognises the ways man may be painfully frustrated
> and victimized in a world with no fixed values or ideals,
> without even a secure sense of what is real and what is not;
> yet through the exercise of an autonomous art the writer
> boldly asserts the freedom of consciousness itself. (Alter, 1975)

For the young reader, the sense of learning through literature becomes a prototype for later experience. Finding out with Barney that
there is a Stig is an early stage in the process which leads the adult to
know what it is to tilt at windmills. Without such early experience,
tomorrow's public may one day find Cervantes out of print.

The primary-school teacher in particular cannot afford to forget that

> Literature for children may be seen as the significant model, the cultural paradigm of subsequent literature in *the experience of the reader*. Children's literature is, undeniably, the *first* literary experience, where the reader's expectations of what literature *is* are laid down. (Meek, 1990)

Finding out that the ground gives way is for Barney, then, seeing things for himself; he is moving into the arena of making things happen, as, in his or her own way, is the imaginative reader. Making things happen in order to learn from that experience is at the centre of more than science attainment targets for the National Curriculum. The 'exercise of consciousness', whether painful or otherwise, is a necessary element in self-definition. The 'active participant' notion predates the narrow concept of a National Curriculum. The mistaken assumption that the experience of reading can be assessed by a Standard Assessment Task (SAT) is grounded in the fashionable assumption that education is in all respects susceptible of measurement along a line or path of progress or by sequential number. Active participation is at least as valid in scientific exploration as in learning through literature in the primary school. The tool of the story is an irreplaceably rich source across the curriculum and must remain central to the models of learning offered in schools. The chart shows how a simple topic model can remain story-centred and also meet the various demands of cross-curricular inquiry made by the National Curriculum.

Having said this, the requirement in earlier versions of the English programmes of study for Key Stage 2 that children should 'be shown how to read different kinds of materials in different ways, for example, "search" reading to find a scientific or geographical fact' (DES, 1990, p. 31) should not distract from the need for a continuing emphasis upon stimulating the desire on the part of the individual child to continue to read through personal choice. Increased levels of personal discrimination can be arrived at only through the exercise of individual judgment. While literature undoubtedly needs to be read for information and while more coherent teaching strategies can and should be devised to this end, the central element of enjoyment through personal reading needs to be continually reemphasized, if development toward different kinds of reading for an increasing range of purposes is to be consolidated.

Fortunately, there is ample evidence to support this view from other areas of humanities. We are reminded, for instance, that visual thinking requires 'the ability to see visual shapes as images of the patterns of forces that underlie our existence — the functioning of minds, of bodies or machines, the structure of societies or ideas.' We also have Applebee's view (1978) that 'the younger child relies on poetic techniques, reexperiencing the story in the process of retelling it', to support our view of the relationship between reading and learning (p. 105). We can also go back to Stig if we need further evidence.

Barney, with nothing to do and nowhere else to go, crawls to the edge of the chalk pit and peers down into its depths:

> Far below was the bottom of the pit. The dump. Barney could see strange bits of wreckage among the moss and elder bushes and nettles. Was that the steering wheel of a ship? The tail of an aeroplane? At least there was a real bicycle. Barney felt sure he could make it go if only he could get at it. They didn't let him have a bicycle.
>
> Barney wished he was at the bottom of the pit.
>
> And the ground gave way. (King, 1963, p. 8)

I believe this passage raises important issues about the desirability of teaching meaning in text, in tension with the need to acknowledge the child's capacity for individual interpretation. We need to remember that effective learning is often learning that takes place when there is no mediation between reader and text; explication has its purposes, but if explication negates or distorts the reader's meeting with the text or implies a hierarchy of readings of that text, into which an individual must be 'initiated', then a common human response is to seek for meaning elsewhere than in that meeting with the text. Children will often then choose not to wish to continue to read for reading's sake, but to rely upon other external forms of motivation. Reading becomes a task rather than a pleasure and moves away from an engagement with primary experience toward considerations of theoretical models of literature irrelevant to and mismatched with the developmental needs of the reader. Thus the ways in which teachers approach and use literature need careful thought in the context of National Curriculum requirements if the act of reading is not to become largely or wholly a reaction to the requirements of some adult readers rather than the expression of choice made by a young reader. This point can be made in another way:

> Art works best when it remains unacknowledged. It observes that shapes and objects and events, by displaying their own nature, can evoke those deeper and simpler powers in which man recognises himself. It is one of the rewards we earn for thinking by what we see. (Arnheim, 1969, p. 315)

Sharing the experience of others takes us into that arena of empathy which is both fiction's cause and its method. Thus an incident in a chalk pit can sensitize the reader to 'this miraculous ability of man to be disturbed by another being's misfortunes, to feel joy about another being's happiness, to experience another's fate as one's own'. The opportunity to move between spectator and participant roles in retelling the story is part of Applebee's more general point about the power of reading in itself.

Tomorrow's readers will, I hope, remain free to make their own assessments, to find out for themselves that if you go too near the edge, the ground gives way.

In making connections between an imaginatively figured (if narrow) social perspective and the world of 'being and doing' which children inhabit, King made an important contribution to our understanding of what it is to 'pretend' or to 'make believe', and significantly reaffirmed the possibility of doing so. Although the world of Barney is of a different order from that of Max and Bernard (Sendak, 1967; McKee, 1980), King signalled the imaginative opportunities available in considering the position of the 'lone' child and highlighted (before Briggs (1978) had the opportunity of doing so most spectacularly) the need for a pretend-friend who could modify and extend experience beyond the normal, literally taking the child to a different order of experience which is wholly personal in character and which has resonances for us all. In engaging in this task, he is among those writers who have examined the relationship between the experience of childhood, definitions of 'the child' and broader issues of 'social order' which are addressed in seminal texts. I should now like to consider some issues arising from other texts which raise broader social implications that teachers may wish to bear in mind when they approach fiction in the classroom and the ways in which it can be perceived in a broader cultural context. Consideration of such issues may well help inform practice at the stage of planning the range of literary experience offered to children as they mature and develop in their reading journeys, and as they move from primary education to the different world of the secondary school.

Childhood: Self — Definition and Social Values

It is not necessary to undertake a study of *The Jolly Postman* to have a sense of the social importance attached to the taking of tea. There is a seminal description in an earlier work which, although much quoted, is worth giving again:

'Well, I'd hardly finished the first verse', said the Hatter, 'when the Queen jumped up and bawled out, "He's murdering the time! Off with his head!"'

'How dreadfully savage!' exclaimed Alice.

'And ever since that', the Hatter went on in a mournful tone, 'he won't do a thing I ask! It's always six o'clock now.'

A bright idea came into Alice's head. 'Is that the reason so many tea-things are put out here?' she asked.

'Yes, that's it', said the Hatter with a sigh: 'it's always tea-time, and we've no time to wash the things between whiles'.

'Then you keep moving round, I suppose?' said Alice.

'Exactly so', said the Hatter 'as the things get used up'.

'But what happens when you come to the beginning again?' Alice ventured to ask.

'Suppose we change the subject', the March Hare interrupted, yawning. 'I'm getting tired of this. I vote the young lady tells us a story.' (Carroll, 1955, p. 79)

Part of Alice's general education in *Alice in Wonderland* is to be inducted into the social mores of the mad tea-party and the new social world in which she finds herself during the course of the story; she is obliged to review her notion of self, her idea of 'manners' and general social behaviour, and she learns that the rationale she lives by in the 'normal' world has to be thoroughly reconstituted in the world of 'wonder' in which she finds herself. Alice's education involves learning the rules of the new game being played. She only partly succeeds. Shortly after the above scene she leaves the table, after what she regards as another instance of the Hatter's 'piece of rudeness' to her. Carroll tells us that 'she looked back once or twice, half hoping that they would call after her'. She then resolves never to go *there* again. As readers, we know that Alice was seen by those at the table as a social transgressor, yet she strongly feels it is she who has been transgressed against. Part of the concern of the book, indicative of an interest displayed in much well-known nineteenth century writing for children, and a theme extensively developed in later children's fiction, is to examine the relationship between the self, value systems and the accepted social order.

The literature of childhood and youth contains many examples of the individual who transgresses the normative social order and who has to deal with the experiences this transgression releases, whether for good or ill. Much of the dramatic interest for the reader of such works lies in the unfolding of and resolution to such dilemmas, centring around major learning experiences of childhood and adolescence. A common twentieth century concern, which I argue is shared by many authors (and eagerly anticipated by many readers), is to present and develop situations in which the reader is invited to share in others' learning experiences in fiction. It is perhaps what helps make modern children's literature a literature *of* children, as distinct from a literature written *at* children, as so much nineteenth century English and American literature was inclined to be.

Here, I hope to develop some tentative suggestions as to a primary and central concern in the literature of childhood and youth. I take this concern to be with the expression, development and redefinition of the self's identity in relation to a broader social or societal value framework. I see the central characters in the literature as operating within or modifying or rejecting such respective social norms as exist in their worlds, testing the bounds of the possible. I believe that this tendency in the representation of childhood may be interestingly linked to earlier developments in fiction, and in particular to the tensions generated in the literature of alienation in the twentieth century.

It is thus possible to argue developments in representation in children's literature as not only socially and culturally conditioned, but as linked to our more general perceptions of the relation between the young learner and the changing world in which the learner learns, that is, to our understanding of cultural relativism in post-modern society.

Modern children's literature is therefore, in Meek's sense, teaching children how to learn about themselves as well as the wider world which they inhabit as part of the social order. What is of interest in this are the techniques and strategies various authors use to handle such concepts. Meek (1988) has, as is so often the case, already made this clear:

> The authors who exploit their art, and the illustrators who make pictures with secrets, link what children know, partly know, and are learning about in the world, to ways of presenting the world in books. These presentations are lifelike, that is, the reader senses their relation to psychological reality. But they are also scandalous, excessive, daring possibilities that the real world, the world of adults, might not endure, but which are real to children (*ibid.*, p. 19).

Examples demonstrating the truth of this are known to us all. Part of the popularity of Salinger's *The Catcher in the Rye* (1951), for example, stems from its central concern with the tensions between the developing adolescent and the social framework which that adolescent is reacting against. To many, Holden still seems 'scandalous' and 'excessive' today, yet he represents a 'fifties culture clash which speaks to other generations. Early in the book he is in trouble again for failing at school. Here we see his cynicism at work as he is questioned by a senior teacher, Mr. Spencer:

> 'What did Dr. Thurmer say to you, boy? I understand you had quite a little chat.'
> 'Yes, we did. We really did. I was in his office for around two hours, I guess.'
> 'What'd he say to you?'
> 'Oh . . . well, about Life being a game and all. And how you should play it according to the rules. He was pretty nice about it. I mean he didn't hit the ceiling or anything. He just kept talking about Life being a game and all. You know.'
> 'Life *is* a game, boy. Life *is* a game that one plays according to the rules.'

'Yes, sir. I know it is. I know it.'

Game, my ass. Some game. If you get on the side where all the hot-shots are, then it's a game, all right — I'll admit that. But if you get on the *other* side, where there aren't any hot-shots, then what's a game about it? Nothing. No game. (*ibid.*, pp. 12–13)

Holden has already begun to accommodate his views to his sense of the social order; he is fully aware of the mismatch between the public and private worlds he inhabits and of the need to present an acceptable persona to that public world, despite any personal doubts he has as to the contrary. Holden thinks he knows the rules, believes he can pull the strings. He plays off his private against his public morality as best he can, trying as he does so to come to terms with, reach a better understanding of, the social conditions which govern his world. In this, he is another in a long line of protagonists for whom self-definition within the boundaries of a broader social framework is an urgent priority. The crises he goes through in this process have an immediate appeal to the reader because they are common crises with which we can easily identify; for his generation Holden as the 'angry young man' takes on a totemic significance.

It is a truism of critical discussion that the representation of childhood in literature for children did not significantly exist before the mid-nineteenth century. By this I mean that the concept of childhood and adolescence was not in the popular arena until this time; there is a sense in which, because it is in book form, it still remains outside that arena even now, in what is becoming a post-book world. The majority of children in the western world do now, however, have relatively easy access to texts, books among them. The chances of their encountering representations of childhood in such texts are high. What kinds of representation are they then likely to find? By looking briefly at some well-known texts, I shall attempt to draw some tentative suggestions.

Over recent years, it is arguable that texts have focussed on the representation of important (if sometimes everyday) experiences of children. If, for example, we think of such texts as *Not Now, Bernard, Nobody's Family is Going to Change, The Snowman, The Turbulent Term of Tyke Tyler,* the Katie Morag series, etc., we can see that what they most obviously have in common is the representation of experience as seen through the eyes of a specific boy or girl living his/her everyday life. There is, in some respects, nothing new in this. Alcott and Twain, it could be argued, were doing the same in their time, as have others before and since. Townsend has shown, however, that the shift from the upper middle class focus to the working class and thence to the 'classless' protagonist focus, which has characterized the development of children's literature over time, has been in part a response by different authors to their notions of the reality of the experience of the 'average' reader, involving a concern to catalogue the changing face of society and the view of the child presented as part of that society.

One important element in the development of modern children's literature, it can be argued, has been a move from the description of childhood, as seen from the perspective of the external adult, to the internalized presentation of experience that we find in many picture and story books produced over the last thirty years or so. This 'psychologically' based representation of childhood, as it may be generally termed for the sake of convenience, is characteristic of a developing strain in children's literature in the period beginning in the 'sixties, and marks a shift in the process of trying to capture the experience of childhood in such a way as to step inside the child, as it were, and to portray the internal emotions, conflicts and drama of the child's felt experience. This is one reason why, though there are many other points of similarity, the writing of Alcott and Twain is quite different in character from that of the modern children's writer, in its manner as well as its matter.

I would wish to argue that other recent texts, such as those I have mentioned, also add to our understanding of the child in its modern or contemporary social context. The way in which the child is constructed informs our perception of that individual personality and also of our relationship as readers to the situation of that child. For example, in one sense Bernard, in McKee's book (1980), seems not to exist for his parents; in another, he is lonely, alienated in a non-comprehending adult world, where he can live only in his imagination. The book is both comic and horrific; Bernard tries to come to terms with 'reality' in his own way, by escaping into his imagination, living out his concerns in a way that is not possible within the 'adult' boundaries of his own home.

Sendak (1963), of course, has been this way before. The wild things we know are inside each of us. Thus we can cross time and space, literally step out of ourselves and become some other thing. With Max in *Where the Wild Things Are*, we can sail off 'through night and day and in and out of weeks and almost over a year to where the wild things are.' You will remember that Max's mother called him 'WILD THING' and that 'Max said "I'LL EAT YOU UP".' Bernard too in McKee's book is eaten up. We are told that 'The monster ate Bernard up, every bit.' Without developing the Freudian interpretations of such incidents, it is relevant that part of the process of becoming our other self involves the temporary destruction of the 'normal', socialized self as a necessary preliminary to the release of inhibitions usually held in check.

The strategies employed in both these texts ensure the encapsulation of the 'beasts' in a broader, normalizing social framework. Part of the tremendous attraction of both books lies in their sustained tension of social challenge, their ultimate testing of the boundaries which enclose their central characters. In this context, one of the questions that is commonly asked, directly or indirectly in children's literature, is whether in fact we do become some *other* thing, or whether, transformed, we merely manifest another face of our real self, another part of the human psyche. Since we must learn to compromise, we learn also to control that unruly, wild part of us, the monster inside. Personally, I can see no easy division to be made in such texts between the 'realistic' portrayal of life on the one hand and the use of 'fantasy' or escapism on the other. I would argue that these books succeed in part because they move between such worlds, between naturalism and dream, across the ordinary and the monstrous contexts.

In his very useful book, Stephens (1992) goes some way to further elaborate such issues:

> In her paper 'The Art of Realism', cited earlier, Jill Paton Walsh remarked that 'A work of fantasy compels a reader into a metaphoric frame of mind. A work of realism, on the other hand, permits very literal-minded readings, even downright stupid ones' (1981, p. 38), and goes on to suggest that the nature of realism is to permit readings of a fictional work as if it were a transcription of actuality which yielded only a single meaning. The kind of over-simplified view of discourse and of world she describes is, it must be suspected, countenanced in some realistic texts, though it can equally be said that metaphoricity is not in itself a guarantee of more complex reading. If fantasy is treated simply as escape, metaphoric utterance will be treated as merely another univocal plane. Conversely, realism has many narrative strategies with which it can as readily 'compel . . . a metaphorical frame of mind'. (*ibid.*, p. 272)

In such works as *Alice, Stig, Where the Wild Things Are* and *Not Now, Bernard*, we are taught to experience the relativity of time as well as of emotion and of the larger social order. With the central characters, we test out the respective boundaries in each in the secure knowledge of an embracing social framework. It may, moreover, be relevant that in the twentieth century texts cited above these central characters are male and the books concerned have quite distinct notions of male ideology attaching to them. Neil Campbell picks up this issue in his chapter.

The ideological context of children's literature, indeed, provides an interesting and developing source of enquiry into the fictional processes at work in the representation of childhood. The construction of childhood in text cannot be viewed separately from consideration of such ideologies (see Stephens (1992) for a recent interesting view of language and ideology).

Looking briefly at some texts to see the ways in which the child is socially constructed in picture and story books, it can be seen that the territory is a fruitful one for further investigation. *The Snowman* (Briggs, 1978), for example, has proved extraordinarily popular since its publication, yet there has been relatively little in the literature that examines the reasons for its popularity. Here a solitary child, having made a snowman, goes to bed at night, then wakes and/or dreams of adventures he and the snowman share when the latter comes to life as the boy's 'friend'. When the boy wakes up the next morning, he finds the snowman has melted away. All that remains are the hat, scarf and pieces of coal the boy used to construct him. Townsend rightly says this book is 'beautiful, moving and sad'. Part of the appeal of the book, as Fry (1985) has shown, lies in the pathos of the ending, the sense of loss the boy feels and the sense the reader has that part of the human condition is to strive for the unattainable. The lesson is wonderfully taught here to early readers through a wordless text. The reader empathizes with the boy because she too has had that experience in her formative years. Metaphorically, the book may be seen as an essay on transience; as such, it has a significance outside of any specific regional culture. The book's success, it seems to me, stems in part from the fact that it draws upon our universal sense of 'if only', that it appeals to the universal desire that things might be different from the way they in fact are.

This wish that things were of a different order has been continually reflected in the history of literature for childhood and youth. With Meg in *Little Women* we can wish to accelerate the process of time, in order that she has her silk, or we can wish to postpone the passing of time, as in *The Snowman*, so that the snowman may live on. Both texts offer a learning experience for the reader that cannot be taught elsewhere. Part of the strength of Briggs' book is that it goes beyond language to strike chords in all of us, to both reflect and condition our social response.

Other texts which have appeared in recent years have similarly raised issues of the child's self-definition. Among the more notable of these is Burningham's *Granpa* (1984) which has deservedly gained much attention for its innovatory style and its treatment of death. By inviting the reader to read between the text and the illustrations, to infer causality in the narrative, the book operates on a variety of levels. For the present, I wish to refer to it briefly as another example of the group of texts investigating the complexities residing in the notion of the self, social relationships, time and loss, which I take to be a central motif in the literature. The little girl's realization that her Granpa was 'once a baby as well' is part of the book's emphasis on the learning their relationship stimulates. The text is centred around both real and imagined worlds of the old and young; through this process the young girl is assimilated culturally to understand and accept new concepts. Among these is the education she receives in the socially acceptable. Learning to understand, for instance, that 'that was not a nice thing to say to granpa' is part of that education. She finally comes to terms with the concept of death at the end of the book. Again here the sense of loss is an educative experience for her, as it has been for other protagonists. The continuity of the life cycle is emphasized in the last caption by the depiction of the little girl pushing a baby in a pram. Hunt has rightly pointed out *Granpa's* originality in the treatment of such issues:

> But I would argue that its very complexity, together with the relinquishing of any authorial control in the verbal text, makes *Granpa* closer to the comprehension patterns of an orally based reader than the vast majority of texts that set out to be 'for children'. As such, it contains serious questions for critics. (Hunt, 1991, p. 195)

One can point to a number of other examples of variations on the theme. Hedderwick's *Katie Morag Delivers the Mail* (1984) is another such. In this book the young Katie helps out her parents by delivering parcels to houses on the Isle of Struay. She slips on a stone in a pool, smudging the addresses on the parcels. She delivers the parcels, not knowing their correct destinations. Finally she delivers a parcel to her Grannie, having been earlier told that Grannie's parcel was the one with the red label. Grannie helps Katie sort out the parcels she has already delivered, restoring them to their rightful owners, and Katie then takes Grannie back home for tea, apprehensive of her reception were she to arrive alone. She is surprised to find a warm reception:

> Katie Morag hid behind Grannie as they walked in the kitchen door but, to her surprise, everyone was smiling. Liam had cut his tooth at last and all was calm. 'Thank you for helping out today, Katie Morag', said Mrs McColl. 'Isn't she good, Grannie?'
> 'Och aye', said Grannie with a smile as she looked at Katie Morag. 'She's very good at sorting things out, is our Katie Morag.' And she said no more. (*ibid.*)

The tacit understanding between Grannie and Katie that is sealed with this social approbation marks Katie's realization that she is dependent on Grannie and can trust her implicitly not to reveal the 'frightened and ashamed' Katie Morag who 'did a silly thing' earlier that day and who had to be rescued by Grannie as a result. Katie learns that adults are not always threatening and hostile, that the social framework is built on mutual understandings of the private and the public, and in this case on love.

A more detailed treatment of the handling of the theme of self and social order in children's literature requires a separate book. I hope, however, I have briefly sketched out the theme's appearance and significance in some recent works in sufficient detail to outline the possibilities arising from further study. Neil Campbell's chapter is, I believe, an interesting example of how texts may be read in more significant and theoretical detail, in terms of the ways in which authors create socially bounded worlds in which fictional characters are located and developed, and in which they can be seen to test the bounds of what is possible in their worlds.

The construction of the child or adolescent is a fascinating area for further comparative work, offering a range of cultural dimensions. *The Catcher in the Rye, Nobody's Family is Going to Change, Your Friend Rebecca. The Village by The Sea* and a host of other texts raise important questions about the social construction of the child and the ideologies of literature for children as developed over recent decades.

It would, moreover, be particularly illuminating to examine in what ways the representation of childhood and adolescence as portrayed through the presentation of Stephen Dedalus in *A Portrait of the Artist as a Young Man* (1915), for example, differs from the portrayal we find in the more recent fiction of childhood and adolescence. Can one, for instance, trace a developmental line in the literature of childhood and adolescence over recent years? In what ways do the authors construct social realities around the self, relationships, time and loss in such texts as *A Kind of Loving, Across the Barricades, Waterland,* or *The Buddha of Suburbia,* and what can one learn from the chronological spread of such texts in terms of the value systems they reflect with respect to youth, as they chronicle the second half of the twentieth century? There can be little doubt that the documentation of the adolescent experience remains central to much quality recent and contemporary fiction, whether targeted at the child or at an adult readership.

Conclusion

In this brief, but relatively wide-ranging chapter, I have quite deliberately extended the treatment of issues beyond the range of material likely to be used at Key Stage 2 in order to emphasize the continuity of theme which underlines much children's literature of the nineteenth and twentieth centuries, irrespective of its social and cultural provenance. In doing so, I hope I have suggested some practical ways in which teachers might organize their work to involve, stimulate and sustain reading interest amongst young children. I hope I have also made it clear that the study of the book is from my perspective only a starting-point on the road to a wider literacy, and that book-based approaches must take account of and be contextualized by wider social issues.

To attempt to emphasize the world of print at the expense of acknowledging the everyday experience of young people is a futile exercise which will fail if narrowly pursued; books must be seen as part of a wider communications network which we inhabit and which informs all that we speak, read and write in schools, as everywhere else. We in education need to constantly remind ourselves that life is larger than the world of formal education; if we cannot find ways of acknowledging this in our primary school practice, we will provide only a limited education to tomorrow's citizens, even if in doing so we claim to be meeting all the requirements of the revised orders for English in the National Curriculum!

Our collective interpretation of 'education' must be both broader and stronger than that contained within the revised English orders for the National Curriculum. It must rest upon collaborative enterprise, shared experience, mutual respect; purposeful but enjoyable exploration, and the development of 'critical readers' engaged in a lifelong journey of analysis, understanding and satisfaction through learning. It is, of course, perfectly legitimate to use established texts from the past alongside more contemporary products, but we must use them to consider our present and our future worlds, rather than as kinds of 'bench-marks' of quality which we assume to have universal and timeless significance.

Books are important, but they cannot *in themselves* be regarded as defining literacy in the modern world. And because books are irreplaceable assets, we need a sharper sense of what we can and cannot do with them, and of where else we can find relevant and important material which should inform good practice in our teaching. To do this, educators need to learn an important lesson which it seems has not yet been learned: we need to be ourselves but we also need to allow others to be themselves:

> As for the duty to educate, it consists fundamentally in teaching children to read, in initiating them in literature, and in giving them the means to judge freely whether or not they experience the 'need for books'. For, while it may be perfectly admissible that someone should reject reading, it's intolerable that he should be rejected — or think himself rejected — by it.
>
> It's an enormous source of sadness, causing a solitude within solitude, to be excluded from books — and that includes those who can do without. (Pennac, 1994)

Notes

1 The concept of the 'reading journey' is developed by Jenny Marum in chapter 6.
2 I am referring here to Margaret Meek's essay (1988) *How Texts Teach What Readers Learn*, Stroud, Thimble Press.
3 I am referring here to versions of the Red Riding Hood story. See Scieszka's picture of granny in bed in *The True Story of the Three Little Pigs*.

References

AHLBERG, J. and A. (1986) *The Jolly Postman*, London, Heinemann.
ALTER, R. (1975) *Partial Magic*, Berkeley, CA, University of California.
APPLEBEE, A.N. (1978) *The Child's Concept of Story*, Chicago, IL, University of Chicago Press.
ARNHEIM, R. (1969) *Visual Thinking*, Los Angeles, CA, University of California Press.
BOOTH, W. (1961) *The Rhetoric of Fiction*, Chicago, IL, University of Chicago Press.
BRIGGS, R. (1978) *The Snowman*, London, Hamish Hamilton.
CARROLL, L. (1955) *Alice's Adventures in Wonderland*, London, Heirloom Library.
CARTER, A. (1979) *The Bloody Chamber*, London, Victor Gollancz.
DES (1990) *English in the National Curriculum*, London, HMSO.
DFE (1995) *The Revised Orders for English in the National Curriculum*, London, HMSO.
FRY, D. (1985) *Children Talk About Books: Seeing Themselves as Readers*, Milton Keynes, Open University Press.
HEDDERWICK, M. (1984) *Katie Morag Delivers the Mail*, London, Bodley Head.
HUNT, P. (1991) *Criticism, Theory and Children's Literature*, Oxford, Basil Blackwell.
HUTCHINS, P. (1968) *Rosie's Walk*, London, Bodley Head.
KING, C. (1963) *Stig of the Dump*, Harmondsworth, Penguin.
LA ROCHEFOUCAULD, F. DUC DE (1959) (trans Tancock, L.) *Maxims*, Harmondsworth, Penguin.

McKee, D. (1980) *Not Now, Bernard*, London, Andersen Press.

Meek, M. (1988) *How Texts Teach What Readers Learn*, Stroud, Thimble Press.

Meek, M. (1990) 'What counts as evidence in theories of children's literature', in Hunt, P. (Ed) *Children's Literature — The Development of Criticism*, London, Routledge.

Pennac, D. (1994) (trans Gunn, D.) *Reads Like a Novel*, London, Quartet Books.

Pinsent, P. (Ed) (1993) *The Power of the Page*, London, David Fulton.

Salinger, J.D. (1951) *The Catcher in the Rye*, Harmondsworth, Penguin Books.

Scieszka, J. (1991) *The True Story of the Three Little Pigs*, Harmondsworth, Penguin.

Scieszka, J. (1993) *The Stinky Cheese Man and Other Fairly Stupid Tales*, Harmondsworth, Penguin.

Sendak, M. (1967) *Where the Wild Things Are*, London, Bodley Head.

Stephens, J. (1992) *Language and Ideology in Children's Fiction*, London, Longman.

Townsend, J.R. (1983) *Written for Children*, Harmondsworth, Kestrel.

Chapter 6

Encouraging Wider Reading: Classroom Strategies (11–16)

Jenny Marum

'There is no frigate like a book to take us lands away'. (Dickinson, E.)

'The main emphasis should be on the encouragement of wider reading in order to develop independent, responsive and enthusiastic readers.' (SCAA, 1994). Where is the teacher of literature who would disagree? Tragically this laudable statement from the revised orders for English in the National Curriculum is followed by a list of pre-twentieth century texts, the prescription of which mitigates against the successful implementation in schools of such an aim. The National Writing Project (1990) developed many successful initiatives in the teaching of writing in schools from an initial consideration of 'What Writers Need'. Perhaps a useful starting point for an investigation into the teaching of reading is a consideration of what readers need.

What Readers Need

Different readers probably have different needs but there seem to be some important common essentials. Developing readers need time to gain experience of reading. They need opportunities to read alone, silently; together in small groups; aloud to the teacher, when there is time for discussion; aloud to the class to share favourite pieces; and together as a whole class for a common reading experience. Readers also need their own choice of reading material; occasions when they can choose to read familiar texts or old favourites and other times when they are challenged by texts which require greater concentration. Readers also need open access to a wide variety of genres: stories, picture books, poetry, graphic novels, newspapers, comics, magazines, information texts. They need access to this material in classrooms, in libraries, in displays, in bookclubs, bookfairs, bookshops and, especially, at home. In summary, readers need the freedom to undertake their own reading journey:

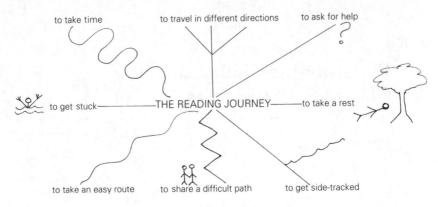

Faced with the contradictions of pupils' needs and the demands of the new orders, what can the teacher do? In this chapter I hope to suggest ways in which teachers can fulfil the requirements for teaching prescribed pre-twentieth century literature and still continue to achieve the first aim of most secondary English departments, to promote reading for enjoyment.[1]

The Class Reader

In the light of the Warwick survey,[2] an examination of current practice necessitates a consideration of the place of class readers in the English curriculum. The debate concerning the use of the shared text in the secondary classroom is long-standing. An early ILEA English Centre publication presented both sides of the argument. 'Some teachers . . . believe that no single book could possibly cater for the diverse interests and levels of maturity and ways of reading in one class . . . On the other hand many teachers . . . felt that the class reader offered the possibility of a shared pleasure involving experience of books (and ways of responding to and thinking about books) which otherwise may not take place' (The English Centre, 1978). A later consideration of the use of class readers in a booklet entitled *Fiction* (The English Centre, 1986) produced the following rationale for shared reading, which I feel would be both understood and supported by the vast majority of English teachers:

1 To assist in the discovery of pleasure in texts;
   — offering support to less confident and reluctant readers who might otherwise not read at all;
   — introducing a variety of books to the independent reader; and thus whetting pupils' appetites for further reading.
2 To provide a shared experience of narrative and a common area of reference from which other classroom work can draw.
3 To provide contexts for pupils to identify and share their own experiences, ideas, emotions, and attitudes and try to make sense of them.

4 To provide contexts for pupils to share and evaluate situations, characters and events outside their immediate experience.
5 To assist in the development of children's understanding of social and moral concerns.
6 To offer texts that represent a variety of settings and characterization e.g. both female and male protagonists, based in a variety of cultural and historical settings.
7 To provide a shared focus for the development of pupils' understanding of literary form.

More recently, the research carried out by the University of Warwick for the National Curriculum Council compared the practice of the teaching of reading in Key Stages 1, 2 and 3.[3] In Key Stage 3, the predominant practice found by the research team was the reading aloud of a shared text, usually preceded and followed by whole class or group discussion. This approach, whilst valuable for the reasons listed above, means many teachers may devote much of a term to the reading of a lengthy text, a practice which those who espouse 'reading for real' would not readily support. In 1993, many heads of department in the survey were complaining that the necessity to study a Shakespeare play and the Key Stage 3 Anthology (SEAC, 1993) had resulted in the abandonment of existing schemes of work and the inability to fulfil all of the requirements of the National Curriculum English Orders. It is not my intention to defend the compulsory study of either the play or the anthology but there is perhaps evidence here that in teachers' concerns to do the best for their pupils, many felt obliged to teach to the test; their reliance upon whole class teaching as a way of working may well have resulted in the sacrifice of their own professional choice of material to meet the needs and interests of their pupils.

There is a danger that the extensive requirements for prescribed reading in the new orders will swallow much of English curriculum time, already eroded in many schools by pressure from other National Curriculum subject requirements. In particular, for the reasons I have given, teachers may now need to review their use of class readers. The reading aloud of poetry and short stories is far less time-consuming than the reading of novels but can fulfil many of the same objectives that teachers value in a teacher-led approach. Similarly, pupils' oral participation in the shared reading of plays contributes both to their understanding of the text as drama and to their enjoyment of it. Consequently, my focus in this article will be upon strategies for introducing pupils to the larger problems posed in the teaching of pretwentieth century novels, whilst simultaneously avoiding the prospect of English classrooms dominated, for example, by the struggle to share all 646 pages of the Penguin edition of Wilkie Collins' *The Woman in White*.

In the Warwick survey, those departments which did not organize schemes of work around whole class shared texts designed units of work around defined themes. This kind of approach at Key Stage 3 helps to familiarize pupils with the thematic approach which is common to several of the literature syllabuses available for study at Key Stage 4. Linking of texts within a theme also helps to prepare pupils for the requirement to make connections and comparisons between texts in order to achieve the higher grades at GCSE. Referring to the teaching of pre-twentieth century novels, the revised orders state: 'Pupils should be encouraged to appreciate the distinctive qualities of these works through activities which emphasise the interest and pleasure of reading them, rather than necessitating a detailed, line-by-line study.' (SCAA, 1994). A thematic approach involving pupils in such activities might be one answer to the problem presented by these texts.

Group Reading

The prescribed lists suggest several themes which might appeal to groups of pupils: the supernatural, villains, mystery, adventure, love, fate, growing up, etc. Such themes could encompass not only the pre-twentieth century requirements but contemporary approaches in teenage fiction, non-literary material and the media. Exploration of a chosen theme by a small group of pupils is a useful way of dividing the workload of an over-crowded English curriculum, and the necessity for groups of pupils to share information and responses provides a real audience in feedback sessions. A group assignment folder can offer suggestions for ways of responding to the texts allocated to pupils and the group can organize its own rota of work for completion of tasks (see appendix 1). Groups can be given responsibility for classroom display areas and given regular opportunities to provide oral updates on the progress of their work for the rest of the class. The organisation of such group work presents a major preparatory task for the teacher and requires considerable classroom management in the initial stages, but once in progress offers the distinct advantage of giving freedom from the class-teaching role and provides the time to support individuals and groups of pupils through the more challenging tasks. In my experience the sense of independence this approach gives to pupils helps to engage their interest and often proves highly motivating.

In 1990, as a newly-appointed Head of Department, I was concerned to set up a system which would provide a bridge between long-established opportunities for private individual reading and teacher-led whole class response to a shared text. It seemed important to ensure that pupils were not given the impression that only literature presented to the class by the teacher was worthy of discussion. When I proposed the introduction of an entitlement curriculum which included at least one group reading experience per year, teachers in the department raised understandable counter-arguments. Their concerns ranged around problems of classroom management, the recording of individual pupils' contributions to a group project, resourcing implications, the provision of suitable activities for a wide range of texts, support for less confident readers and, not least, a clear understanding of their own role in such a project.

Departments will find their own ways of dealing with these concerns. My department decided to devote the first half of a seventy minute lesson to silent reading or writing activities and the second half to collaborative tasks of various kinds. This was simply a way of providing pupils who were unused to this method of working with a sufficiently disciplined structure to ensure that all pupils spent time reading, even if they were reluctant or unable to complete the reading at home. A system which required pupils to log their own contributions to the project in a self-assessment record completed at regular intervals solved the monitoring problem and a pooling of teachers' ideas soon produced a bank of materials from which pupils could select those activities most appropriate for the texts they were investigating. Resourcing is often not the problem it appears. Most departments will find their stock cupboards full of little-thumbed novels which never quite worked as whole class readers but which might well appeal to selected groups of pupils, and investment in a few copies of the classic texts listed in the revised orders will make far smaller holes in department budgets than would the purchase of sufficient numbers for whole class reading. The problems faced by less confident readers can be solved to some extent by imaginative expenditure of the Special Educational Needs budget, which is now to be clearly identified in schools' expenditure budgets, as specified in the legislated Code of Practice (DFE, 1994).

A recent, extremely successful initiative in my own authority has exploited teachers' willingness to capitalize upon the ever-increasing numbers of audio-books for use with less confident readers. The aims of the Enhanced Reading Project (Humberside LEA, 1993/94) were to extend pupils' interest in books and to broaden their experience by departing from the private, silent reading lesson. In this scheme, pupils rotate around a series of reading activities which involve them in individual, paired and small group reading, sometimes supported by an audio-tape recording of the text. When reading aloud, pupils make their own decisions about how the reading is to be shared, for example, by simultaneous or alternating readers, or by dividing the text into narrative and dialogue. Pupils also tape-record their reading in order to engage in self-assessment of their own delivery. This has been a particularly successful way of supporting less confident readers and engaging reluctant readers in purposeful activities related to texts.

Investment in a few sturdy tape-recorders with headphones (or a loan from a friendly modern foreign languages department) can give groups of pupils access to texts which they might find difficulty in reading unaided. The paucity of the language used in any graded reader edition in comparison with the original classic text makes this approach with such pupils infinitely preferable. For example, teachers investigating the place of the supernatural in literature might be tempted to use a recently published script adaptation of *A Christmas Carol*. A comparison of the original text with the scripted version of the section describing the arrival of the Ghost of Christmas Yet to Come illustrates what is lost in such a dilution:

The Phantom slowly, gravely, silently approached. When it came near him, Scrooge bent down upon his knee; for in the very air through which this Spirit moved it seemed to scatter gloom and mystery.

It was shrouded in a deep black garment which concealed its head, its face, its form, and left nothing of it visible save one out-stretched hand. But for this it would have been difficult to detach its figure from the night, and separate it from the darkness by which it was surrounded.

He felt it was tall and stately when it came beside him, and that its mysterious presence filled him with a solemn dread. He knew no more, for the Spirit neither spoke nor moved.

'I am in the presence of the Ghost of Christmas Yet to Come?' said Scrooge . . . (Dickens, 1991a)

Perhaps pupils could be asked to explain what is lost in this version:

Scrooge is utterly cast down. Church bells become distorted and a slight mist begins to rise. Chilling music as a hooded robed figure starts slowly to enter. It should have a blind man's mask hooding its eyes. If we see anything it is only the mouth. From the robe a thin figure beckons.
Scrooge: I am in the presence of Christmas yet to come? (Holman, 1994)

How much better to allow a group of pupils to read or hear the original text and write their own dramatized version or filmscript in response to it!

Audio versions of less freely available texts can easily be 'home-made' by sixth formers, visiting students, colleagues and pupils' parents. Their value in terms of the independence given to less confident readers is enormous.

Boys and English

Another concern which many teachers raise when faced with the prospect of teaching the prescribed lists at Key Stages 3 and 4 is the specific issue of boys' attitudes to and achievement in English in secondary schools. The latest GCSE and 'A' level results are testament to the fact that English is no longer the only subject in which girls have more examination success than boys. Nonetheless, teachers of English are understandably unwilling to allow half of their clientele to perceive themselves as reluctant readers and anxious to interest them in what, in the revised orders, appears to be an even more alienating curriculum. The pamphlet, *Boys and English* (OFSTED, 1993), raises many questions relating to the criteria for setting in schools which invariably places more boys than girls in lower English sets. The conclusion to the report blames teacher expectations for the lower achievement of boys and lists amongst the ingredients for boys' success a greater emphasis on: speaking and listening activities; the use of computers for word-processing and desk-top publishing; lessons about language use and variety; research and retrieval skills; media education and the use of non-literary texts. The report found 'potential in all of *these areas* for improving boys' performance in English' (*ibid.*, paras 123 and 124). A warning note was sounded in the report's penultimate paragraph: 'However, these new emphases should enhance rather than replace a central concern for wide reading of high quality, including pre-twentieth century literature. The continuing need is to ensure that boys benefit from the affective aspects of the English Curriculum. This should be a central issue for policy-making in English departments.' (*ibid.*, para. 125).

Not surprisingly, the inspection also found differences between the reading preferences of boys and girls. Horror, science fiction, fantasy and adventure were some of the obvious choices of boys, though it was found that girls shared an interest in adventure books and 'books dealing with strange and unusual events' (*ibid.*, para. 37). What is important about the choice of a suitable theme for the study of literature, however, is not its propensity towards stereotypical gender bias but its capacity to provide opportunities for both boys and girls to 'discuss the more affective aspects of experience' and 'scope for writing with conviction about personal feelings' (*ibid.*, para. 50).

The Pre-Twentieth Century Novel

With these aims in mind, I would like to explore one or two of my suggested themes and how they might be employed in the classroom. Villainy certainly lends itself to study in a wide range of literary and non-literary contexts. Pupils could start by exploring the roles of favourite villains from their reading histories and try to categorize their villainy: those who prey upon particular victims, those with criminal tendencies, those who have supernatural powers, etc. Particular categories could then be investigated by separate groups of pupils. Teachers can add to pupils' lists of early encounters with villains who prey upon 'damsels in distress' (the wicked queen, the big bad wolf, Bluto, etc.); other notables such as Bill Sikes from *Oliver Twist*, Alec Durbeyfield from *Tess of the d'Urbervilles*, Peter Quint from *The Turn of the Screw*, Sir Percival Glyde from *The Woman in White* might also be considered. Pupils can be asked to compare physical descriptions, first encounters, relationships with their chosen 'prey', motivation, fate, etc., and, of course, their own reactions to the villains.

The devising of classroom activities to promote pupils' exploration of these texts needs careful thought, if interest is to be sustained. The revised orders provide a basic list of the key skills pupils need to be helped to acquire in relation to reading but teachers need to address the development of these skills alongside their overall provision for pupils' development in speaking, listening and writing. The skills cannot be taught in isolation. The importance of pupils' awareness of the interrelationship of the language modes, was clearly articulated in the Cox Report:

> The profile components are interrelated. For example, group discussion may precede and follow individual writing; writing may be collaborative; and listening to stories is often a preparation for reading . . . Because of the interrelationships between the language modes, the programmes of study will necessarily and rightly be integrated in good classroom practice. (DES, 1988)

It is, in my view, regrettable that this important principle of English teaching has now been relegated to one easily missed sentence at the start of the programme of study for each key stage: 'Pupils' abilities should be developed within an integrated programme of speaking and listening, reading and writing' (SCAA, 1994). A current document which gives clearer guidance for teachers which also echoes the Cox Report is the OFSTED *Handbook for the Inspection of Schools*: 'Where standards are high, pupils are aware of the interrelationship of all these skills. They regularly use their proficiency in one of them to improve the quality of their work in the others, as when they do more reading so as to raise the standard of their written work or engage in reflective discussion to clarify their thoughts on what they have been reading.' (OFSTED, 1994). Whilst my focus in this article is primarily on strategies for developing pupils' reading, it seems important to emphasize, as the OFSTED Handbook does, the necessity for teachers to provide opportunities for pupils 'to write in a wide variety of styles for real motivating purposes' (*ibid.*). The investigation of a theme in literature by a group of pupils need not always involve them in the onerous task of continuous writing in exercise books when, for example, the production of charts to illustrate findings will suffice or when a more imaginative way of presenting the information can be found. To fulfil the requirements for analysis and comparison of writers' use of language, for example, pupils can be asked to extract the adjectives and verbs which create unappealing characters from authors' descriptions and present them as a graffiti board of villainous characteristics.

Ideally, as indicated earlier, much of the work should be designed for display purposes so that groups of pupils can benefit from other groups' work on different aspects of the theme. In a search for more attractive finished products, teachers will find that many of the 'old favourites' sit well in a list of activities designed to present information about villains: physical descriptions and 'crimes' can be incorporated into 'Wanted' posters; settings can be presented as brochures for unattractive holiday destinations; distressed damsels can write letters to problem pages; villains' viewpoints can be presented as alternative accounts using D.J. Enright's *Other Version* poems (1981), Jon Scieszka's *The True Story of the Three Little Pigs* (1992) or the Ahlbergs' *Jolly Postman* (1986) as models; and their fates can be detailed in news articles or broadcasts with editorial comment.

Non-Literary Material

Teachers will also find abundant non-literary material to link with this topic. An examination of the treatment of villains on television, for example, both in documentaries and in programmes which use reconstructions of real crimes, could be compared with pre-twentieth century accounts. An examination of public attitudes to villains might lead pupils to consider the Reverend John Skinner's account of a public hanging in 1828:

> The females pressed even to the foot of the gallows to witness his mental pangs and his bodily torments, which in all probability were very violent, for the executioner held by and pulled down the legs of the sufferer for two minutes in order that his convulsive pangs might be shortened. Yet, notwithstanding this, even when *ten* minutes had elapsed the limbs were still convulsed. (Brett, 1989, p. 290)

In the same volume, Henry Machyn's description of the punishment meted out to a villain in 1561 would lead into another area for discussion, pupils' views of today's justice system, and also provide teachers with an opportunity to discuss 'how usage, words and meaning change over time' (SCAA, 1994).

> The xxxj day of January the sam man was sett on the pelere and ij grett peses of the measly bacun hangying over ys hed, and a wrytyng put up that a ij yere a-goo he was ponyssed for the sam offense for the lyke thyng. (Brett, 1989, p. 38)

A creative activity for a Key Stage 3 project might involve groups of pupils in the production of a narrative which includes some of their favourite villains. The ideal model for such a project is *The Mystery of the Russian Ruby* by Iain Smyth (1994), a recently published pop-up whodunnit. The book provides top secret information about the suspect villains in the form of pull-out factual dossiers of their character profiles and previous activities. Its final page provides a booklet of the accumulated evidence and a wheel which changes the final clue and results in a choice of alternative endings. This book would also provide a model for work on the related theme of the supernatural element in fiction.

Female Writers

For teachers concerned to find a place for women writers in a National Curriculum in which they are apparently peripheral, an exploration of the origins of tales of the supernatural is an ideal place to begin. As Manley and Lewis indicate in *Ladies of the Gothic* (Manley and Lewis, 1975), the routine of home and housekeeping led many women of the eighteenth century to seek outlets for their romantic imagination. Links with the gothic tradition unite several of the authors on the prescribed lists and the influence of Ann Radcliffe and her contemporaries can be examined, for example, in the works of Emily Bronte, Wilkie Collins, Conan Doyle, Charles Dickens, Henry James, Mary Shelley, R.L. Stevenson, H.G. Wells and, my own addition, Susan Hill (Radcliffe, 1991). The violence and sheer terror depicted in the scene in which Cathy's spirit first appears at the window as Lockwood sleeps soon dispel the belief that *Wuthering Heights*, for example, can be read as a mere love story:

> The intense horror of nightmare came over me; I tried to draw back my arm, but the hand clung to it, and a most melancholy voice sobbed,
>
> 'Let me in — let me in!'
>
> 'Who are you?' I asked, struggling, meanwhile, to disengage myself.
>
> 'Catherine Linton', it replied, shiveringly (why did I think of *Linton*? I had read *Earnshaw* twenty times for Linton). 'I'm come home, I'd lost my way on the moor!'
>
> As I spoke, I discerned, obscurely, a child's face looking through the window — terror made me cruel; and, finding it useless to attempt shaking the creature off, I pulled its wrist on to the broken pane, and rubbed it to and fro till the blood ran down and soaked the bed-clothes: still it wailed, 'Let me in!' and maintained its tenacious grip, almost maddening me with fear. (Bronte, 1994, pp. 21–2)

Pupils could compare this extract with the opening of chapter 5 in *Frankenstein*, when the inventor has fallen into a nightmarish slumber only to be awoken by the 'miserable monster', his jaws open as 'he muttered some inarticulate sounds, while a grin wrinkled his cheeks' (Shelley, 1994, p. 56). Such comparisons will help pupils to begin to appreciate the use of night-time visitations as a characteristic device of the genre. A further dimension is added by a reading of extracts from Mary Shelley's diaries:

> 6 March 1815   Find my baby dead. Send for Hogg. Talk. A miserable day . . .
>
> 9 March 1815   Read and talk. Still think about my little baby. Tis hard indeed for a mother to lose a child . . .
>
> 19 March 1815   Dream that my little baby came to life again; that it had only been cold, and that we rubbed it before the fire, and it lived. Awake and find no baby. I think about the little thing all day. Not in good spirits. (Brett, 1989, pp. 83, 87 and 101)

The use of such non-literary material at Key Stage 4 will assist pupils in an understanding of authorial viewpoint, in this case the parallels between aspects of Mary Shelley's own life and her protagonist's obsession with the creation of life itself.

Most pupils will certainly enjoy Mary Shelley's challenge to think of a story 'which would speak to the mysterious fears of our nature and awaken thrilling horror — one to make the reader dread to look round, to curdle the blood, and to quicken the beatings of the heart' (Shelley, 1994, p. 7). Pupils' additions to work in the genre will be much improved, however, by a preliminary study of the essential ingredients of the tale of terror in the work of the 'masters': the importance of setting in Anne Radcliffe's *The Mysteries of Udolpho* (1991) with her heroine's discovery of 'the desolation of the place — the rough stone walls, the spiral stairs black with age, and a suit of ancient armour, with an iron visor, that hung upon the walls'; the creation of atmosphere and mood inside the castle's torture chamber as 'it struck her that some poor wretch had once been fastened in this chair, and had there been starved to death. She was chilled by the thought; but what was her agony when, in the next moment it occurred to her that her aunt might have been one of these victims, and that she herself might be the next!'; the effects of descriptions of weather and landscape, as in Susan Hill's *The Woman in Black*: 'I came out of my reverie, to realize that I could no longer see very far in front of me and when I turned around I was startled to find that Eel Marsh House, too, was invisible, not because the darkness of evening had fallen, but because of a thick, damp sea-mist that had come rolling over the marshes and enveloped everything' (Hill, 1984). The modern novelist's choice of the Victorian era as the setting for her ghost story can also be discussed with pupils to focus attention upon narrative technique.

Links with Contemporary Teenage Fiction

Whilst it is obviously important not to give pupils the impression that novels are written merely to exemplify particular themes, teachers can exploit individual works to suit their own strengths and their pupils' interests. Notions of good and evil are inherent in many of the prescribed texts. However, if novels are to 'offer perspectives on society and community and their impact on the lives of individuals' (SCAA, 1944), it would seem essential for teachers to include in the English curriculum literature which explores such issues in contemporary society, the world their pupils inhabit. Robert Cormier's recent novel, *Tunes for Bears to dance to* — (1994), contains none of the explicit violence of many of his earlier depictions of American society but nonetheless places its central character, Henry, in a position in which he encounters evil for the first time and tries to understand it:

> Henry said, with dawning recognition of a truth too incredible to understand, 'You wanted me to do a bad thing.'
> The grocer smiled, not his inside-out sneer behind his customers' backs but a ghastly smile, like the smile on a Hallowe'en mask.

Astonished, Henry thought:

It was me he was after all the time . . . He didn't want me to be good anymore.

The grocer regarded him with affection, as if Henry were a favourite son. 'You see, Henry, you are like the rest of us, after all. Not so innocent, are you?' . . . (*ibid.*, p. 88)

Teachers can draw pupils' attention to the parallels between Henry's experience with a contemporary employer and Fagin's exploitation of Oliver's goodness in *Oliver Twist*. Non-literary material can be found in factual accounts of the exploitation of child labour such as Mayhew's description of the Farringdon watercress market where 'some of the boys have brought large hand-baskets, and carry them with the handles round their necks . . . ; others have their shallows fastened to their backs with a strap, and one little girl . . . stands shivering in a large pair of worn out Vestris boots, holding in her blue hands a bent and rusty tea-tray' (Mayhew, 1851).

Anne Fine's *Flour Babies* is a novel many Key Stage 3 pupils will enjoy and again deals with a feature of contemporary society and its impact upon a particular teenager. Asked what he was like as a baby, Simon's mother replies:

. . . 'No doubt about it, you were the most beautiful baby in the world.'

He knew she wouldn't want him to spoil things by saying it, but he couldn't help himself.

'So why did my dad push off so quickly?'

His mother tried her usual tack of making a joke of the whole business.

'Be fair, Simon. He did hang around for six whole weeks.'

But she could tell from the look on his face that the answer wasn't working the way it usually did. So she tried throwing in her Old Crone imitation.

'And there be those who say he could see into the future . . .'

But still Simon wouldn't smile. . . . He felt sour all over suddenly. Suppose his dad was able to see into the future. Did that make up for Simon not being able to see the past? Anyone who'd ever met their real dad could put it together somehow. Take out some middle-aged spread. Wipe out a few wrinkles. Add a bit of hair. But if you'd never so much as seen the man —

'Why aren't there any photographs? I know you didn't have a proper wedding or anything, but why aren't there any other photos?' . . . (Fine, 1992, pp. 33–4)

The passage makes an interesting comparison with an earlier version of a similar dilemma and illustrates 'the variety of language use in fiction'. (SCAA, 1994)

My father's family name being Pirrip, and my christian name Philip, my infant tongue could make of both names nothing longer or more explicit than Pip. So I called myself Pip, and came to be called Pip.

I give Pirrip as my father's family name, on the authority of his tombstone and my sister — Mrs. Joe Gargery, who married the black-smith. As I never saw my father or mother, and never saw any like-ness of either of them (for their days were long before the days of photographs), my first fancies regarding what they were like, were unreasonably derived from their tombstones. The shape of the letters on my father's, gave me an odd idea that he was a square, stout, dark man, with curly black hair. From the character and turn of the in-scription, '*Also Georgiana Wife of the Above*', I drew a childish conclu-sion that my mother was freckled and sickly . . . (Dickens, 1991b, p. 1)

A class study of the all-encompassing theme of 'Growing Up' could also include the Brontes' *Jane Eyre* and *Wuthering Heights*, Joyce's *A Portrait of the Artist as a Young Man* and other Dickens novels. Pupils will also be able to choose from a number of contemporary novels which offer perspectives from other cultures, including those which have earned a long-standing place in secondary classrooms: Rosa Guy's *The Friends*, Mildred Taylor's *Roll of Thun-der, Hear My Cry*, Julius Lester's *Basketball Game*, etc.

In *Flour Babies*, towards the end of the flour baby experiment, Simon writes in his school diary:

Last night, when I was rocking her in my arms, Mum said I re-minded her of someone. She didn't say who, and I didn't have to ask. But it was good to know he used to rock me like that when I was a baby. Maybe he really did love me, in his way. . . .

He just wasn't very good at showing it, running away like that. But I can't talk, can I? My flour baby ended up such a mess, I prac-tically got my ears torn off. But I really did care about her. I really did. (Fine, 1992, p. 135)

This novel offers a highly accessible example of a tough teenage boy coming to terms with his feelings and an important opportunity for male pupils to engage in the affective domain. Another recent example is *Telling the Sea* by Pauline Fisk which tells the story of two teenagers in Wales and their separate struggles against the lives their parents had planned for them. Nona and Owen are drawn together when she finds his secret journal on the beach:

'I'm the wrong boy inside the wrong body . . . I'm not like the rest of them. I never get the chance to be the sort of boy I really am, except down here. It's as though I'm living out somebody else's life instead of mine . . .'

> Nona slammed the book shut. She could have written those words herself. They were more than she could bear. (Fisk, 1993, p. 138)

Teachers need to find ways of ensuring that as well as being able to 'read, analyze and evaluate' (SCAA, 1994), pupils still have opportunities to simply enjoy their reading, empathize with characters and reflect upon their own experiences. The prescribed reading lists for Key Stages 3 and 4 will be welcomed by few teachers of English. It is important, however, for teachers to be aware of the vast number of choices they are still able to make both to exploit their own strengths and to suit the needs of their pupils. This article has attempted to contribute to the exploration of those choices, in the hope that reading in the English curriculum will remain a source of enjoyment for pupils rather than become a mere nightmare for their teachers.

Notes

1 Idea borrowed from *The Writing Journey*, Pat D'Arcy, Educational Consultant.
2 Research for the NCC by the University of Warwick (1994) *Evaluation of the Implementation of English in the National Curriculum at Key Stages 1, 2 and 3* (1991–1993), London, SCAA. I refer to the findings of this survey later in the chapter.
3 Research for the National Curriculum Council by the University of Warwick (1994) *Evaluation of the Implementation of English in the National Curriculum at Key Stages 1, 2 and 3 (1991–1993) (3.5.3 Key Stage 3, Policy and Practice in Schools)*, London, SCAA.

References

AHLBERG, J. and A. (1986) *The Jolly Postman*, London, Heinemann.

BRETT, S. (Ed) (1989) *The Faber Book of Diaries*, London, Faber and Faber.

BRONTE, E. (1994) *Wuthering Heights*, Oxford, Heinemann New Windmill Classics.

CORMIER, R. (1994) *Tunes for Bears to Dance To* —, London, Lion.

DES (1988) *English for Ages 5 to 11*, London, DES, November.

DFE (1994) *The Code of Practice on the Identification and Assessment of Special Educational Needs*, London, DFE.

DICKENS, C. (1991a) *A Christmas Carol* (Stave Four) in 'The Christmas Books', London, King Penguin.

DICKENS, C. (1991b) *Great Expectations*, London, Mandarin.

ENGLISH CENTRE (1978) *Class Readers*, London, ILEA.

ENGLISH CENTRE (1986) *Fiction*, London, ILEA.

ENRIGHT, D.J. (1981) *Collected Poems*, Oxford, Oxford University Press.

FINE, A. (1992) *Flour Babies*, London, Hamish Hamilton.

FISK, P. (1993) *Telling the Sea*, Oxford, Lion.

HILL, S. (1984) *The Woman in Black*, London, Penguin Books.

HOLMAN, D. (1994) *A Christmas Carol* (Act 2, Scene V), London, Heinemann Plays.

HUMBERSIDE LEA (1993/94) *Enhanced Reading Project*, Hull, Humberside LEA.

MANLEY, S. and LEWIS, G. (1975) *Ladies of the Gothic*, New York, Lothrop, Lee and Shepard.

MAYHEW, H. (1851) 'The Farringdon watercress market', in CAREY, J. (Ed) (1989) *The Faber Book of Reportage*, London, Faber and Faber.

NATIONAL WRITING PROJECT (1990), London, Nelson.

OFSTED (1993) *Boys and English*, London, DFE.

OFSTED (1994) *Handbook for the Inspection of Schools* (Part 4, 6.2, Standards of Achievement), London, OFSTED.

RADCLIFFE, A. (1991) *The Mysteries of Udolpho*, Oxford, Oxford University Press World Classics.

SCAA (1994) *English in the National Curriculum*, London, SCAA, November.

SCIESZKA, J. (1992) *The True Story of the Three Little Pigs*, London, Penguin.

SEAC (1993) *Key Stage 3 Anthology*, London, SEAC.

SHELLEY, M. (1994) *Frankenstein*, London, Penguin Popular Classics.

SMYTH, I. (1994) *The Mystery of the Russian Ruby*, London, Orchard Books.

Example of a Rota Drawn up by a Group of Four Pupils — Tasks Chosen by Pupils According to their Suitability to the Particular Text Studied

(Some of these tasks can be completed before the group has finished reading or listening to the whole novel but the programme of work can also be supplemented by tasks designed to encourage close reading of particular sections chosen by the teacher.)

Pupil A interviews pupil B as the main character immediately after a significant event in the novel. Tape-record for radio programme.

Pupils C and D collaborate on the rewriting of the most dramatic incident in the novel in script form.

Pupils write diary entries describing the same events from different characters' viewpoints, each pupil taking responsibility for the collation of the thoughts of a particular character.

Whole group decision on most appropriate sections of novel to rewrite as a picture book for children aged 5 to 7. Sections divided between individual members of group.

Pupils collaborate on the writing of a visitors' guide to the region and time in which the novel is set — pupil A climate and physical geography, pupil B important centres, pupil C significant historical events, pupil D social conditions. Library research activities to be allocated accordingly.

Visual representations of aspects of the text, for example, pupil A family tree or relationships chart, pupil B map of area where main incidents take place, pupil C photo album of main events in a character's life, pupil D time line of events.

Pupils collaborate on the writing of a newspaper supplement reporting the main events of the novel and editorial comment, using a desktop publishing package.

Whole group designs publicity and marketing material for a film version of the novel — pupil A poster, pupil B badge, pupil C t-shirt, pupil D character doll; whole group involvement in planning and presenting trailer for local cinema.

Extension of text to recount minor characters' stories, each pupil developing a different individual's story.

Pupils collaborate on the writing of a pupils' guide to the language of the novel, focussing upon dialect, archaic usage, the idiosyncratic language use of particular characters.

Pupils collaborate on the scripting of an edition of *This is Your Life* for the main character in the novel — individual pupils take responsibility for the documenting of the reactions of other major characters.

Chapter 7

Coping with Assessment: An Approach to Recent Developments (11–16)

James Pattenden

'Examinations are formidable, even to the best prepared, for the greatest fool may ask more than the wisest man may answer!' (Colton, C.)

Introduction

With the election of a new Conservative government in the spring of 1992 it was anticipated that the forthcoming school year could well be one of 'disturbing consequences for those concerned with the well-being of English teaching in our schools' (John Johnson, NATE, 1992). Attempts to politicize the curriculum and assessment arrangements in schools were chiefly responsible for the difficulties experienced by examination boards as well as by English departments. New syllabuses and new ways of testing them caused problems for both resourcing and teaching. As a result a key issue that teachers continue to have to address is how effective assessment may take place, given the statutory arrangements imposed. It will be important to take note of these as well as subsequent developments, as they have an important bearing on what is the essential issue in assessment — the need to trust in the professional judgment and practice of English teachers who actually work with children in the classroom.

More recently (November 1993) Sir Ron Dearing's request for views on the curriculum and its assessment gave some measure of hope that someone out there was listening. The subsequent Dearing Report, however, has not been greeted with universal admiration by professional educationalists and its attempt to trim an unwieldly curriculum and its testing arrangements has missed the point of the chief concern of most English teachers, which is a professional disapproval of a form of assessment that appears to lead rather than follow an even more prescriptive curriculum. The attempt to compromise by narrowing the content to create less assessment affords no comfort since it limits the range of tasks available for assessment. It is this 'misplaced generosity' that has ultimately frustrated teachers who are already attempting to fulfil a variety of roles as well as take on the work load of new initiatives such as the National Curriculum and record-keeping together with the traditional demands of marking and preparation.

In general there is conflict between well-tried positive assessment approaches and the more recent demands of National Curriculum testing where, for example, the ten levels of attainment are mismatched with the principles of negotiation and self-assessment that many English teachers consider to be indispensable elements in the whole process of teaching. What I shall be concerned with here will be to define what I mean by assessment and to consider *why* it is a necessary part of our teaching, before going on to suggest ways in which an imposed assessment framework may impede an appropriate and meaningful evaluation of pupils' achievements. It will then be pertinent to describe briefly a consensus of the general principles that recent commentators have discussed in some of the available literature, before considering some practical approaches that have been employed by schools in an attempt to come to terms with statutory demands and find a balance which, whilst perhaps not perfect, will at least afford the teacher some sense of professional credibility at a time when dearly-held principles are in danger of being compromised.

It is always going to be difficult for an 'arts' subject like English with its 'progressive accumulation of a broadening range of generic skills and understandings' (Furlong, 1992) to fit a national system designed to measure the acquisition of knowledge. Some basic criteria for assessment would include a pupil's reading, writing, talking and listening abilities as well as, Evans (1982) has suggested, such qualities as 'initiative, tolerance, cooperation, perseverance, conscientiousness and enthusiasm'. The primary requirement of classroom assessment should be to help understand how the pupil has made and can also best make progress. This implies a policy that not only addresses individuals but makes clear that the criteria for assessment are known beforehand by the pupil. Some would extend this knowledge to parents and other involved groups. Such a policy will assess processes in English work as well as 'end-products'. Progress, Evans continues, should be assessed in 'personal relations, cooperation, organization and reference skills, use of time available, ability to seek and act on advice, perseverance, discrimination as well as . . . originality, accuracy, delivery'. Well over ten years later these criteria will still be recognized, endorsed and celebrated by a majority of English departments; but, unfortunately, as I have intimated, such criteria do not fit neatly into today's statutory assessment framework, which is closer to a traditional model that will be of more use to examiners and politicians than it is to pupils, since the guiding principle seems to be measuring of performance rather than formative evaluation.

It has been noted (Brook, 1994) that the Dearing consultation document on English in the National Curriculum (1994) places more emphasis on what should be taught rather than on learning itself; and teachers have been made to feel accountable for steady linear progression through the levels of attainment when many largely accept that achievement in English cannot be judged in such quantifiable terms. Accountability, in its broader sense, should be a perfectly acceptable concept; parents have a right to know the progress of their offspring and teachers should be given the resources to monitor development, diagnose problems and indicate directions that might be taken to improve skills. This will ideally be through 'task-specific' situations wherein the teacher will take note of the achievement of particular children by observing specific features of a given situation. When assessing English we are taking account of all the elements of language development and we will not be able to deduce progress from an isolated task or assignment.

Such an approach necessitates setting up and reporting on a wide variety of situations with sensitivity to the particular context. Most secondary English teachers with a sense of responsibility and experience of GCSE coursework processes would judge such an approach as 'good practice'. David Allen (1987) has noted the importance of the development of the GCSE for establishing criteria and expressed the need to inform 'parents, governors and politicians' of these basic principles at a time when those groups were receiving much of their information through the convenient slogans in newspapers and television, where the debate on 'standards' was being encouraged. The domain of accountability had extended far beyond the classroom and far from the crucial dialogue between teacher and pupil. Parents and governors will have their own requirements from assessment but politicians, Allen alleges, want assessment that evaluates the system or that measures the child against accepted norms. Thus there is a choice between a narrow and inexpensive system or a comprehensive, time-consuming and expensive system. What we ended up with in 1993 and 1994 was a narrow, time-consuming and expensive process that resulted in widespread boycotting of tests for 14-year-olds. The urgently commissioned Dearing Report — 'a face-saver after the debacle of external testing' (Martin, 1994) — misjudged teachers' concerns despite its strenuous listening. Allen's report (1987) was based on 'first hand observation' and his own direct appraisal of English departments so that he was confident in saying that the above recommended processes 'match the best work in secondary records of achievement and GCSE coursework'. This confidence was qualified by the recognition that politicians would look to cheap and simple tests but that society will eventually learn there is no substitute for a complex and detailed classroom assessment of language development. The alternative would be judgments based on limited information and the erosion of good practice.

Teachers have not always helped themselves on this issue; Allen reports that too often in-school testing has been inadequate; reading tests, for example, have provided a convenient yardstick for language development, assuming that writing and speaking skills are commensurate with reading ability. This lack of detail results in the accidental matching of tasks and a distorted picture of achievement can be the only result. Some of these points have been reported by the Office for Standards in Education (OFSTED, 1993) based on inspections of schools by HMI during the first three years of English as a National Curriculum subject. They begin their account of Assessment, Recording and Reporting by, not surprisingly, identifying a 'clear link between achievement and the introduction of the National Curriculum'; due to the need to meet National Curriculum requirements, schools are revealing greater evidence of good practice. Marking is not always sufficiently diagnostic and there are not always 'planned opportunities for achieving levels'. Putting it another way, they say that 'assessment is often made without reference to specific criteria and without follow-up'. These summaries, albeit repetitious and always keeping an eye on attainment levels, do however contain some of the chief elements of what should be written into the policy of an English department. Where the OFSTED is less fair to schools is when it comments on developments in 1992–93 at the time when Standard Assessment Tests were being introduced into the curriculum:

> In the best English departments the pupils were being prepared for the end-of-Key Stage assessments without undue distortion to the syllabus or to the processes of teaching and learning, but in many schools a distortion of the year 9 curriculum occurred, as too much time was taken up preparing for the Key Stage 3 tests . . . (OFSTED, 1993, p. 17)

This does not take into account the lateness of the arrival of the orders and the urgent need to purchase resources in order to meet statutory assessment requirements, including a Shakespeare text for each pupil, for example. For OFSTED to imply that the tests for 14-year-olds would be a natural consequence of good practice is somewhat disingenuous and contradicts the formative philosophy previously cited, at the same time that it ignores the mismatch between the original Programmes of Study and the nature of the tests themselves.

Indeed, it is the pace of events that has impeded the kind of progress in assessment developments that Allen referred to and that were recommended implicitly by the inspectors for OFSTED in their 1993 report. We recall that Allen suggested that debates surrounding the introduction of the GCSE considerably determined the way that English assessment was going, and the processes involved in producing and assessing coursework may have been responsible for the growing consensus on this issue by the main body of English teachers. Robert Protherough (1991) has pointed out how ironic it is that English teachers, often strongly opposed to the formal examination of their subject, are responsible for one of the most important and popular examination subjects; and further, how developments in examining English at the age of 16 have paralleled developments towards more appropriate and meaningful assessment practices. Before, and perhaps during, the introduction of the CSE, 'O' level English language was seen by many parents, pupils and employers as '*the* stable test of literacy and accuracy in an apparently unstable world of slipping standards and widespread permissiveness' (Evans, 1982).

It represented the 'terminus' of English teaching, but by today's standards it appears a flawed model with its familiar pattern of essay, summary and comprehension for language and the study of about four texts for literature. Protherough and Atkinson (1991) have brought to our attention the harm such examinations can bring since what they are testing 'has little to do with the real nature of the subject'. At the same time they appreciate that the move from 'O' level to GCSE may be responsible for 'genuinely new approaches'. Running alongside the 'O' level examination and preceding the GCSE was the CSE examination. Although originally designed to cater for those pupils insufficiently capable of sitting 'O' level, most CSE syllabuses had compulsory coursework and 'oral' elements. The CSE folder of pupils' work revealed how a final, formal examination was an unrealistic and unrepresentative indicator of their ability to use language in a number of ways and in a variety of circumstances. As far back as 1973 the Consultative Committee on Examinations in Secondary Schools reported that the alternative 'terminal' examination did little other than examine a candidate's ability to write under pressure. Teaching towards this kind of examination emphasizes 'the power of merely reproducing other peoples' ideas', and induces the pupil to 'aim at absorbing information' (in Evans, 1982), whereas the GCSE broke down divisions between pupils in school and between schools and created a 'new unity of English teachers'. (Protherough and Atkinson, 1991).

Grade criteria for the new syllabuses were developed to make explicit in positive terms educational targets that are achievable and to increase the motivation of children. National criteria required that schemes of assessment should be selected on the basis of 'fitness for purpose', i.e. the form of assessment should be appropriate to the subject, its aims and assessment objectives. Thereby the validity of the assessment is increased in that it measures what it intends to measure. English may be unique as a subject in that its very nature demands an 'accumulation of a broadening range of generic skills' (Furlong, 1992) and contains a 'rich variety of . . . concepts and attitudes which should not be seen as separate, unconnected parts of the curriculum' (Allen, 1987). Coursework would therefore seem to be one of the most appropriate methods of assessing this variety since it allows for open-ended tasks, a formative approach and helps us to understand how the pupil can best make progress. In a recent article David Martin (1994) has condemned the new limits placed on coursework for GCSE in English and English literature as 'a tragedy'; the discussion and moderation of pupil folders not only ensured more reliable results but also helped to identify what was being assessed in terms of language skills and how a pupil's understanding develops over a period of time. Other advantages include the sharing of ideas for purposeful assignment work and a growing appreciation of a child's achievements other than those presented as written responses. Research had suggested that the former GCSE helped to foster the 'new unity' of English teachers into a consensus of opinion regarding the integral nature of teaching, learning and assessment and records of achievement, (Protherough and Atkinson, 1991).

The main emphasis in GCSE has been on positive evaluation of pupil outcomes and the development of 'conferencing', negotiation and self-assessment in the recording of achievement. However, the same research also reveals anxieties that these commonly-shared principles may be compromised by the statutory demands of National Curriculum testing. OFSTED seems to suggest that disruption of the curriculum and its assessment should have been avoided and did not occur in the 'best' departments, yet it is difficult not to see conflict between the ten attainment levels and the principles of self-assessment. This conflict may, ironically, be linked to the origin of the national criteria which in many ways were so liberating for English assessment. In 1984, as Secretary of State for Education, Sir Keith Joseph stated he was in favour of criterion-referencing as opposed to norm-referencing since the former gives 'a measure of achievement in absolute terms'. Although claiming not to be interested in 'the relative standards between candidates' (in Mobley *et al.*, 1986) he was surely pointing to national norms and unwittingly, by using the language of calculation, anticipating league tables based on National Curriculum levels of attainment. The Draft Proposals for English (May, 1994) replaced Statements of Attainment, with Level Descriptions aimed at making summative assessments on a 'best fit' basis, in order to avoid mechanical assessment linked to the number of statements acquired by the pupil. This move has been welcomed not only because it seems a step in the right direction but also because

> it reveals unambiguously the folly of policies which seek to claim that precise measurements may be hitched to language performance and which invoke the accountant's notion of value added where it is incapable of indisputable application. (Frater, 1994)

But the same writer warns us that the new impressionistic descriptions with their accumulation of diverse skills can only be of use for the kind of norm-referenced grading that was applied to GCSE coursework, and will be of very little benefit in identifying Sir Keith's 'absolute' standards. Most importantly, the new level descriptions, with their need to balance one element against another, should cause us to question the need for short tests and strengthen the argument for assessment by coursework.

Issues Arising

Apart from administrative and managerial disruption to entitlement, resourcing and organization caused by the revisions to assessment at the ages of 14 and 16, what distressed a number of English departments was this conflict of commonly-held principles with the new statutory requirements. Perhaps most had satisfactorily come to terms with GCSE coursework and benefited from its influence on teaching processes, as they had equally come to terms with accommodating and delivering the programmes of study recommended by the original Cox committee. Indeed, there is evidence that adherence to those programmes had been to the advantage of departments and pupils. The report of a NATE survey published in May 1992 concluded that 'planning had improved and was becoming more detailed . . . and . . . more thought was given to the selection of literature offered'. Also, it was noted that

> the experience of the assessment procedures called for by the National Curriculum had assisted many teachers in taking closer account of their pupils' strengths and weaknesses.

but,

> the pilot standard assessment tasks though helpful in this regard, had been heavily time-consuming. The required element of teacher assessment was similarly beneficial and demanding. (NATE, 1992)

Between the time of the pilot and the final statutory exercise the 'tasks' became 'tests'. Schools involved in the piloting experiment reported concerns that argue against the above, mainly positive, statements. They echo familiar concerns expressed urgently by teachers when a campaign began to alert interested parties to the dangers of these conflicts of interest, following the publishing of assessment orders late in November 1992. Apart from the divisive and difficult exercise deciding 'tiers' of entry for candidates, it was found that the assessment of reading was now reduced to preparing pupils for answering comprehension exercises; planning and drafting were incompatible with the nature of written tasks and presented little opportunity for demonstrating flair, creativity or interest. Summary remarks record that, as OFSTED has reported, teachers found themselves working towards the tests rather than to programmes of study; levels produced in tests were lower than those arrived at by teacher assessment and the validity of concentrating three years' language experience into three hours in terms of real achievements in a range of reading and writing activities over a period of time was repeatedly questioned.

Problems with assessing 14-year-olds were compounded with those surrounding new examination syllabuses for children aged 16. As already recorded, the chief concern of teachers has been the significant reduction of coursework as well as the requirement to separate candidates by tiers of entry; departments realized they were being nudged into a situation where setting by ability was a sensible response. The fact is that many English teachers 'are wedded to mixed-ability teaching in the interests of a common culture and find the notion of distinguishing among their pupils . . . highly distasteful' (*TES*, 15 February 1993).

The requirement of the new syllabuses to read set texts was a throw-back to pre-GCSE syllabuses when it was necessary to study three to four texts, one of which was inevitably a Shakespeare play. The CSE syllabus, catering for less-able students, often recommended as many as sixty texts, offering a broader range and a richer variety from which the teacher could choose at his/ her professional discretion. Students were then given a wider range of opportunities for writing and speaking and listening tasks. GCE students, on the other hand, were sentenced to close textual study of a narrow range of books, most of which would be taken from the canon of acknowledged 'great' books. The GCSE national criteria, as well as the Cox working group, had recommended lists of possible texts, but it was anticipated that teachers would use their professional judgment on what they considered to be most appropriate for the development of students in their own teaching groups. This would avoid a situation whereby able candidates 'failed' due to not having revised selectively; nor would it be necessary for staff and students to guess likely examination questions on the basis of what had appeared in previous years. It would also be less likely that the less-able candidate, on the strength of CSE coursework, would do better than the GCE candidate who had a 'bad day'.

As a result of changes made, examination boards were subjected to a rigorous weighting requirement of 70 per cent terminal examination and no more than 30 per cent coursework, which for English Literature implied a return to a close study of a narrow range of texts which would include a compulsory study of a Shakespeare play and largely pre-twentieth century authors. Wider reading, covering a variety of genres and cultures, is encouraged but, as with the SATs, teaching towards the examination is inevitably going to occur when coursework appears to account for so little and departments and individual teachers feel that results in external examinations are a measure of their accountability. Too often the examination boards, whilst listening to and no doubt understanding the concerns of the English constituency, have been forced to compromise ideals to satisfy the demands of their political bosses. To allow common coursework for both English and English literature reflects a sympathy for the unitary approach. Syllabus requirements for English that include, for example, evidence of personal writing, research and drafting, knowledge about language and response to literature suggest an understanding of the breadth of language performance. However well-intentioned and perceptive these requirements may be, the teacher needs to be reminded that we are concerned with only 40 per cent of the assessment pattern — 20 per cent of which, although not necessarily divorced from these areas, must be based on the pupils' speaking and listening. Examination boards encourage the setting of assignments which cover more than one of the requirements; this will often be inevitable, but teachers will need to ensure that this forced economy does not generate artificial tasks that remain a sideshow to the real business of examination preparation. I argue that breadth and balance in the planning of curriculum and assessment do not have to be sacrificed for terminal examination expediency.

There have obviously been attempts by the boards to 'market' their vehicles for assessment whilst showing a sensitivity to the principles and practices of the teaching profession. It has been pointed out by one English Subject Officer that the 30 per cent coursework element for English literature still allows oral assessment and gives teachers the choice of setting assignments in the manner to which they are accustomed, or they may set fewer, more 'focused' assignments which will elevate the unit in the eyes of the students (*TES*, 13 November 1992). The good sense of these comments will be expanded upon further but unfortunately the same article avoids, indeed ignores, the question of the significance of the 70 per cent terminal examination which must significantly determine a candidate's final grade. Neither is it suggested how marks from the different assessment elements will be aggregated to award the final grade or how coursework might be integrated with preparation for the final paper. Despite the soothing and reconciling noises of interested parties we cannot avoid the fact that reduced coursework and the prescription of a narrow range of reading texts means that professional judgments about the curriculum and learning are being taken out of the hands of teachers.

But what has been valuable in GCSE English and English Literature need not be surrendered. Students need the opportunity to explore at length imaginatively, as well as through straightforward analysis, a range of texts carefully selected by the supervising teacher. Geoff Barton (1992) has noted that the experience of teaching GCSE has made the profession aware that children *are* reading widely, although the books may not always be considered 'appropriate' or 'worthwhile'. GCSE allowed for this to take place and also ensured that childrens' reading was not left to chance and could be extended to include a range of quality fiction as well as allowing for an increased awareness of each individual pupil's reading interests and habits. Of fundamental benefit to this approach is that the 'continuum of a child's reading is visibly maintained'. Reduction of coursework in English literature could lead to a breaking of that continuum. This is bad enough; the amount of prescribed literature in the Draft Proposals (May 1994) could see the end of English literature as a separate examinable subject.

Principles and Assessment

Before turning to some practical approaches to the kinds of problem I have briefly described it may be profitable to review more concisely some of the principles for assessing English that have already been touched on. It is widely accepted that assessment in education will generally be of two kinds: formative and summative. The Dearing Report (SCAA, 1993) recognizes formative assessment as 'day to day assessment . . . undertaken according to policies decided by individual schools'. Many would suggest it was the more significant and more valid form of assessment since it exclusively involves the teacher/pupil relationship and is integral to the learning and teaching process, in that it identifies the strengths and weaknesses of students and may set targets for further achievement. Dearing defines summative assessment as 'tests and summaries (teachers') which provide an overall judgment on a pupil's achievements and contribute to reports on progress to parents'. Dearing makes no judgment as to which he considers the more important process, although from the tone of the extract formative assessment is routine, whereas summative assessment is a record of the teacher's accountability to other interested parties. John Blanchard (1986) has pointed out that some of the dangers inherent in stressing the summative method include using the conclusions for our own purposes, which may have little to do with the child's learning, and that by emphasizing a final test or examination we may subvert the purposes of education.

Assessment should 'develop and enrich' children's learning and should be regarded as 'unfinished business'. At the same time however, certain parties will need information about genuine attainment from summative assessment in order for decisions to be made about future courses and careers — so they need to be compatible. Blanchard makes the useful distinction that formative assessment takes into account the elements of performance and competence, whereas summative assessment is descriptive and judgmental and assumes that specific performances are representative and is somehow regarded as a universal measure of competence across any range of tasks for all time. Very little depends on criteria by which judgments are made, so that pupils may not be able to use comments constructively and interested outsiders will not be in a position to know what value to attach to the assessment. Dearing (SCAA, 1993) accepts that 'ongoing teacher assessment is central to the assessment of the performance of the individual child' but insists that this form of assessment 'needs to be complemented with information from short well-conceived national tests' and quotes the Office for Standards in Education which has reported that 'teacher assessment and statutory testing have both played a part in improving teachers' understanding of the National Curriculum and of the standards that are expected'. There is very little justification supplied for statutory testing apart from OFSTED's contention that as a result teachers are 'setting more demanding targets for learning', which does not necessarily mean that better learning is taking place; teachers aware of the demands of programmes of study and the needs of individual pupils will know what targets there are — Dearing makes this particular form of statutory assessment sound like a mechanism for goading teachers to push youngsters towards universal standards that might not be appropriate for individual children. Dearing's justification for statutory tests is 'accountability to parents and society' in exchange for 'increased trust' in 'the professional judgment of teachers', thus bringing the assessment of children into the sphere of bargaining (SCAA, 1993).

Blanchard, on the other hand, would prefer to promote what would now be recognized as an ongoing record of achievement, supplying pupils and other interested parties with appropriate information that

> supplies the evidence and an interpretation of the work undertaken so that judgment may reasonably and ultimately be reached by those whom assessment is intended to benefit. (Blanchard, 1986)

Blanchard opposes any form of norm-referencing, since it means that those who succeed do so at the expense of others and the process relies on pre-determined levels of attainment. Writing in 1985, Blanchard was perhaps not to know that such terminology would become part of the rubric for a National Curriculum.

The Dearing Report (SCAA, 1993) acknowledges that during the review process there was considerable discussion regarding the retention of a ten-level scale and that some witnesses giving evidence thought it impossible to measure pupil achievement with unambiguous criteria definitions or to have objective criteria for different levels. Dearing further suggests that the current plethora of statements has led to a fragmented assessment-led approach to teaching, with an emphasis on counting the numbers of statements of attainment achieved through elaborate 'tick lists'. Also, the ten-level scale approach cannot indicate 'value added' but only the number of pupils at particular levels. To this extent the report has shown sympathy with commentators who have identified with Blanchard's organic 'differentiation by outcome' model. Where they would part company once more would be in response to the report's contention that 'progress . . . is characterized by an increasing mastery of skills'; this suggests a hierarchical and linear model of language development which fails to acknowledge the interrelationship between the skills of speaking and listening and reading and writing. The report, however, insists that levels will facilitate curriculum planning and assessment and help 'evaluate learning needs and assess pupil progress'. The recommended level descriptions based on a cluster of the main statements of attainment have been seen as a preferable alternative in that they may prove more manageable, although they contain 'in-built hurdles (that) will disadvantage pupils with special needs' (Brook, 1994). The NATE has called for the abandonment of the ten-level scale precisely because of its in-built hierarchical implications and would prefer to see an end-of-key-stage grade based on the principle that 'assessment criteria can only be derived from actual performance' (NATE, November 1993). Part of that performance should be reflected on through self-assessment, encouraging pupils to become participants in the assessment process rather than passive consumers of education.

With an open and individual discussion of syllabus aims and the knowledge, understanding and skills under review, pupils will become more conscious of strengths and weaknesses and be able, with encouragement, to evaluate the development of their competence. In order that effective assessment may take place the programmes of study should be so designed that a complete range of abilities is reflected in syllabus terms, together with a statement of aims. Teachers, pupils and other interested parties also require what might be called a course descriptor, indicating what is achievable in the subject, so that achievement is interpreted through the evidence in the assessment. This open approach is crucial to Blanchard's argument since it is only by 'explicit, publicly agreed, curricular definition and regular, systematic, accredited and validated assessment that an informed account and interpretation of pupils' learning can be made'. All interested parties require a summative assessment without the detail of the syllabus if the wider needs of social recognition are to be met and clients are to be informed clearly and accurately. Finally, in setting out his key principles for assessment, Blanchard asserts that they should involve an equal opportunity and that all pupils are entitled to this process, not only because it is intrinsic to learning but also because 'whatever a pupil's performance, it requires description and deserves qualification' (Blanchard, 1986).

In considering the recent history of English I have suggested a number of problems that surround the current situation with regard to the way that the subject is assessed and how it is likely to be assessed in the future. These problems or concerns might be summarized as an insistence by curriculum designers on an hierarchical and linear model of progress through skills, knowledge and understanding, when it might be argued that such skills require a recursive model that does not see skills in isolation but rather as incrementally achieved through an appreciation of the interrelatedness of language development. I have expressed doubts with regard to the short isolated testing of limited skills but have not been in receipt of satisfactory reasons for their maintenance. We should recognize that the Dearing Report entered into lengthy debate on these issues and at least recognizes the complexity of the subject. Its conclusions with regard to what children should be taught and how learning might be assessed may remain unsatisfactory but I have noted that some commonly-held principles were profiled along the course of the discussion. Most important is the principle of formative teacher assessment; although not retaining exclusive judgment it at least shares tacit equality with statutory testing up to the age of 14. Summaries of consultations carried out at local authority level (for example, Derbyshire, July 1994) appear to suggest that there is broad agreement among English departments that these principles are acceptable and appropriate. My task now is to suggest some practical strategies for coping with this dual system of assessment — or at least making them compatible — whilst maintaining the good practice which grew from preparing students for the GCSE examination.

Issues for the English Department

In its policy review an English department will probably want to draw attention to the variety of demands for assessment that might exist in any one school. These demands could be identified at different levels depending on for whom the collected information is intended — in most cases simply that for departmental use and assessments made for wider publication and national accreditation. At departmental level care will need to be taken to ensure that assessment from programmes of study, whether in the shape of modules, themes or whatever curricular structure is agreed, is compatible with the agreed approach to formative assessment, which will generally be based on the collection of evidence of achievement over a given period of time and across a range of language activities.

Secondly, there will be assessment for the school's purposes: summative statements and perhaps grades or levels for use in reporting progress and attainment to parents, careers officers and other interested parties. Thirdly, there are the statutory tests and public examinations which provide accredited qualifications for students and have assessment prescribed, and partly carried out, by outside agencies. When one further considers that assessments will need to be documented for recording and reporting purposes it is clear that a considerable amount of time will need to be reserved and planned for. This is a particularly heavy workload if the department is in a school where a form of reporting already exists that is based on statements with National Curriculum terms of reference, so that much duplication is demanded to satisfy different purposes. Ways of avoiding complexity and achieving clarity and facility may only be discussed and agreed at the level of school management. Many schools have considered developing their records of achievement in a coordinated way in order to achieve this end; but it is difficult to consider how a satisfactory document could be brought into being without transcription and time-consuming duplication. Difficulties are compounded for those departments that strongly agree with David Allen that 'there is no substitute for the complex assessment of language development' (1987) and that this will necessitate fairly elaborate documentation, as well as recognition from school management that time must be found for this valuable work.

It is important to repeat the principle expressed above that departments should have ownership of the chosen system of the curriculum and its assessment. By consensual agreement on its aims, objectives, content and delivery of programmes of study and purposes and methods of assessment, departments will not only give themselves the 'unity' that Protherough remarks on, but also the shared ethos and integrity that will authenticate their work. There has been wide recognition of the benefits derived from the implementation of the GCSE, particularly so for English; Broadbent and Moger (1992) have asserted that 'we know that 14 to 16-year-olds thrive on the motivations and tangible evidence of progress and development that the coursework ethos of English lessons has allowed in recent years'. This was written at a time when it had become clear that the coursework element in final GCSE assessments would be substantially reduced. For some time before, GCSE commentators had maintained that a language file is the only way of collecting a true perspective on a child's progress and more recently it continues to be claimed that grading in a training session of teachers is most secure 'where schools had established a folder system containing best work, rather like a GCSE folder' (Derbyshire, 1994). The content of a language folder may vary considerably but would probably at the very least contain evidence of achievement across the areas of speaking and listening, reading and writing which, of course, correspond to the attainment targets of the National Curriculum. The Dearing Report itself cautions against a 'complex bureaucratic process which eats into teaching time and involves a great deal of effort'; in keeping with its 'lean' approach it suggests a minimum content — referenced reading and writing records with attainment levels and a 'brief note' of any significant progress made in speaking and listening.

An alternative and more 'elaborate' model might include records passed on from feeder schools, pupils' personal statements, skills checklists and planned and sequenced self-assessments as well as teacher statements. This is obviously the full treatment that a subject like English requires. Unfortunately the deluge of commitments faced by today's teachers make it physically impossible to fulfil this kind of commitment. Departments will inevitably have to decide where they are going to draw the line; it is difficult enough developing new schemes alongside those extant in the school without also having to combat innovations such as testing at the age of 14 and drastically revised syllabuses for 16-year-olds. The perhaps well-intentioned advice from Dearing mentioned above once again misses the point of keeping a language file and records. The NATE organization has offered one of the most thorough rationales for developing such a policy (NATE, 1986).

Such an approach will involve a longitudinal record of development that is capable of providing evidence and comment upon a broad range of language activities. It will serve the double purpose of giving encouragement through the accumulated evidence of achievement but at the same time will reveal concerns that may be acted upon following discussion between pupil and teacher. In this sense it demonstrates what Blanchard (1986) describes as 'concern for the pupil's developing consciousness and for the fostering of mutual respect between teacher and pupil'. The file will provide evidence to help in discussions with parents and anyone else who requires information about the pupil. However, we are reminded that words can be ambiguous and that it is very difficult to avoid subjectivity when judging language work. With regard to levels of attainment, therefore, it will be crucial to provide standardization and moderation opportunities for all members of the department. This has been recognized in the Dearing Report but must also be acknowledged, as must the whole system of assessment, by evidence and recording; the school managers need to be made aware of relevant issues. It is surely not reasonable that management should be divorced from the processes of assessment; neither should it assume that standardization may be carried out in departmental meeting time or in the teachers' own time.

For some years it has been difficult for departments to find standardization time, mainly because this system of assessment, because of the special nature of English, has been 'out of step' with most other subjects. As a result there has been lack of equality between schools with regard to the time negotiated and also therefore to the quality of the moderation exercises carried out for GCSE coursework. With the need to agree on pupils' achievement 'levels' at the age of 14 the problem has doubled although there seem to be few schools where finding time for this crucial exercise has been a management priority. Since one of its end-products is a summative grading or levelling which often satisfies the assessment expectations of schools in general, and since the government has called attention to the need for 'an effective system of moderated teacher assessment' (SCAA, 1993), there may be hope for some developments in this line. In the meantime it is up to individual departments to negotiate for time in a very busy year, using arguments for staff development and training along with those for arriving at and maintaining standards.

With other subjects adopting coursework elements during the flourishing years of GCSE, the notion of standardization has become less alien for schools and the communities that they serve. It has been suggested that keeping parents informed of assessment processes is a desirable objective of a whole school policy and would certainly be a useful preparation for discussions held at parents' evenings. If parents and governors are informed of these developments then they are more likely to add their collective 'voice' in demanding reasonable time allocation for what they would consider to be an extremely valuable exercise.

It will be necessary for individual departments to decide the nature and content of the language folder; any integration with whole school policies will influence the extent of the information provided and the extent of detail will depend on the agreed number of criteria and the amount of time a department feels will be available for its effective development. In considering time it will be imperative to consider the collecting of evidence, writing comments, recording other information, discussing or 'conferencing' with individual pupils. It is easy to underestimate the amount of time required for negotiation with each child in a group. Departments must be prepared to change the model of assessment once it is trialled, modifying details in the light of experience; most will inevitably wish to simplify the process but must be alert to the lesser value of convenient tick-box alternatives. At all costs the system must be manageable within the terms of reference for individual departments. There must, however, be minimum requirements for a folder if it is to retain any credibility and be of service for formative and summative purposes.

If the folder is to provide 'growing evidence' of a pupil's language development there should be sufficient examples of written work and the drafting and revision process. How much is required will be a department decision. The NATE (1986) has suggested six pieces per year, representing one piece of writing per half-term in the first three years of secondary education (11–14). This should represent a growing range of types of writing, in keeping with the statutory requirements of the National Curriculum programmes of study. Some departments may wish to include a common assignment for comparative purposes in view of 'testing' requirements; this would probably be the outcome of a controlled conditions exercise set at the same time for a whole year group, perhaps replacing the traditional end-of-year examination, which has in any case reappeared now that the assessment wheel has turned full circle.

Particular schools that have been through such development processes have often begun with an elaborate and unmanageable system, itemizing too many skills (often in response to National Curriculum statements of attainment) and attempting to cram every single piece of writing into increasingly fragile folders. This not only raises time management and storage issues but creates a bulk of work and information that is not always necessary for making realistic and meaningful judgments that could as easily be made by more selective procedures and more concise commentary in the teacher's written records. One school with a similar history, after experiencing the above problems and realizing that records that merely reflect the curriculum are inadequate, has now adopted a 'minimalist' model of collecting a piece of personal writing; a piece of writing for a purpose other than narrative; a non-literary response; a 'common' assignment produced in controlled conditions, and evidence of drafting. In addition, the documentation will include an index of a range of activities undertaken in speaking and listening, reading and writing and a further document allowing for brief comment on particular activities which should be formative and shared with individual pupils (see appendix I). The remaining documents are sheets on the various skills areas completed by the pupils themselves and consisting of 'can do' and 'hope to do' statements that he or she is invited to check with a tick.

Pupils are also invited to write lengthier comments reflecting on their progress, attitude and further intentions. For these to have value, time will of course need to be found for individual discussion; self-assessment, although important, is prone to invite an overbalance of subjective comment. The NATE believes that this exercise could be carried out twice a year, perhaps formally by a group of children, although it may be necessary to discuss the process first and it may be expedient to offer a series of questions to act as guidelines for their written comments. John Blanchard's *Out in the Open* (1986) gives a number of examples as appendices to the book for all ages of pupil from 12 to 16. Standardization and moderation exercises will be obligatory for national tests and for GCSE coursework, but it will be useful to rehearse this exercise at least once a year in the less formal setting of the departmental meeting where sample folders may be discussed not only for grade or level purposes in respect of reporting, but also as a forum for exchanging ideas and solving problems, monitoring the progress of the scheme with the understanding that it may be necessary to adapt and modify certain practices or procedures (see appendix II).

Whereas an English department may be clear in its approach to assessment and have a number of strategies in place for dealing with its implementation, it may, as has been suggested, find itself at odds with school practices as a whole. With any luck the school will have a general assessment policy that will take into account the particular needs and methods characteristic of its various faculties or departments, following on from a careful investigation. There are many opportunities for accidentally duplicating information. It frequently happens, for example, that students returning from work experience placements will encounter invitations to similar exercises of self-assessment in both their English and Personal and Social and Careers lessons. It would again be the responsibility of the school managers to ensure that such evaluation, self-assessment or feedback is coordinated, so that work is not duplicated, time not wasted and students not confused.

Elsewhere we have seen events turn almost full circle. In the early 1980s, when assessment through a profile of student achievement across a range of language skills began to develop momentum, many English departments found themselves at odds with general school policies that for a number of purposes required the results of assessment in the form of grades and percentages. For most non-English departments this simply meant the setting of a common examination with 'cut-off' thresholds, sometimes loosely related to GCE percentage boundaries. It then became the task of English departments to argue against the common end-of-year examination and promote the introduction of a system more suited to the specific nature of learning in the subject and the organization through mixed-ability groupings. More fortunate departments were allowed to go their own way and the school reporting system was adjusted appropriately. In other cases departments found themselves attempting with some difficulty to marry two systems of assessment and reporting. It would make the most sense if the English department progress report and the annual English report to parents were one and the same thing. Before this can happen there is a need to implement whole school discussion so that traditional models of education — i.e. teach, examine, report — may be addressed and evaluated. It may be that the progress report/record of achievement, backed up by evidence of coursework, will be recognized for a more honest and frank form of assessment that is understood and approved by parents, thus helping the 'demystification' process at the consultation evening.

Curriculum-Led Practice

Departments should be urged to debate issues and not be assessment-led. Careful attention to a programme for the content of an English syllabus will probably reveal a consensus that includes all of the statutory requirements drawn up and slimmed-down by the politicians and their advisers; it will also probably be a wider, more meaningful and appropriate syllabus than this. Similarly, with assessment, departments must ask fundamental questions about *what* is to be assessed, as well as *why* and *how*. It is crucial to the integrity of the department that these principles are agreed upon and it is important also that these principles are presented in a palatable form to pupils, senior school managers and parents. It may well be found that patterns of formative and summative statutory assessment may be established that are both manageable and compatible. It is most important that commonly-held principles are not compromised by the statutory requirements; indeed I have noted that OFSTED has criticized departments taking up too much time in preparing for tests. The issue of testing children at the age of 14 remains controversial at the time of writing (1994); however it is to be resolved we must resign ourselves to the inevitable fact that some preparation must take place. There is no reason, however, why some of this preparation should not be fully integrated into schemes of work and assessment, including the assessment style of the current SAT, whatever that may be, without disruption or a sense of inconsistency. Research shows that more departments are organizing English work in modules which allow for greater flexibility, adapting teaching to the needs of pupils. Since experience has shown that a Shakespeare play is likely to feature largely in any statutory test, it may be worth considering building a module around the chosen text or at least featuring this text significantly in a more general 'drama' module; assessment would thus be carried out according to departmental policy at the same time as taking care of preparatory requirements for formal testing. Assessment will be built into each module following the principles outlined in the first part of this chapter. The majority of this assessment will need to be of the formative approach bringing together statements drawn from negotiation, the teacher's 'competence/judgment' observations and the student's own judgments (see appendix III).

Previously, the 'problem' of a lack of an end-of-year examination was overcome by some departments by virtue of the fact that all GCSE syllabuses required that some assignments were undertaken in controlled conditions. This became generally an exercise in using already prepared materials for a specific writing purpose within a given time. Literature examinations, on the other hand, could take the form of an 'unseen' criticism or the compiling of an assignment against the clock. Whatever the merits or demerits of the controlled conditions piece, it often made some managers feel better that there was some form of terminal examination.

With the statutory revision of English syllabuses in 1993 and the reduction in the amount of coursework permissible, the setting of an examination for practice became a standard feature for the first cohort of students to sit the paper. Since teaching and assessment are so integral many felt it was necessary also to alter classroom methods quite radically, thus abandoning such fiercely-held principles as mixed-ability teaching. Perhaps the message to these departments should be that it is possible to continue normal practice with GCSE work and prepare for the examination at the same time, so long as the coursework is recognized as being preparation for the terminal examination. Departments will continue to set 'controlled-conditions' style assignments but will also need to place considerably more emphasis on the significance of its weighting. The nature of the controlled pieces will reflect the particular style of the examination syllabus; in most cases these will be directed writing assignments inviting candidates to complete a task for a specific purpose and audience, often as a response to pre-released stimulus material (see appendix IV). Sadly, some departments have had their thinking done for them and students have returned to sets based on ability to correspond with tiers of entry. It is to be hoped that these students will benefit from as broad and rich a curriculum as that enjoyed by their more fortunate peers, although when this has happened to younger children set in preparation for national tests, pupils in lower ability sets 'were not always taught the full range of the National Curriculum' (OFSTED, 1993). There must also, inevitably, be a return to diminished motivation and its attendant problems when groups are organized in this way:

> Mixed ability teaching is likely to be one of the few ways in which student motivation, teacher morale and student attainment are maintained. (Broadbent and Moger, 1992)

It will be necessary for terminal examinations to inform some planning, but if we accept that the preparation of coursework is also preparation for the examination, then there need be no sense of disjunction between course and assessment. As when planning courses with younger children, it would be expedient to devise a series of modules that cover all the requirements of the National Curriculum but also reflect the assessment pattern for the terminal examination. A controlled piece might be built into each unit as a standard feature. Departments with a number of staff teaching English literature may find it advantageous for colleagues to work in pairs on specific texts, devising modules of work that can be shared with other teachers working on the same novels, plays and poetry. Those departments maintaining a unitary approach to English teaching would wish to devise a non-literary unit ensuring that the requirements for 'English' were being met, although a necessarily wide range of language activities could still be supplied where the emphasis remains literature-based. At their best modules will bring together all the necessary elements of the National Curriculum, the examination syllabus, school resources and recording and assessment requirements. The beauty of 100 per cent coursework was that it not only brought coursework and assessment together but also provided continuing evidence of progress and development. Adopting the above approach will help teachers to continue to motivate students and at the same time provide a practical balance between coursework and examination. The pattern for the ensuing five-term course need not be unfamiliar.

It will be necessary as usual to begin in a positive manner, drawing attention to the more sophisticated areas of personal and social experience that will be under consideration. Beginning the course with an autobiographical unit, supported by relevant texts, has been found to be an excellent approach to identifying areas of interest appropriate to the age of the students. The theme also lends itself to a variety of literary texts that could be explored, as well as to a range of written and spoken activities. Running a 'short story' unit separately or concurrently is often a useful way of introducing or reviewing more specific literary areas of study before perhaps tackling the more demanding syllabus texts at a later date. The half term before Easter in the final year of the course will continue to be a period of intense activity, finalizing the contents of folders, commencing the internal and external moderation process as well as, perhaps, dealing with tests for 14-year-olds.

Some professionals have claimed that the oral element of language is unexaminable, but oracy has been described as 'the expression of the whole cultural development of emotion and general intelligence' (Knowles, 1983), and it is argued that it is therefore impossible to isolate the act of speaking for examination purposes. In addition, by formalizing oral assessment it is possible to deaden language activity. Once again, practice instigated by the development of the GCSE has established a very useful 'pyramid' model of assessment. This means that standards agreed by a group of representative moderators are filtered down to guide the judgment of individual teachers. The revised assessment arrangements for 14-year-olds and 16-year-olds still require reference to speaking and listening performance and it is possible to retain the good practice established in earlier years, especially if a department has appointed one member to be coordinator for spoken language. Subjective judgment may be offset if certain categories are defined by criteria; if the use of criteria is appropriate for written assignments, then criteria may also be drawn up for spoken utterences. Such a model based on agreed standards may be applied to a variety of opportunities for speaking and listening (see appendix V).

Written work, either in the form of an examination script or as part of the folder of coursework, is more easily quantifiable in terms of assessment than are speaking and listening activities. To the regret of many English teachers, the percentage allowable for assessment was reduced to 20 per cent in the 1994 examinations. There were fears of pre-GCSE concerns on a number of points regarding the reliability of external markers, previous evidence of discrepancies and emphasis on orthographic features. The unfairness of timed examinations for slow but bright pupils and the difficulties they present in assessing true performance are familiar arguments, many of which are known and understood by parents.

The assessment of childrens' reading at the age of 16 is another area of deep concern. The revised GCSE syllabus prohibits dual certification and the proposed (1994) National Curriculum orders with their prescriptive list of texts suggest there is going to be little time left for teaching English literature as an additional GCSE. What remains necessary is that we continue to create what Barton (1992) has called a 'reading ethos' providing a sense of purpose and challenge to children as readers. Young children may obtain a whole range of reading strategies only in a contextualized reading programme. Our assessment should indicate the development of independent reading enjoyment and critical appreciation. Referring to Blanchard's 'performance/competence' model of assessment mentioned earlier, I would also be identifying the range of reading expected to be undertaken by pupils, the clarity of understanding and the degree of response and perception related to it. Simple tests will not adequately reflect such developments in a child's reading; although statutory assessment arrangements will have to be considered, it must not be at the expense of such key elements of reading development. Evidence collected should include reading aloud and a variety of written responses which may include 'sequels, parodies, critical essays, comparative studies, etc.' (Brook, 1993). Central to this approach is the need to be more aware of each pupil's reading interests and habits. Reading records listing author, title and evaluative comment give a continuum of a child's reading from junior school to the sixth form and help identify the need to read from different genres. Opportunities for discussing reading with peers as well as with the teacher will help to engender what Barton calls 'a common critical vocabulary' including genre, viewpoint, metaphor, plot, character, etc., in order to foster the skills of comparison and discrimination (see appendix VI).

These features of good practice might be considered synonymous with the provision of a coherent reading and assessment policy (see appendix VII), in spite of the imposed testing and examination arrangements. Teachers have the responsibility to improve reading skills, encourage a genuine liking for reading and to deepen the pupil's understanding of the power of writing through differentiated styles and viewpoints. Prescribed reading lists adjusted to specific 'levels' intimate streamed classes and limited testing: a rich range and variety of reading cannot be assessed within the strictures of a one-and-a-half hour examination.

Conclusion

The question of assessment in the 1990s has been characterized by a conflict of interests; on the one hand the assertion by professionals that the only valid means of assessing language development is by a necessarily complex process covering a range of skills; on the other hand the imposition of a narrow system of assessment by timed tests. Dearing's compromise, arising from a desire to placate burdened teachers, seeks to minimize unnecessary work but, unwittingly perhaps, cuts out a lot of the good practice. In the context of the past thirty years or so we have experienced some radical changes: we go from one extreme to another and the cycle begins again. In particular we have seen how the development of the GCSE informed approaches to assessment through moderation, against a range of criteria, with an emphasis on the celebration of achievement.

The increasing drive by the government has been towards a more utilitarian curriculum assessed by narrow tests, the aim of which was to produce 'results' along a normal distributive curve, allowing for comparative assessments between individuals, schools and LEAs. This remains the agreement that Dearing wishes the profession to undertake in exchange for whatever he understands teacher assessment to be. It is hoped that some key principles and practices have been outlined with sufficient clarity and will be recognizable by the number of English teachers who have been concerned at radical alterations to a system that was working very well for schools and their constituencies and proved to be so consistent. This is where we are today and there is still much to be done.

Parents, headteachers and governors need to be informed of the negative outcomes of limited types of national curriculum assessment which fail to define adequately achievements in language development as well as take no account of the different interests of boys and girls, social and cultural backgrounds and the needs of children with special educational needs. The examination results of the first cohort of students to sit the papers of the revised GCSE were provisionally published in August 1994. The fact that they were generally better than anticipated and in some cases better than grades recorded for 100 per cent coursework in previous years did not alter the concern of English teachers: indeed it will still be argued that the coursework, properly standardized and moderated and covering a wider range of achievement, is the more reliable, valid and rigorous means of assessment.

The arrival of generalized 'level descriptions' and their requirement that strengths are weighed against weaknesses should be bad news for those supporting the unrepresentative evidence of short tests and further justify the reintroduction of a greater proportion of evidence through coursework. We are told there will be no further alteration to the National Curriculum and its assessment in English for five years after new orders are made statutory in January 1995. This will not be a period of passive acceptance; English teachers must continue with their good practice and protest at attempts to deny opportunities to demonstrate what is at the heart of the matter

a concern for the pupil's developing consciousness and for fostering
a mutual respect between teacher and pupil. (Blanchard, 1986)

References

ALLEN, D. (1987) *English, Whose English?*, London, NAAE/NATE.
ANWYLL, S. (1992) 'KS3 English pilot 1992: Evaluation — Sheffield LEA', *NATE News*, autumn.
BARTON, G. (1992) 'Personal response to literature', *Use of English*, summer.
BLANCHARD, J. (1986) *Out in the Open: A Secondary English Curriculum*, Cambridge, Cambridge University Press.
BROADBENT, S. and MOGER, R. (1992) 'Holding on to good practice', *The English and Media Magazine*, **28**, autumn.

BROOK, D.G. (1993/94) *Responses to National Curriculum Consultation Document*, English, Derby, Derbyshire County Council, July.

CATTY, M. (1992) 'KS3 English pilot', *NATE News*, autumn.

EVANS, T. (1982) *Teaching English*, London, Croom Helm.

FURLONG, T. (1992) 'CATS tales: Assessment and government policy', *The English and Media Magazine*, **26**, spring.

HMI/OFSTED (1990/91, 1991/92, 1992/93) *The Implementation of the Curricular Requirements of the Education Reform Act: English*, London, HMSO.

JOHNSON, J. (1992) 'Introduction', in *NATE Made Tongue-tied by Authority*, London, NATE.

KNOWLES, L. (1983) *Encouraging Talk*, London, Methuen.

MARTIN, D. (1994) 'Myopic masquerade', *The English and Media Magazine*, **30**, summer.

MOBLEY, M., EMERSON, C., GODDARD, I. *et al.* (1986) *All About GCSE*, London, Heinemann.

NATE (1988) *The English Curriculum: Writing*, London, NATE.

PROTHEROUGH, R. (1983) *Encouraging Writing*, London, Methuen.

PROTHEROUGH, R. and ATKINSON, J. (1991) *The Making of English Teachers*, Milton Keynes, Open University Press.

SCAA (1993) *The National Curriculum and its Assessment: Final Report*, London, SCAA, December.

TIMES EDUCATIONAL SUPPLEMENT, Leader article, 15 February 1993.

WELDON, H. (1992) 'Writers blocked', *Times Educational Supplement*, 13 November.

Folder Work: An Example of Index Sheet

ENGLISH DEPARTMENT

INDEX TO COURSEWORK ACTIVITIES

TEACHER:

GROUP: YR 10

DATE: 1993–95

CENTRE NO.:

Number	Date	Activity/texts/audience	ATs covered
1.	14 Sept. '93	Talking about a memory	2
2.	21 Sept. '93	Autobiographical writing	2, 3
3.	8 Oct. '93	Short Story assignment based	2, 3
		on 'The Fury' by S. Barstow &	
		'Strike Pay' by D.H. Lawrence	

Oral and Written Coursework

ENGLISH DEPARTMENT

ORAL AND WRITTEN COURSEWORK

Teacher: _____   Student: _____   Group: 10Y

Date: 1993–94

Number of Activity	Speaking and Listening Level/Grade	Reading Level/ Grade	Writing Level/ Grade	Teacher's Comments
1	7+			*A lively, fluent and amusing account; should try to talk for longer period.*
2.			7	*Some good descriptive writing; but needs to vary sentence structure.*
3.		7+	8-	*Very good literature assignment, well-organised and showing a good understanding of the issues. Need to check paragraphing.*
	LEVEL AWARDED AT THE END OF THE YEAR OR COURSE			

Folder Work: Notes on Moderation Procedure

Either

1 Each teacher selects five (or as appropriate to size of candidature) folders covering a range of ability within his/her group.

2 Internal Moderation Meeting
   (i)   Folders are placed on tables appropriate to teacher-assessed level or grade, i.e. the 'C' table; 'D' table, etc.
   (ii) Pairs of teachers read and assess all folders on their table looking at content; syllabus requirements; range of activities, etc.
   (iii) Folders are passed between tables for consultation as 'standards' are established.
   (iv) Plenary session where decisions are confirmed and 'problem' folders are discussed.

3 Further period of time allowed for pairs to exchange remaining folders awarding grades/levels based on standardization meeting. Experienced teachers matched with those less-experienced.

OR

   (i)   Teacher in charge selects approximately 20 folders covering whole range of ability.
   (ii) Reading time given (one, two weeks) for all teachers involved to assess folders.
   (iii) Internal moderation meeting to standardize levels/grades calling up individual folders.

The first method tends to cover more folder assessment.

Approaching a Shakespeare Text (Macbeth), Based on Evans (1982)

The following outline of a scheme of work for *Macbeth* suggests a variety of activities and related assessment opportunities.

— need to demystify and make relevant to the modern world;
— important that the first lessons in the unit have an impact. Look at a key speech with different varieties of register/dialect;
— important to relate the text to the stage/theatre;
— try to find modern texts on the same themes;
— choose a dramatic incident to arouse interest;
— use drama and improvization techniques to 'get into' the text;
— the only way to gain a 'feel' for the language is to read the play, although recent examinations and statutory tests may detail specific scenes or allow concentration on an area of study;
— always concentrate on plot and 'tone' before character, theme and language study;
— plot summaries provide scope for group activities and 'peer' assessment;
— a wide range of writing activities should be made available for a variety of purpose and audience.

English Department: Policy Statements on Assessment

(Developed by Derry Twomey, Teacher in Charge of Lower School English, Eckington School)

Assessment and Personal Records

Aims

(a) To identify the strengths and weaknesses of an individual pupil's work.
(b) To maintain an up-to-date professional assessment that can be used to discuss a pupil's progress with either the pupil, or his/her parents, or other colleagues who may need a report on a particular pupil's English work.
(c) To illustrate how an individual pupil is being catered for in a mixed ability teaching situation.
(d) To help the support teacher quickly organize a programme of work for a pupil, if required.
(e) To help other colleagues, within the English department, to become quickly acquainted with a pupil's work when they take over a class at the beginning of a new academic year.

Objectives

(a) Each teacher will keep a record of assessment for every group she is in charge of. A folder, with a recording sheet for individual pupils, will be provided.
(b) The folder will be used to record the pupil's progress in writing, reading and oral work.
(c) The general guidelines for assessing these skills, and which are provided with the folder, should be used.
(d) Teachers should study the guidelines for assessment and make constructive notes on these areas of a pupil's English work. These comments may be added to by colleagues from other subject areas. For example, a science teacher could record that a pupil is unable to reproduce the findings

of an experiment in a table form, or a history teacher may remark that there is no logical development in a pupil's discursive essays.
(e)   A pupil's personal interest in certain aspects of writing, reading and oral work, should also be recorded.

Self-assessment for Students Answering Part Two of GCSE Paper, 1994: Directed Writing (Based on Anthology of Pre-released Material)

Sense of *character*:
   have you written as if you are presenting the character's point of view?
Sense of *situation*:
   does your writing show a real understanding of the character's feelings about his/her relationships?
Sense of *style*:
   have you written in the appropriate style for a diary, report, letter, etc.?
   can you write vivid descriptions of people, places and things?
   have you used short sentences and longer sentences where they fit in with your ideas and description?
Sense of *drama*:
   can you make your writing exciting and can you create tension?
dialogue:
   can you punctuate speech?
proof-reading:
   have you checked everything?
   have you time to write a second draft?

The Assessment of Oral Work

General Considerations

Does the pupil:
(a)   Participate in oral situations? Pair/group/class discussions.
(b)   Speak clearly and effectively?
(c)   Show a sense of audience?
(d)   Order ideas effectively?
(e)   Use a range of appropriate language?

Instructions and Directing

Is the pupil able:
(a)   To give clear instructions?
(b)   To clearly follow instructions?

Giving and Interpreting Information

Can the pupil:
(a) Relay information?
(b) Convey information based on personal knowledge?
(c) Convey information based on observation?
(d) Summarize and convey information from notes and other sources?
(e) Answer questions?
(f) Report the outcome of a collaborative task?

Narrating

Is the pupil able to:
(a) Retell a story?
(b) Tell a personal anecdote?
(c) Construct a story?
(d) Summarize the plot of a book?

Describing and Specifying

Can the pupil:
(a) Describe a picture?
(b) Relate information in a tabulated form?

Discussion

Is the pupil able to:
(a) Collaborate with others?
(b) Evaluate evidence with others?
(c) Build an hypothesis based on a discussion?
(d) Persuade others?
(e) Reevaluate his/her views as a result of discussion?

The Assessment of Reading

Practical Considerations

(a) Does the pupil normally read a book?
(b) Does the pupil know where to procure a book? Library/reading boxes/ school bookshop/class reader/personal sources.
(c) What is the pupil's attitude to reading? Reads regularly/sometimes/only when necessary/never.

(d)   Does the pupil read a variety of books? Various authors/fiction/non-fiction/diverse themes.
(e)   Is the pupil reading at the correct level?
(f)   Cfr. *The Assessment of Reading*, a Special Needs booklet, for a more detailed assessment of the reading ability of a pupil.

Fiction

(a)   Does the pupil read fiction books?
(b)   Is the pupil familiar with the Fiction section of the Library?
(c)   Is the pupil able to locate a fiction book?
(d)   Has the pupil a knowledge of fiction authors?
(e)   Does the pupil complete the reading of fiction books selected?
(f)   Does the pupil understand the main story elements of plot, character and theme?
(g)   Is the pupil's first impression of a book modified after reading?
(h)   Does the pupil pay close attention to detail?
(i)   Does the pupil understand meaning conveyed in connotations?
(j)   Does the pupil respond to structure and style?
(k)   Is there any empathy with characters?
(l)   Is the pupil utilizing reading for extending vocabulary, concept . . . ?
      Points (g) — (k) are especially relevant for Third Year groups.

Non-Fiction

(a)   Is the pupil familiar with the non-fiction section of the library?
(b)   Is the pupil able to use table of contents, indices and glossaries relevant to the information required?
(c)   Is the pupil able to scan and read selectively?
(d)   Is the pupil able to locate and extract necessary information?
(e)   Does the pupil relate information?
(f)   Does the pupil relate pictures and text?
(g)   Is the pupil able to evaluate and reevaluate evidence?
(h)   Does the pupil make relevant notes?
(i)   Is the pupil able to summarize material and sequence the evidence?

The Assessment of Writing

Content

(a) Personal experience
(b) Observations
(c) Given material
(d) Books, plays, films
(e) Imagination
(f) Memory

If the intention of the writing was based on one, or more, of these *content* areas, how has the writer responded?

Organization

(a) Structure: genre, layout, tables, etc.
(b) Continuous prose
(c) Paragraphs
(d) Tables
(e) Diagrams
(f) List of points

Appropriateness and Style

(a) Sense of audience, knowledge and interest
(b) Register: formal, informal
(c) Variety of sentence structure
(d) Specificity of vocabulary
(e) Colloquialisms and dialect
(f) Non-standard forms

Knowledge of Grammatical Conventions

(a) Coherence of whole text
(b) Coherence of each section
(c) Sentence
(d) Clause
(e) Phrase

Grammatical/Punctuation Markers

(a) Full stop, question mark, etc.
(b) Pronouns

(c)   Time and tense sequences
(d)   Singular and plural

Knowledge of Orthographical Conventions

(a)   Typographical errors/systematic experiments
(b)   Spelling
(c)   Word division: internal punctuation, apostrophe

Capitalization

(a)   Sentence position
(b)   Upper/lower case
(c)   Proper names, titles

Non-Grammatical Punctuation

(a)   Superfluous commas
(b)   Commas in lieu of full stops
(c)   Incomplete speech marks

Developing a *Reading Journal*

The following notes and self-assessment scheme are taken from a reading journal developed by Jacqui Cutts and colleagues at Fortismere School, Mill Hill, London.

Purpose

The Reading Journal provides an imaginative and structured approach to engaging with a wide range of texts throughout the lower school years.

It encourages independent reading and acts as a *record of achievement* in reading.

It creates the right conditions for the discussion of progress and ideas between students and adults (both teacher and parent).

Contents

— an index of books read throughout school life (home and school);
— 'useful terms', for example, 'plot', 'theme';
— reviewing: students are encouraged to give personal responses rather than repeat the plot;
— writing a synopsis;
— discussion of use of language in groups;
— recording most exciting incident/episode; most interesting character/ development;
— discovering new vocabulary;
— opportunity to read with adult or peer and discuss problems and achievements.

Reading Journal Assessment Scheme

1 I can read aloud fluently and vary the tone (suggesting character, feeling or mood).
2 I have expressed opinions about what I like/dislike.
3 I can explain why I hold those opinions.

4 I have chosen my own texts.
5 I have read:
      a range of stories
      a range of poems
      a modern novel
      a play
      a non-fiction text
      a text(s) written before the twentieth century
      a text written from another culture.
6 I can read silently and concentrate for . . .
7 I have made predictions about what happens later on in the book based on my understanding of what I have read so far.
8 I can relate what I have read to my own experiences.
9 I have made a personal or creative response to the text.
10 I have talked/written about the plot, setting and characters. (That is the storyline, the places where the story takes place and the people whom this story is about.)
11 I have used chapter headings and illustrations to bring out the meaning of texts I have read.
12 I have looked at the 'mood' of texts I have read.
13 I have looked at the themes in the texts I have studied. (That is the idea or message which we receive from the events and characters in the book.)
14 I have considered the structure of texts I have read. (The way in which the book is organized.)
15 I have studied the particular way an author uses language (and chooses words and phrases) in the text for particular effect.
16 I have studied the sound of the language used; rhyme, alliteration, figures of speech, etc. (for example, poetry).
17 I have seen evidence in my reading of how language (grammar and vocabulary) changes with time.

Appendix VI

Self-assessment Sheet for Students Answering Part One of GCSE Paper, 1994, 'What Causes Conflict?'

— Have you read the question carefully?
Do you *know* what you are expected to do?
Have you planned your answer carefully: does your writing have a *beginning, middle* and *end*?
— Need to link ideas: are the points you are making linked together and have you used *paragraphs* to separate the main ideas?
— Have you really presented an argument or are you 'telling a story'?
— Have you come to a conclusion?
— Reading skills: have you shown an understanding of the texts?
: have you answered the question or just given a summary of a few of the texts?

General Points

TONE: is this right for the *purpose*?

Sense of AUDIENCE: who are you writing for? What kind of language would you use for a teen magazine, for instance?

PROOF-READING: check sentence structure, punctuation and spelling?

PRESENTATION: how clear is your handwriting considering that you are writing against the clock?

USEFUL PHRASES: If you are presenting an argument have you used any of the following phrases?

'Several people think . . .'
'Many believe that . . .'
'It is often said . . .'
'It is my belief . . .'
'I disagree . . .'
'However, . . .'
'This may be true, but . . .'

Self-assessment (Developed by Jacqui Cutts & Colleagues at Fortismere School)

Please write about yourself (things you like, things you have learnt, things you would change) and the work you have done; be as honest as you can but make sure you are *fair* to yourself.

These questions are to help you do this; you do not have to answer all of them, just those which seem relevant at the moment. You may add anything you feel is not covered by them. Try to answer them as fully as you can.

1 How have you been working this half-term/term in English? Can you give reasons for your answer?
2 How much effort have you put into the following: reading; talking; listening; writing; homework? Can you suggest why this is so?
3 Do you feel you have progressed in any of the categories in question 2? Again, can you suggest why?
4 Which skills and ideas do you think you have learnt about?
5 Is there any piece of work with which you are particularly pleased? Can you explain how it differs from your other work?
6 What parts of English do you really enjoy? Why is this?
7 Is there any aspect of English you do not enjoy? Can you say why?
8 Have you found any work difficult? If so, what could you do to avoid problems in the future — what could your teacher, your friends, *you*, do to help?

9 Is there anything new or different you would like to see covered in English?

10 Finally, make a list of things you have read both in and out of English; make a note of any films, videos, and plays you may have seen.

'Carrie's War'

A *Characters*

Why is *Miss Evans* described as 'a small frightened mouse?'
What do the following phrases tell us about Mr. Evans?

(i)   'the children heard the roar of his voice'.
(ii)   'they heard the heavy tread of feet down the passage'.
(iii) 'they heard the bang of the door'.

B *Understanding the story*

(i)   In what ways was Mr. Evans a bully?
(ii)   Describe the first meeting with Mr. Evans. Did it go well or badly?
(iii) What do the following phrases mean:
       'his bark is worse than his bite' (p. 29)
       'he won't stand to be crossed' (p. 29)
(iv)   Why did Mr. Evans threaten to beat Nick?
       Why did he change his mind?

C *Assignments*

(i)   Imagine that you are either Carrie or Nick. Write a letter to a friend
       back home in London describing your first few days in Wales. You
       need not worry about addresses; just think up a name for the friend.
(ii)   Look at the pictures below. What is happening in the pictures?

Example of a Shakespeare unit for year 10 (age 14/15)

MACBETH

First half-term: practical/oral activities

Begin reading the play

Students devise headlines summing up each scene in Acts 1 and 2

Students act out situations and relate to play

Design a set for the opening scenes of the play

Discussion on atmosphere

Discuss how particular scenes might be directed

Identify key quotations

Write diary entries for Lady Macbeth over the first two acts.

Determine the pros and cons of having the ghost of Banquo visible in a production

Macbeth quiz

Interview characters — mock trials

Second half-term: mainly written assignments

Detailed analysis of Lady Macbeth's sleepwalking scene, finding references to earlier scenes

Compare Duncan's sons' response to his death with that of Macbeth and Lady Macbeth

Show how Macbeth/Lady Macbeth relationship develops through the play . . .

Ideas of light and darkness in the play

'The Empty Space of Not Knowing': Childhood, Education and Race in African-American Literature (14–19)

Neil Campbell

I will come forward and sing from memory songs they will need once more to hear. For it is the song of the people, transformed by the experience of each generation, that holds them together, and if any part of it is lost the people suffer and are without soul. If I can only do that, my role will not have been a useless one at all. (Walker, 1976)

Who will compute the lonely nights made less lonely by your songs, or the empty pots made less tragic by your tales? (Angelou, 1969)

My tribe never practiced any magic arts, but storytellers all, they cling very close to my ear and tell softly what I have forgotten or have never known. (Davis, 1992)

Contexts: Teaching African-American

Current and future 'A' level syllabuses in literature show a growing interest in the literature of African-Americans, both as individual set texts, and as thematic topics.[1] Writers like Toni Morrison appear on almost all the syllabuses now being prepared, alongside Alice Walker, Maya Angelou and James Baldwin. At GCSE and within the English National Curriculum, there are also Angelou and James Baldwin. There are also recommended texts such as those by Mildred Taylor and Rosa Guy, writing about the experience of African-Americans. It is with these innovations in mind that I want to examine some of these writers in a wider sociohistorical context linked to a thematic approach that teachers would find both interesting and useful for their own discussions of the African-American experience. I am not going to suggest a step-by-step approach to the texts, but instead I will explore some key ideas and the context in which they emerge, and provide a starting point for more detailed examinations of the books. I will suggest in the appendix some specific classroom approaches that may be useful to follow up the ideas within this chapter.

I have deliberately chosen a structure which will theorize certain aspects of the African-American experience, and then examine the implications of this through the work of significant writers. I have tried to demonstrate the arguments by adopting three authors' works of varying degrees of complexity; Mildred Taylor, Maya Angelou and Toni Morrison, and in so doing indicating the ways in which their works can be interconnected and cross-referred around specific themes; childhood, education and race. For example, I will show how in childhood, when education and school are seen as priorities, African-American literature has stressed an alternative current of learning which questions the official education of white America and emerges through aspects of everyday life. Indeed, it is through this process of learning that black history has been passed on from generation to generation. The texts I examine give voice to this process from different points of view and are placed within their cultural context in order to stress their interrelationship to African-American history. Although I am primarily concerned here with the 'A' level student and teacher, I have in mind the wording of the document *English in the National Curriculum: Draft Proposals* (May 1994) when it calls for literary study to encourage a 'breadth of reading' which will (a) 'offer perspectives on society and community and their impact on the lives of individuals'; (b) examine 'other cultures and traditions'; and (c) inspire students' 'engagement with the ideas and themes of the literature they read'. My purpose is to suggest an approach to these objectives, stimulate ideas about how these books may be studied within a wider context, and raise important political and social questions relevant to any minority cultural group.

Lawrence Levine's *Black Culture and Black Consciousness* (1977) quotes an ex-slave as saying,

> If you want Negro history . . . you will have to get it from somebody who wore the shoe, and by and by from one to the other you will get a book. (p. 443)

The statement suggests a tension in the way black history has been recorded and transmitted which centres on the difference between lived, dynamic experience conveyed from generation to generation, and the represented versions found in books. For the speaker here, the more authentic and reliable is that 'from somebody who wore the shoe' because it is unmediated by the impulse of historians to organize, construct and explain in a 'grand narrative of legitimation'.[2] Instead, individual narratives from those who lived and felt the experiences are significant and valued, since, as Toni Morrison has said, 'people crave narration . . . That's the way they learn things' (quoted in Clayton, 1993, p. 93). This knowledge is 'unauthorized' (*ibid.*, p. 95), because it comes from an unofficial source and does not carry the sanction of the educational norms of American mainstream society, but draws on vernacular traditions, oral tales and folk wisdoms rather than upon a more conventional and legitimated mode. Such a tension reveals an important point about African-American culture and its mistrust of given history and of its expression in institutions of education. Too often education articulates history through the discourse of the dominant culture to the detriment of other groups, so that their own histories and traditions are diminished or silenced. Ralph Ellison (1952) expresses this very concisely:

> For history records the pattern of men's lives, they say . . . All things, it is said, are duly recorded — all things of importance that is. But not quite, for actually it is only the known, the seen, the heard and only those events that the recorder regards as important that are put down, those lies his keepers kept their power by. (p. 353)

This discourse acts to verify, authorize and sanction views and opinions about African-American life and culture within the larger society and enshrines a particular view of the historical process (a grand, single narrative). A useful definition of discourse suggests it is

> the means by which institutions wield their power through a process of definition and exclusion . . . A discursive formation consists of a body of unwritten rules which attempt to regulate what can be written, thought and acted upon in a particular field. (Storey, 1993, p. 92)

A racial discourse built upon a precise and persistent means of defining the African-American in prescribed and limited terms of reference, was dictated and controlled by the 'master-culture' of white America beginning with slavery, thereby creating what has been termed 'enslaving fictions' (Benston, 1984, p. 151) because of the way language, so used, can enslave through setting discursive limits on the subject. In this respect, it is as if the master 'authored' the slave by means of ordering, defining and writing them in the precise manner determined by him, and not by the individual. This cultural domination and positioning of the African-American as subject, persisted in the control over education and learning that was available after emancipation. Much of the authorized education was aimed at disciplining African-Americans to accept a prescribed place and role in society, or as Raymond Williams (1958) puts it 'of leading the unenlightened to the particular kind of light which the leaders find satisfactory for themselves' (p. 234). One danger of this approach is that it denies, as slavery had denied speech to the slave, any sense of African-American history, and so any individual relationship to a past outside of the imposition of the slave system.

A similar argument is taken up in W.E.B. Du Bois's 'The Freedom to Learn' (1949):

> But if at any time, or for any long period, people are prevented from thinking, children are indoctrinated with dogma, and they are made to learn not what is necessarily true but what the dominant forces in their world want them to think is true, then there is no aberration from truth and progress of which such a people may not be guilty. (Du Bois, 1970, p. 230)

His terms are clear and rehearse contemporary critical ideas about dominant discourse and its authority over the framing of knowledge and power 'by making statements . . . authorizing views . . . describing . . . teaching . . . dominating, restructuring, and having authority over' (Said, 1978, p. 3) a specific area. Education holds the key since it has the capacity to give credence to preferred stories and their attendant ideologies. Edward Said's recent work on culture and imperialism begins with a very similar wariness about how such discourses are 'woven into the very fabric of education, where children . . . are taught to venerate and celebrate the uniqueness of *their* tradition (usually and invidiously at the expense of others)' (Said, 1993, p. xxix). He argues that his work is a 'corrective . . . a patient alternative' to such 'uncritical and unthinking forms of education', and this is precisely how I would view one of the functions of the texts I am going to examine in this essay. They attempt to do with fictional and autobiographical narratives what Said achieves with his theoretical studies of marginalized groups, which is to acknowledge and voice the 'counter-discursive' elements of African-American culture (Said in Couzens Hoy, 1986, p. 153) and assert 'self-creation and reformation of a fragmented familial past' (Benston, 1984, p. 152).

By employing the 'unauthorized knowledges' of African-American tradition, its stories, rituals, folk culture and songs, these texts present what Said (1993) calls 'another way of telling' (p. 405) the readers about American history and its people. Education and schooling as such are not devalued or cast aside in these works, nor in black life, where it has always been valued highly, but it is supplemented by an other education, by what I have termed, borrowing from Said, a counter-discourse. This runs alongside mainstream education or enters into dialogue with it, sometimes complementing, challenging or even contradicting its assertions through the provision of an alternative model of knowledge and learning.

Children are the recipients of both normalized education and this alternative version and, therefore, have a unique position in much African-American literature, for they represent the point of connection between the past and the future, the private / domestic space (home) and the public / social space (school). Crossing between these spaces gives them a special sense of educational duality, and therefore provides writers with an opportunity to explore the collisions and contradictions that occur in the border territory of childhood.

As with much writing that employs the child as narrator or protagonist, an adult writer can examine a point where both self and society are being encountered in new and challenging ways. For the black child, there is the very prescient sense of a past shaped by slavery, but also the very real issues of living towards some kind of future outside of its shadow. This is one reason why so many African-American writers return, via autobiography or fictional recreations of the past, because they are seeking a 'sustained conversation with ancestral origins' (Benston, 1984, p. 167), an 'exorcism' of the past [3] and 'access to a new understanding of self' (*ibid.*). As Anthony Walton has written:

> We need to help every black child learn, as a matter of course, that being a black American involves a way of looking at the world, a philosophical position. We need a new story — . . . that gives them a teleological place to exist in the here and now. (in Early, 1993, p. 260)

The child's role in the texts is varied, but they share an important and dynamic relationship with the passing on of tradition and history through stories and experiences that are distinct from the source of learning provided by schools. I will show, for example, how Cassie Logan in *Roll of Thunder, Hear My Cry* grows as a result of her contact with the lived experience of racism and the struggle to overcome it in her familiy's life. As Walton argues, children are essential to the 'new story', and it is important that they do not simply inherit the accepted view, but establish 'a way of looking at the world' which is different and relevant. They must gather knowledge, rather than rely only on what is presented to them, and sift the many stories and lessons, creating for themselves a version of who they are, based upon the ideas of where they have come from.

Children are at a crossroads in the texts I examine, between childhood and adulthood and between accepted versions of history and the ability to question those views. For this reason, the books are concerned with identity, both as children and as African-Americans, and this gives the texts their power in the classroom with readers of various ethnic groups. As Kimberly Benston writes, 'self-creation and reformation of a fragmented familial past are endlessly interwoven' (1984, p. 152), and so as children shape their identities, they also unravel their histories too. These texts interrogate the ways of learning that inform the history of African-Americans through the explorations of the self and the urgent need for the protagonists to move closer to some sense of self-definition and identity outside of the definitions given by white society. Thus there is a double passage of learning which concerns the individual, but also something larger, what Levine called earlier 'Negro history'.

For teachers, this combination of a dual education, of what one might term the 'classroom' and the 'home', and double learning, of the individual and the communal group, is very exciting for it invites a detailed study of the texts, but within an historical, social context. This opens the way for interesting interdisciplinary connections between different types of texts, here confined to autobiography, essays and fiction, but which could include the relationship of written materials with film and television.[4] The possibility inherent within these texts is suggested in my title, borrowed from Toni Morrison, 'the empty space of not knowing', for it relates, in part, to a goal of teaching texts of this kind, which is to expand and challenge accepted ideas about people of colour in all cultures, and also to show how some writers have sought, in a variety of styles, to fill 'the space of *not knowing*' with perceptive and exciting knowledges previously hidden or erased from the general view, in ways that permit the reader to reassess and revise their own thoughts about how history is itself constructed and passed on. For example, as the children learn through experience of the world, so too do the readers placed in a parallel position of enlightenment, and are able to empathize with the revelatory knowledge that ensues. So as Maya Angelou (1969) writes, these texts explore 'the general darkness just beyond the great blinkers of childhood' (p. 74) by entering into it and permitting the readers to discover what lies there. Thus both the reader and the protagonist are affected by the process of knowing, and in varying degrees, by filling in the 'empty space of not knowing' that preceded the journey.

Contexts: Beyond Slavery

African-American history has been too often dominated by the sense of 'not knowing' which has its roots in slavery and a system of denial which forbade education, and any kind of self-knowledge. The slave, rather like the child, was expected to be seen and not heard, obedient, not questioning and generally considered to be without authority and knowledge. As Frederick Douglass wrote in his narrative of slavery:[5] 'I know nothing; the means of knowing was withheld from me' (Douglass, 1845, p. 48). One of the 'means' was language and the right to speak freely, and this too was clearly denied:

> To all these complaints, no matter how unjust, the slave must answer never a word. Colonel Lloyd could not brook any contradiction from a slave. When he spoke, a slave must stand, listen, and tremble; and such was literally the case. (*ibid.*, p. 61)

Under slavery, the only approved learning was within the regime of the Master who controls, through violence and denial, the 'education' of the slave so as to create the subject that he desires; obedient, passive, silent. This model of repressive 'education', or of what Michel Foucault would call a 'disciplinary system', shapes the subject/slave through the discourse of slavery.[6] Any other form of learning beyond this control was dangerous:

> it was unlawful, as well as unsafe, to teach a slave to read . . . 'If you give a nigger an inch, he will take an ell'. A nigger should *know*

nothing but to obey his master — to do as he is told to do. *Learning would spoil the best nigger in the world. . . .* (*ibid.*, p. 78, my emphasis)

For Douglass, 'the white man's power to enslave the black man' was revealed in this moment as the authority over learning, and his 'pathway to freedom' was connected to the acquisition of knowledge other than that prescribed by the master. For Douglass it is a personal quest and a communal one, hence his setting up of the 'Sabbath school':

> They came because they wished to learn. Their minds had been starved by their cruel masters. They had been shut up in mental darkness . . . it was the delight of my soul to be doing something that looked like bettering the condition of my race. (*ibid.*, p. 121)

The 'education' of the master-discourse of denial, obedience and control is countered by the potential for another kind of learning provided from within the racial group/community and concerned with self-definition formulated by their language, in order to find their own voice within a framework of appropriate communal values. The word 'education' derives from two meanings; 'educare' which means 'to rear' and 'educere', 'to lead', and to an extent it is the original senses of the word that are important since the kind of rearing and leading comes not simply through an institutionalized system, but in diverse, pragmatic ways. Bell Hooks (1991) has written of this tradition in black life as part of what she terms the 'counter-hegemonic', which surfaces in

> habits of being that were a part of traditional black folk experience that we can re-enact, rituals of belonging . . . (the) sharing of stories that taught history, family genealogy, and the facts about the African-American past. (p. 39)

In this type of education 'memory (is) . . . a way of knowing and learning from the past' (*ibid.*, p. 40), as it reclaims a history 'whitened', as Malcolm X wrote, by years of it only being told in white versions, so that a 'decolonization of the black mind' could take place (*ibid.*, p. 79). A past constructed to follow the lines of white history could be challenged through the voicing of an alternative perspective which might empower and enable an active vision for the future. One function of the texts I examine is to enable this process, for example in Toni Morrison's commitment to a fictional reconstruction of slavery in *Beloved,* or Thulani Davis's child's view of the struggle for civil rights in the 1960s in her novel *1959.*

African-American literature has provided this kind of memory and alternative perspective, and like Douglass's slave narrative, suggested a form of resistance, a counter-narrative to the dominant 'story' being told about the ignorant and lazy black in the 'master-narrative' (which I take to mean both the story told by the master about the blacks and the dominant, emergent history within America itself).

In this tradition, Richard Wright's autobiographical *Black Boy* (1945), shows a boy growing up in a world of racism and inequality still defined by the 'discourse of slavery': 'acting in conformity with what others expected of me even though, by the very nature and form of my life, I did not and could not share their spirit' (p. 31). Wright records, like the works of Taylor, Angelou and Morrison, that the first battle is with the established assumptions that fix identity into set patterns and expectations, like the woman who on hearing he wanted to become a writer replies, 'You'll never be a writer . . . Who on earth put such ideas into your nigger head?' He comments 'she had assumed that she knew my place in life, what I felt, what I ought to be and I resented it with all my heart' (p. 129). The language that defines the African-American *positions* them into a set role, a prescribed place from which no other path can be followed, for to do so would intrude upon the routes established from the dominant group. Just like the slave, Wright felt denied and part of 'a white man's system' (Malcolm X, 1965, p. 380) that restricted and limited his progress. His quest was for an alternative to the pattern laid down by others:

> I hungered for a different life, for something new. The cheap pulp tales enlarged my knowledge of the world more than anything I had encountered so far . . . they were revolutionary, my gateway to the world. (Wright, 1945, p. 112)

Echoing Douglass's discovery of his 'pathway to freedom' bound up with learning, Wright saw the necessity of gaining knowledge wherever he could, even if it was in the most unconventional ways. What Toni Morrison (1981) would later call 'alternate wisdom' (p. 43) persists in Wright's work as the 'yearning for a kind of consciousness, a mode of being that the way of life about me had said could not be, must not be, and upon which the penalty of death had been placed'. It is, in the eyes of the dominant culture, the 'wrong track' for him to follow because it is 'different' and 'new' and would be seen to upset the 'natural order' of white hierarchical power and authority:

> The white South said that it knew 'niggers', and that I was what the the white South called a 'nigger'. Well, the white South had never known me — never known what I thought, what I felt . . . (they) said that I had a 'place' in life. Well, I had never felt my 'place'; or rather my deepest instincts had always made me reject the 'place' to which the white South had assigned me . . . as I had lived in the South I had not had a chance to learn who I was. The pressure of Southern living kept me from being the kind of person I might have been. I had been what my surroundings had demanded, what my family — conforming to the dictates of whites above them — had exacted of me, and what the whites had said that I must be. Never being fully able to be myself, I had slowly learned that the South could recognize but a part of a man. . . . (Wright, 1945, pp. 227–8)

Wright explains what I have termed the 'racial discourse' at work in the positioning and formation of the 'subject'. This latter term is appropriate for it carries the meanings of being both an individual subject and yet 'subjected' by the powers that surround and shape. This process is what Richard Wright terms 'my Jim Crow education' (Wright, 1989, p. 8), named after the laws that governed the lives of African-Americans, and best summarized in the line 'I must never again attempt to exceed my boundaries' (*ibid.*, p. 8).

The autobiographical work of Richard Wright emphasizes the 'dual role which every Negro must play' (*ibid.*, p. 13) in terms of two educations; the official discourse of the society and the school, and the alternative learning process that comes from other sources.[7] Survival with pride and a sense of self-worth is linked to the latter route, with its emphasis upon communal history and knowledge, and through this to a resistance and a counter to the definitions that are imposed from the dominant group. The alternative learning is a necessary process which empowers the African-American by asserting their own voices and stories alongside, or over, those established and socially sanctioned, authorized versions coming through the prevailing discourse.

Edward Said (1993) has written that,

The power to narrate, or to block other narratives from forming and emerging, is very important to culture and imperialism, and constitutes one of the main connections between them. (p. xiii)

And goes on to say that,

centrality gives rise to semi-official narratives that authorize and provoke certain sequences of cause and effect, while at the same time preventing counter-narratives from emerging. . . . (*ibid.*, p. 393)

In a world where a master-narrative dictates, authorizes, controls what you can be, say, do, think and so on, there is an important need to intervene in the process and 'un-block' the imperialist grip on a single version, and to 'progress beyond a number of assumptions that have been accepted uncritically for too long' (Levine, 1977, p. 444). Thus in African-American writing there has been 'a strong centripetal urge which continually drew them back to central aspects of their traditions even as they were surging outward into the larger society' (*ibid.*, pp. 444–5) with its dominant, imperialist discourse.

In Michele Wallace's comments on Toni Morrison's novel *The Bluest Eye*, she writes that the book's use of Dick and Jane stereotypes of perfect white family life,

lays out the world as classless, lily-white, sexually stratified but sexless, timeless and without history — as the single path to learning, to the achievement of knowledge. (Wallace in Gates, 1990, p. 64)

What this correctly identifies, in relation to normalized education, is its tendency to prescribe or set boundaries around knowledge and by so doing indicating what is acceptable and what is not. In this case, where race, class and gender issues are underlined, the education is demarcating a world very different from many people's experiences of family. Wallace and Morrison are showing the need for more than a 'single path to learning' in order that such stereotypes are challenged and questioned by other voices and images. This has been a central concern in black literature and relates closely to the historical debate about education in African-American life which goes back to the work of Booker T. Washington and W.E.B. Du Bois. For example, Washington believed in the education of the race as a means of securing the prosperity and prospects enjoyed by whites and set up colleges with that specific aim. Du Bois, who questioned Washington's acceptance of the American Dream myth as the right course to follow for the black American, wrote of something more which he saw in the young.

> There were however some . . . whose young appetite had been whetted to an edge by school and story and half-awakened thought. Ill could they be content, born without and beyond the world. And their weak wings beat against their barriers. . . . (Du Bois, 1961, pp. 67–8)

His attention to more than a single path, to 'school and story and half-awakened thought' suggests a recognition that learning comes from different quarters for the African-American and cannot be limited by official education. The 'barriers' are, after all, intrinsic to the very education system that controls and disciplines knowledge of both self and world.

I am going to concentrate on the work of three female African-American writers who have, in different and similar ways, charted this territory; Mildred Taylor, Maya Angelou and Toni Morrison.[8] It is significant that women writers have taken forward this argument about knowledge and learning in such a forthright manner, but it is not surprising since they have, as Zora Neale Hurston and Alice Walker have both commented, been the subjects of double oppressions as black and as women in a sexist and racist culture. Perhaps for this reason, women writers have paid attention to the demands of new learning, of re-defining the African-American so as to give worth to the 'unwritten history'[9] and the stories that present black tradition as important and strong. It is also very often a culture passed on through the women, in the private space of the home rather than the public space of the classroom where, as we have witnessed, other discourses dominate. In this space, women 'author' stories which they pass on to their children, being what early black feminist Anna Julia Cooper called 'the fundamental agency under God in the regeneration and retraining of the race'.[10] With women lies the possibility of countering the received, master-discourse, and breaking down some of the boundaries through which it prescribes black life.

Essential to the transcendence of the boundaries of dominant narrative is what George Lipsitz (1990) has called 'counter-memory', a term, although not a definition, he borrows from Michel Foucault.[11] He explains it as

> a way of remembering and forgetting that starts with the local, the immediate, and the personal. Unlike historical narratives that begin with the totality of human existence and then locate specific actions and events within that totality, counter-memory starts with the particular and the specific and then builds outward to a total story. (It) looks to the past for the hidden histories excluded from dominant narratives . . . (and) forces revision of existing histories by supplying new perspectives about the past . . . Counter-memory focuses on localized experiences with oppression, using them to reframe and refocus dominant narratives purporting to represent universal experience. (*ibid.*, p. 213)

The process is a necessary antidote to the accepted 'memory' provided through authorized history. I see it as part of what I call counter-discourse in order to suggest the wider process of learning which includes memory and its application in various forms of expression aimed, not to the past, but to the future. It is 'literary archaeology' visiting the 'site to see what remains were left behind and to reconstruct the world that these remains imply' (Morrison, 1987b, p. 112) in order to provide a sense of racial continuity in a culture structured on its denial.

Mildred Taylor, *Roll of Thunder, Hear My Cry* (1976)

Mildred D. Taylor's novel *Roll of Thunder, Hear My Cry* (1976) is a recommended text for use in the classroom both in Britain and the USA, and yet in many respects it is a subversive exploration of the nature of educational discourse and its relationship to the structures of power. The novel, which is never mentioned in 'adult' studies of African-American literature, contains within it a helpful dramatization of many of the threads of my argument about counter-discourse. Using the child-narrator, Cassie Logan, Taylor (1976) takes the reader into the world of 1930s Mississippi where 'though seventy years have passed since slavery, most white people still think of us as they did then — that we're not as good as they are — . . .' (p. 107). This racial discourse is prevalent in Cassie's world and the novel's main dramatic purpose is the gradual education of the young girl into its realities, whilst permitting her to grow into greater wisdom as an individual. She encounters some of the worst aspects of a divided community, such as violence, prejudice, discrimination and the abuse of power, often directly, and sometimes through the specific workings of discourse, but at all times she is learning. Discourses, in a more detailed explanation than the one earlier in the chapter, are about what can be said and thought, but also about who can speak, when, and with what authority. Discourses embody meaning and social relationships, they constitute both subjectivity and power relations. (Ball, 1990, p. 2)

The discourse is dependent, for its proper maintenance, on the often concealed presence or exertion of power. The people involved in the discourse can be characterized as the 'subjects' of discourse — and they will take up particular positions in relation to its power . . . The power of discourses exerts control over oral statements, over what gets written, how it gets written, and, equally, over what and how things get read and interpreted. (Peim, 1993, pp. 38–9)

The workings of discourse are most apparent in the education system which subjects and positions Cassie Logan in relation to a powerful framework of concepts and beliefs, particularly those to do with race. Again and again this double web of discourse, educational and racial, is exposed by Taylor's prose. For example, in an important early section of the book, the children are presented by the school authorities with 'new' textbooks, which are soon revealed to be recycled from the white school system. Inside the cover, the label designates the books as 'very poor' and so suitable for 'nigra' students only. This establishes hierarchy, power, and positions the black recipients in very precise ways as second-rate, worthless and dependent. The teacher punishes the child who rejects the book, Cassie's brother, Little Man, and so upholds the system's authority and power. She tells us she was to 'plan to base all my lessons around' the book (p. 30) as if to reinforce the authority of the powerful object and the whole formation it stands for. But Cassie's mother, who is also a teacher, refuses to accept the 'labels' and pastes over them as a mark of her resistance to the 'county', only to be told she is 'biting the hand that feeds (her)' by another teacher, who believes the label has taught an important lesson to the class of children and 'they've got to learn how things are sometime' (p. 30).

Mary Logan resists this racial discourse saying 'that doesn't mean they have to accept them . . . and maybe we don't either'. As the 'disrupting maverick', she represents the possibility of an alternative way of seeing and it is, therefore, important that she is a teacher who refuses to conform to the precise nexus of power/knowledge that the educational discourse provides. Embodied in Mary Logan is the counter-discourse, the alternative education that she imparts to her daughter, and through the novel, to the reader. Unlike the disciplinary power of the institutionalized education which seeks to produce 'docile bodies',[12] Mary expects more for her pupils.

Mildred Taylor echoes slavery's aim to create the 'docile and dumb, to be big and breeding . . . to be turkey / horse / cow, to be cook / carpenter / plow . . . to be bed bait . . . to be nothing human nothing family nothing from nowhere . . .' (sic June Jordan, in Russell, 1990, p. 2). But Mary Logan resists, determined to define herself and not be defined by others, and to pass this message on to her daughter. Thus when the racist shopkeeper tells Cassie that her 'mammy (should) teach her what she is' (p. 94), the issue is made plain, and since Mary refuses to impose such a discourse on her children, she cannot remain in the school system. In the most significant scene in the novel she is fired for refusing to teach the school's authorized version of history, echoing Malcolm X's famous description of a school history lesson whose 'textbook section on Negro history . . . was exactly one paragraph long' and how the teacher read aloud that the blacks 'were usually lazy and dumb and shiftless' (Malcolm X, 1966, p. 110). She also echoes James Baldwin by assert-ing that African-Americans have to 'accept one's past — one's history — (which) is not the same as drowning in it; it is learning to use it' (Baldwin, 1981, p. 71), thus suggesting the need to rediscover a history hidden by the textbooks and utilize it for the future.

Mary's class on slavery refutes the school book version presenting instead a history learned from her ancestors and the stories they told, as an exchange in the class shows:

'I don't see all them things your teaching in here (holding the book).'
'That's because they're not in there.'
'Well, if it ain't in here, then you got no right teaching it. This book's approved by the Board of Education and you're expected to teach what's in it.'
'I can't do that . . . Because all that's in that book isn't true.' (p. 150)

This scene is mirrored almost exactly in a much more recent novel, Thulani Davis's outstanding *1959*, wherein a black schoolteacher, Mrs Taliaferro (ap-propriately the 'T' in Booker T. Washington), refuses to teach a whitened version of history. The following conversation between her and the white school inspector makes the parallel clear and reveals through its language familiar ideas about the need to challenge the dominant discourse.

'Just where did you get that material about the so-called "twenty-nigger law"? *That's not in our texts.*'
'I do some studying on my own. I have to supplement the books provided by the state because they simply are not adequate, and in the case of my children, the books are often biased.'
'*That material has not been authorized by anyone*', said Burleigh.
'It doesn't have to be!' said Mrs T. 'If I had to get everything author-ized that I give those children, they'd be months behind!' (Davis, 1992, pp. 150–1 — my emphasis)

In both scenes the event is viewed by the child-narrator, also the daughter, Cassie, in Taylor's novel, piecing their educations together like Frederick Douglass symbolically using the old copy-books of his Master's son and 'writing in the spaces left' (Douglass, 1845, p. 87), or like the folk-tradition quilts that Alice Walker used as a symbol of African-American strength and creativity, stealing scraps of information in order to reveal a 'known pattern' (Walker, 1976, p. 239). Cassie is constantly seen just 'close enough to hear' (p. 217) the adult world, but having to work hard to see the pattern of the society in which she lives.[13] This is one of the enduring strengths of the novel for adolescent readers, since it acknowledges the peripheral role they often have, and yet gives them a point of identification with the determined and wilful character of Cassie Logan.

This is a device used by both Angelou and Morrison too, as we shall see later, and suggests a further reason for the interest in the child-narrator in African-American fiction. The child is marginal to adult society, standing at its edge, being gradually socialized and disciplined to accept its rules and regulations, and thus resembles the position of the African-American infantilized by a paternalistic social order whose discourses have the effect of restricting and circumscribing the world of the black subject. The parallel may have influenced the use of the child as central to black writing as if to underline the necessity of the struggle to be more than 'seen and not heard' in American culture.[14] So when Toni Morrison (1970) writes

> We do not, cannot, know the meanings of all their words, for we are nine and ten years old. So we watch their faces, their hands, their feet, and listen for truth in timbre. (p. 10)

she is asserting the position of the child on the edge of 'meanings', but also the desire to know the 'truth', through whatever means, as much as is possible, and to piece it together by watching and listening.

Taylor presents, through the child, the clash of learning, between on the one hand, those forces that seek 'to show us where we stand in the scheme of things' (p. 186) and, on the other, a range of resisting energies which together constitute counter-discourse, opposing and challenging the normative view.

Mildred Taylor's introduction to *Roll of Thunder, Hear My Cry* suggests her awareness of the importance of this process at work in African-American life, when she writes of her father's stories from which she 'learned a history not written in books but one passed from generation to generation on the steps of moonlit porches' (p. 7). Although he 'did not have an excellent education', he had 'wisdom . . . strong moral fiber . . . and plain common sense' (Taylor, 1977, p. 402), that conveyed a history of 'many simple things . . . (and) the complex things too' through which she 'learned to respect the past, to respect my own heritage and myself' (pp. 7–8). As Mildred Taylor (1977) wrote, 'those were hard things for a child to learn' (p. 102), but her father 'tempered' this knowledge with the belief 'that we were somebody, that we were important and could do or be anything we set our minds to do or be' (*ibid.*).

What is significant here is the distinction that her father made between the formal education and the alternative wisdom that came through stories, self-respect and principles. Taylor writes,

> He was not the kind of father who demanded A's on report cards . . .
> He was more concerned about how we carried ourselves, how we
> respected ourselves and others, and how we pursued the principles
> upon which he hoped we would build our lives. (*ibid.*)

All through her long celebration of her father, Taylor emphasizes his role as 'teacher' in a 'discriminatory society', and his passing on to her, through his stories, the capacity 'to question, to reason' (*ibid.*, p. 403). In summarizing the influence of this upon her novels about the Logans, she concludes that it gave her the impetus to demonstrate both their 'spiritual heritage' and to show them as 'contrary' to the normalized view of the black family as 'disintegrating' (*ibid.*). The urgent need to rewrite African-American history through her fiction is this 'contrary' push against a discourse that had for so long presented her race as:

> a history of a docile, subservient people happy with their fate who
> did little or nothing to shatter the chains that bound them, both
> before and after slavery. (*ibid.*, p. 404)

This gave rise to a

> terrible contradiction between what the books said and what I had
> learned from my family, and at no time did I feel the contradiction
> more than when I had to sit in a class which, without me, would have
> been all white, and relive that prideless history year after year. (*ibid.*,
> pp. 404–5)

Her fiction exposes this 'terrible contradiction' by emphasizing the disciplinary power determining what should be thought, known, said and expected, and all those contrary forces which run against it. A history lesson or text book-governed authorized meaning is a single narrative version of events which cannot be permitted to exist as the sole representation of 'truth'. Unchallenged, it becomes part of the hegemony of white history:

> Hegemony contributes to or constitutes a form of social cohesion not
> through force or coercion, nor necessarily through consent, but most
> effectively by way of practices, techniques, and methods which infil-
> trate minds and bodies, cultural practices which cultivate behaviours
> and beliefs, tastes and desires, and needs as seemingly naturally occur-
> ring qualities and properties embodied in the psychic and physical
> reality (or 'truth') of the human subject. (Smart in Couzens Hoy, 1986,
> p. 160)

Mildred Taylor's fiction, like the work of Maya Angelou and Toni Morrison, identifies the process of hegemony in the discourses of education and racism that cohere to 'make subjects' of African-American children, and seeks to present a resistance to its power and a way forward for her people. It involves recognizing the boundaries of the discourse and then counteracting it with an alternative telling of the 'truth' which encompasses a revision of history and 'what can be told', as well as a rethinking of the actual boundaries themselves. Bell Hooks sees this kind of resistance as vital and describes it as 'counter-hegemonic cultural criticism . . . honed and developed in black living rooms, kitchens, barber shops and beauty parlours . . .' (Hooks, 1991, p. 4). All these voices contribute to a 'long black song' that locates the importance of progress and liberation within the problematics of education and learning.

Appropriately, Houston Baker's book *Long Black Song* (1972) states that,

> Education — the process of developing knowledge, mind, skill, and character — has played a vital role in the black American experience. (Baker, 1972, p. 84)

and demonstrates the contrasting views of leaders like Booker T. Washington and W.E.B. Du Bois, and later Malcolm X, about what constituted that 'experience'.[15] Washington, for example, equated education with 'getting into paradise', and the sight of school as 'the promised land' (in Lauter, 1994, pp. 984–1008), but his idea of black education was limited to manual skills and crafts, and to a view of his race which seems limiting and accepting of the discourse of the white system of government and marketplace. Du Bois, however, was highly critical of Washington's views, seeing in this approach the problem of the 'double-consciousness, this sense of always looking at one's self through the eyes of others, of measuring one's soul by the tape of a world that looks on in amused contempt and pity' (Du Bois, 1961, pp. 45–6), which he saw as central to the 'history of this strife'. The emphatic use of terms such as 'measuring' and the idea of 'the eyes of others' invoke slavery and the power of the master-discourse to channel and control the making of the black subject within a white society, and yet DuBois refused to accept this double-bind, calling for a journey towards change and progress. A particular passage is relevant to the fictional quest of writers like Taylor, Angelou and Morrison:

> (The journey) changed the child of Emancipation to the youth with dawning self-consciousness, self-realization, self-respect. In those sombre forests of his striving his own soul rose before him, and he saw himself, — darkly as through a veil — and yet he saw in himself some faint revelation of his power, of his mission. He began to have a dim feeling that, *to attain his place in the world, he must be himself, and not another.* (ibid., pp. 47–8 — my emphasis)

Du Bois urges self-education for pride, dignity, self-worth and power, causing a major shift in African-American attitude, away from the compromises of Washington towards the ideas seen in later writers like Mildred Taylor. This is the root of the counter-discourse, as I have called it, which emphasizes the rejection of a prescribed world, where prescribed literally means 'to write before' and so suggests the history already constructed for the race by the 'master'.

If African-Americans did not seize the opportunities to write their own history and *inscribe themselves* then the system would continue to mould and construct docile bodies and unquestioning minds. This is illustrated in Nella Larsen's *Quicksand* (1928) which begins by describing a black school, Naxos, based in part upon Booker T. Washington's Tuskegee College:

> (Naxos) had grown into a machine . . . It was . . . only a big knife
> . . . cutting all to a pattern, the white man's pattern. Teachers as well
> as students were subjected to the paring process, for it tolerated
> no innovations, no individualisms. (Larsen, quoted in Carby, 1987,
> p. 170)

The school's 'pattern' embodied what Hazel Carby calls, 'the narrow-minded adherence to the dictates of white Southern expectations of Negro passivity' (*ibid.*, p. 171) whilst the work of Du Bois and earlier African-American feminists like Anna Julia Cooper and Frances Ellen Watkins Harper, stressed the need for self-assertion and dignity. Recent autobiographical and fictional black writing has encompassed this tension, whilst calling for an education from within, or what Toni Morrison has called 'the unwritten interior life' (Morrison, 1987b, p. 111) of African-American history.

Maya Angelou, *I Know Why the Caged Bird Sings* (1969)

In James Baldwin's essay 'My Dungeon Shook' (1963), which is addressed to his young nephew, he passes on his learning about living in a society dominated by others' discourse and explains how that might 'cage' the African-American. He tells of his grandfather 'defeated' because 'he really believed what white people said about him . . . spelled out with brutal clarity' (Baldwin, 1981, p. 13). Baldwin's awareness of the way language structures lives is implicit in the phrase 'spelled out', which suggests the mechanisms of prescription at work to write the single narrative of black history. Baldwin goes on to advise,

> Take no one's word for it . . . but trust your experience. Know whence
> you came, there is really no limit to where you can go. The details
> and symbols of your life have been deliberately constructed to make
> you believe what white people say about you. (*ibid.*, p. 16)

Baldwin's advice to 'trust your own experience' rather than the 'spelled out' version of it offered elsewhere, echoes the constant search in African-American life for a voice not determined by the other (white discourse). This is, as elsewhere endorsed by black literature, 'something . . . no school on earth . . . can teach' (p. 84), but is crucial to the search 'to become myself' (p. 59) which is at the heart of Baldwin's writing. His fear is of 'never being allowed to go behind the white man's definitions . . . never being allowed to spell your proper name' (p. 17), but of being 'spat on and defined and de-scribed and limited' (p. 29). Such an individual quest is, however, a political gesture since 'the power of the white world is threatened whenever a black man refuses to accept the white world's definitions' (p. 62) and assert his own alongside theirs.

Baldwin's autobiographical essays are in a long tradition going back to the slave narratives concerned with 'the schism between what one thinks of oneself and what others expect one to be' (McPherson, 1991, p. 121), and it is to this line that Maya Angelou's work belongs. *I Know Why the Caged Bird Sings* charts the child's growth through 'lessons in living' (Angelou, 1969, p. 97) very similar to those of Cassie Logan in *Roll of Thunder, Hear My Cry*, piecing together an education 'filched from those hushed conversations' (*ibid.*, p. 36). Like Cassie, 'the truth had to float to me through the kitchen door' (*ibid.*, p. 146) because real education had to come from a variety of sources and not just the school-house. It is from her church, her mother, her Grand-mother Henderson and from Mrs Flowers, as well as from all the trials of everyday life that Maya sees her learning shaped. Indeed at one point she notes that 'education (was) quite different from the education of our white school-mates' because it included 'the streets and . . . homes' (p. 219).

Mrs Flowers makes Maya aware of the importance of these alternative sources of learning, calling them 'lessons in living', and reminding her

> some people, unable to go to school, were more educated and even more intelligent than college professors . . . to listen carefully to what country people called mother wit . . . (because) in those homely say-ings was couched the collective wisdom of generations. (p. 97)

This counter-discursive knowledge, that includes the history and traditions of the race, becomes central to Maya's growth, and as Angelou comments, 'I knew I knew very little, but I was certain that the things I had yet to learn wouldn't be taught to me at George Washington High School' (p. 264).

The conflict between the two educations is captured best in a scene rather like Mildred Taylor's classroom scene discussed earlier, namely Maya's gradu-ation. This is what Selwyn Cudjoe has termed the scene of 'ideological unveilment' (in Gates, 1990, p. 288) when the values of the racist society are revealed to the expectant Maya through the graduation speech of Mr. Edward Donleavy. It is 'the ancient tragedy (of oppression) being replayed' through the assumptions and positioning of African-Americans in the white discourse as athletes and boxers, and as Maya Angelou writes, 'what school official in the white-goddom of Little Rock had the right to decide that those two men must be our only heroes?' (p. 174):

> We were maids and farmers, handymen and washer-women, and any-
> thing higher that we aspired to was farcical and presumptuous . . . It
> was awful to be a negro and have no control over my life. It was brutal
> to be young and already trained to sit quietly and listen to charges
> brought against my color with no chance of defense. (pp. 175–6)

Echoing the slaves' silence and powerlessness, she adds 'we couldn't *be*', and adjusting Hamlet's soliloquy, comments 'there's the erase', as if to summarize her feelings at the lowest point in the book. It is as if her self and her race have been erased from the history of America. Part of Angelou's quest as a writer, and something she has in common with all the writers discussed here, is her desire to correct this erasure through her act of writing. The words she pro- duces and the voiced heritage, both personal and cultural, that they represent, are counter-discursive acts of resistance and statements of empowerment. As *author*, she denies others' control over her existence, and asserts both self and race against the dominant culture.

This contrary impulse offers hope for the future through the agency of the community 'of the wonderful, beautiful Negro race' (p. 179) who raise up their voices against the humiliations of racism. The combination of commu- nity, with its strong depth of family, tradition and shared experience, and the voice / expression of the group posit a counter-force to the seemingly all- powerful presence of the social order, giving Maya, and the reader, a sense of survival and solidarity.[16] As Cudjoe writes, Angelou is able to 'subvert those institutional discourses and practices that were meant to ensure her mental enslavement' (Gates, 1990, p. 286) by disclosing her awareness of them in her writing, and by the evocation of some alternative, benign forces from within the community.

Maya Angelou's project as an autobiographical writer can be closely linked to the work of Malcolm X, whom she knew well and wrote about in *All God's Children Need Travelling Shoes* (1986). She records a particular comment by Malcolm X which is relevant to my argument; 'a person must make the effort to learn, and growing is the inevitable reward of learning' (*ibid.*, p. 130). This is in keeping with Malcolm X's own autobiography, which also emphasizes his 'self-correcting' (Malcolm X, 1965, p. 382) and the search for 'true knowledge' (p. 256) through education and experience. In the same way that Malcolm X presents himself as a model for his race, 'a testimony of some social value' (p. 497), so too does Maya Angelou, who uses her life as a 'broadening of vision' (in MacPherson, 1991, p. 140), 'to inform and educate people . . . with the hope that an informed oppressed society would swell the voices of protest and hasten the coming of a more just system' (*ibid.*, p. 1). In this manner, autobiography, or what Angelou has called a 'kind of story-telling' (*ibid.*, p. 140), can contribute greatly to the process of filling up 'the empty pots . . . by our tales' (Angelou, 1969, p. 180), because it both enables the individual to discover and express her own worth, as well as contribute to the greater 'history' of the people. In these works the personal truly becomes the political for they are touched by the same forces and together trace an important pattern, which helps us understand the significance given by Angelou to the saying, 'He who does not learn from his history is doomed to repeat it' and then qualify it with, 'I think that . . . if you could just learn, you might not have to repeat *all* the experiences. But I'm afraid that many will'.[17]

Toni Morrison, *Beloved* (1987a)

Learning about and from history is at the heart of Toni Morrison's fiction, which claims specifically 'to bear witness to a history that is unrecorded, untaught, in mainstream education, and to enlighten our people' (in Wisker, 1993, p. 80) through the telling of stories too long unspoken. Her novels want 'to part the veil that was so frequently drawn, to implement the stories that I heard' in order to 'fill in the blanks that the slave narratives left' and to reposition the African-American into 'the discourse that proceeded without us' (Morrison, 1987a, pp. 111–2). Hers is the goal of a 'reconstruction of a world . . . (and) exploration of an interior life that was not written and to the revelation of a kind of truth' (*ibid.*, p. 115). Her writing continues and extends the work of the other writers considered in this chapter, placing black history, identity and education in a wider frame in order to suggest that the counter-discourse is a method in the process towards enlightenment and power. As she wrote in her first novel *The Bluest Eye* (1970),

> Being a minority in both caste and class, we moved about anyway on the hem of life, struggling to consolidate our weaknesses and hang on, or creep singly up to the major folds of the garment. Our peripheral existence, however, was something we learned to deal with . . . (Morrison, 1970, p. 11)

Morrison's novel is for all her young characters about 'learning' in a variety of ways, Claudia and Pecola especially, who experience life in a world governed by 'the eyes of other people' (*ibid.*, p. 35). One section reiterates almost exactly the lessons of all the texts I have considered:

> They go to land-grant colleges, normal schools, and learn the white man's work with refinement: home economics to prepare his food; teacher education to instruct black children in obedience; music to soothe the weary master and entertain his blunted soul. Here they learn . . . how to behave. . . . In short, how to get rid of funkiness.

The dreadful funkiness of passion, the funkiness of nature, the funkiness of the wide range of human emotions. (p. 64)

It is the powerful presence of white bourgeois values that modifies 'funk' by teaching it out of black life, displacing it with correct training and 'refinement'. The alternative 'funkiness' is closer to the rightful self-determination desired by all the figures considered in this essay. Susan Willis argues that 'Funk is really nothing more than the intrusion of the past in the present' (in Gates, 1984, p. 280), and if this is true then what the white world fears is precisely the project that Morrison has set herself as a writer, to remember the past and to reconstruct it in her fiction. What Morrison calls eruptions of funk are the threads of an alternative narrative of African-American life that refuse to be sealed and hidden away under white discourses. Indeed, this whole idea is metaphorically staged in the novel *Beloved*, wherein the past returns to the present in the form of a family ghost in order to bring others to certain recognitions about their past lives and their racial history.

In discussing *Beloved*, I am going to concentrate on two elements; the narrative tension surrounding the central figure of Denver and the terrifying presence of the schoolteacher. These are crucial aspects of the novel and yet curiously ignored in many discussions of the book. Denver is 'the daughter of hope' (Rushdy, 1992, p. 578) representing Morrison's sense of the future as reaching beyond a past, with all its terror and brutality, which is appropriately conveyed by the man of 'learning', the schoolteacher.

Denver has some 'formal' education, with Lady Jones, and this is clearly important to the girl, but Morrison is drawing the contrast with other, and perhaps, greater knowledge gained elsewhere and in different forms. As Morrison (1987a) comments, most blacks '*learned* and died at home' (p. 247 — my emphasis), but that place, as Bell Hooks has written, is the seat of great education:

We could not learn to love or respect ourselves in the culture of white supremacy, on the outside; it was there on the inside, in that 'homeplace', most often created and kept by black women, that we had the opportunity to grow and develop, to nurture our spirits. (Hooks, 1991, p. 42)

Sethe tries to 'keep . . . the past at bay' for herself and for Denver because it is painful to confront, however,

What Denver must do is remember, and she must do so by revising her memory — her history and her mother's history — in a collective anamnesis. (Rushdy, 1992, p. 580)

It is not an easy education for Denver, who at one point in her life stops hearing (just as Maya Angelou stopped speaking), as if to indicate an unwillingness to receive the messages from the past that are so painful, but it is part of her role to reawaken and filter the past so that her mother, Sethe, might carry on. As with so much African-American literature, the child who must learn becomes the symbol of the possible future and the community's strength.

As Malcolm X tells us, history had been 'whitened' and reduced so that black history was 'covered in one paragraph' (Malcolm X, 1966, pp. 268–9), and Morrison adds that even slave narratives tended to omit the interior lives of slaves and, as a consequence, there is a need to activate memory and to fill in the gaps as a counterbalance to the process of reduction. This is best represented by the schoolteacher, who links education and violent denial together, suggesting the very worst aspects of learning when it is turned into a closed and intolerant discipline. He demonstrates that 'definitions belonged to the definers — not the defined' (Morrison, 1987a, p. 190) and therefore that the command over knowledge and learning permits enormous power and authority. Here the idea of authority is again linked to 'authoring' to suggest the ways by which he literally 'writes' their existence as slaves by charting and recording them in his 'book'. The slaves are the objects of the study, with their 'characteristics' divided into 'animal' and 'human', their bodies measured and recorded in pseudo-scientific ways, all aimed at dehumanization as a means of social control. This educational-scientific method and discourse positions Sethe as powerless subhuman without recourse to language, thus

> turning . . . real lives into writing is no longer a procedure of heroization; it functions as a procedure of objectification and subjectification. (Foucault, 1977, p. 192)

A real life has become a 'collated life' (*ibid.*) under the gaze of the master who writes his version of the narrative into his 'notebook' and thereby excludes all other stories:

> First his shotgun, then his thoughts, for schoolteacher didn't take advice from Negroes. The information they offered he called backtalk and developed a variety of corrections (which he recorded in his notebook) to reeducate them. (Morrison, 1987a, p. 220)

What is 'recorded' by schoolteacher is reflective of the single, authorized narrative about black life that must be countered by 'funkiness', the 'homeplace' and the other knowledges which exist outside the normalized system.

Denver has to learn about schoolteacher and all he represents for the present as well as the past, through the stories she is, at first, reluctant to hear from her mother, grandmother, Paul D and Beloved. Only through these is Denver released into the world and able to reengage with the black community in a way that further aids her healing. Denver's learning, as a proactive process of remembering, is preempted in an earlier exchange with Baby Suggs, her grandmother, who instructs her to 'Know it, and go on out of the yard.

Go on.' (p. 244). She must listen to her ancestral voice, not so she can dwell in the past horrors, but so that she can both know who she is and use this to move forward with greater certainty. The growth of Denver from the sheltered and protected daughter of Sethe to her final position in the novel is shown when Paul D says,

'Well, if you want my opinion —'
'I don't', she said. 'I have my own'.
'You grown', he said. (p. 267)

If African-Americans have sought to redefine themselves in a discourse of their own making and based it upon an education drawn in part from the 'lessons in living', then it is expressed here in Denver's assertion of independent thought and opinion. She has indeed 'grown', both from childhood and also into a new knowledge of her self within a community which comes together at the end of the novel to exorcise the ghost of Beloved, a community described as 'voices of women (that) searched for the the right combination, the key, the code, the sound that broke the back of words. Building voice upon voice until they found it . . .' (p. 261).

Denver's process is echoed in the words at the novel's end; 'she gather them and give them back to me in all the right order' (pp. 272–3), for her growth has depended upon the 'pieces I am' being told and brought out into the open, rather than being evaded or hidden from view. Out of the pieces of the (hi)story, memory and wisdom, Denver reconstructs a self which is not reliant upon the schoolteacher's discourse, or indeed even Paul D's, but comes out of her 'familial past' in order to provide her with 'some kind of tomorrow' (p. 273). Denver's going out of the yard is the step into the future based on 'knowing' rather than ignorance, and is her effort to fill 'the space of not knowing' as a positive gesture of resistance and reconstruction of self and community.

Conclusion: '. . . like a sealed letter' (Alice Walker, *Meridian*)

Such a positive gesture has been the quest inherent in all the texts I have discussed, but it is in Toni Morrison's work above all that the profound importance of what she calls 'alternate wisdom' (1981, p. 43) finds its true value. This wisdom, that I have called counter-discourse, is the education that comes to the child from beyond normalized institutional routes; from 'the ancestor' and the 'village', and it must 'defy the system, be cautious . . . and establish and sustain generations in a land . . . (for) Without this presence and recognition there is no life' (*ibid.*). Such ideas challenge the way we read or accept versions of history or stories without question, and Morrison (1989) has written that into the 'spaces' she leaves in her work, like the underlying assumptions conveyed through white discourse, 'should fall the ruminations of the reader and his or her invented or recollected or misunderstood knowingness' (p. 29). This clash of views provides the great challenge of African-American literature as it engages in a process of 'disentangling received knowledge from the apparatus of control' (*ibid.*, p. 8), impelling its readers to reeducate themselves as part of the process of reading and learning undertaken within the books. This suggests the double-edged effect of these texts, for on one hand they tell the story of children who must learn to question received views of history and to see their own place within the wider frame of things, and yet, on the other, the texts are written to educate the reader in a process of rethinking their own values and ways of seeing. The 'space of not knowing' is as real for the reader as it is for the protagonist in the text itself, and both must become part of the counter-discursive process so that knowledge is challenged and increased.

It may be that these texts confirm the need for what Cornel West terms 'the new cultural politics of difference' wherein the African-American

> stays attuned to the best of what the mainstream has to offer — its paradigms, viewpoints, and methods — yet maintains a grounding in affirming and enabling subcultures of criticism . . . simultaneously position(ing) themselves within (or alongside) the mainstream while clearly aligned with groups who vow to keep alive potent traditions of critique and resistance . . . rooted in nourishing subcultures that build on the grand achievements of a vital heritage. (West, 1993, p. 27)

This is not compromise, but an acceptance of the power of the black community and its 'vital heritage' within a larger social group, America itself, towards which the dual educations in these texts lead. Neither is complete on its own, but like the text and the reader, need each other as part of the process of understanding which might lead to filling up 'the space of not knowing' until each individual admits her role in the whole pattern. As Alice Walker (1976) has written, it is important to see 'this existence extended beyond (the) self to those around' (p. 204), for then one can begin to connect the education of the self to a wider, more universal learning about the 'One Life' and the possibility of healing the wounds of history. These examples of African-American literature reinforce and inform Michael M.J. Fischer's view that

> Ethnicity is not something that is simply passed on from generation to generation, taught and learned; it is something dynamic, . . . it is something that institutionalized teaching easily makes chauvinist, sterile, and superficial, something that emerges in full — often liberating — flower only through struggle. Insofar as ethnicity is a deeply rooted emotional component of identity, it is often transmitted less through cognitive language or learning . . . than through processes analogous to the dreaming and transference of psychoanalytic encounters. (Fischer in Clifford and Marcus, 1986, p. 195)

These texts are akin to this process and their young protagonists engaged in a vital, dynamic gathering of 'alternate wisdom', intertwined with the dual struggle of growing up and growing into a racist society. As James Baldwin wrote, 'each of us, however unconsciously, can't but be the vehicle of the history which has produced us. Well we can perish in that vehicle, children, or we can move on up the road' (Baldwin, 1985, p. 556). In different ways, these works reach forward, regarding struggle, to use Fischer's term, as an essential element in the dynamic process of formulating self and communal identity, whilst questioning many of the conventional forms of discourse through which identity is traditionally shaped. Their collective aim is to open up 'the sealed letter' of African-American culture so that it might take its place as a truly dynamic force within a plural, multicultural America.

Notes

1 For example, the AEB syllabuses for 1996 and beyond includes Toni Morrison, *Beloved*, Maya Angelou, *I Know Why the Caged Bird Sings* as set texts on their English 0623 Paper, and its 0660C/0660W Paper suggests *Beloved* as a prose selection, whilst offering in its 'Literary Themes' paper for 1999 'Black America', to include Angelou, Beecher Stowe's *Uncle Tom's Cabin* and suggested choices from Baldwin, Walker or Morrison. *Beloved* is also listed in the Oxford and Cambridge Schools Examination Board syllabus for 1996, and Angelou, Walker and Morrison are listed in the 'Studies in Contemporary Literature' paper for 'AS' level with the University of London Board. Mildred Taylor is recommended in all the English National Curriculum documents for Key Stages 3 and 4.
2 This phrase is taken from Jean-Francois Lyotard (1984) *The Postmodern Condition: A Report on Knowledge*, Manchester, Manchester University Press.
3 This is Toni Morrison's point about *Beloved* being an 'exorcism of the past', which is never an easy or painless process, but is one through which the past is brought out into the open and confronted so that the future can be entered. She argues this in *The South Bank Show* interview with Melvyn Bragg, London Weekend Television, 1987.
4 For example, one might apply some of these framing-ideas to a discussion of other representations of African-American life such as film or television. The British Film Institute teaching materials are useful for classroom activities, and include extracts from some unusual films portraying African-Americans in a range of ways. This could be up-dated to include discussions of contemporary materials such as *The Cosby Show* or *A Different World*, or films like *Boyz n the Hood* or *Do the Right Thing*.
5 I use Frederick Douglass, *The Narrative of the Life of a Slave*, as the most accessible and discussed example, but one should also consider a number of female slave narratives in the same critical light; for example, Harriet Jacobs, *Incidents in the Life of a Slave Girl; Written By Herself*, Oxford: Oxford University Press.
6 Michel Foucault, *Discipline and Punish: the Birth of the Prison* (1977) sets out this concept of the 'disciplinary society' which I find helpful to understand the lasting power of slavery on the lives of modern African-Americans, and the ways in which its discourse works within society to determine and control those lives.

7 Notice how Richard Wright echoes the work of Du Bois here by repeating the sense of duality at the heart of black life. The 'double-consciousness' permeates the process of education and learning too and forms the basis of my argument in this chapter. Wright's influence is still significant on contemporary writers like Rosa Guy who has said 'I understood Black America because of Richard Wright' (Chamberlain, 1988, p. 8).

8 These three works are the most often used in syllabuses and represent a range of complexity as well as a number of points of similarity which I explore here. I cannot discuss at length the importance of African-American women writers and their unique role in contemporary literature, nor do I intend to discuss their work as purely feminist texts. Instead, I have followed a theme in their works and located them within a tradition of African-American writing and history.

9 Anna Julia Cooper, 'Woman Versus the Indian' in Lauter (1994) p. 791. Cooper was a contemporary of Du Bois and dedicated her life to the education and social improvement of African-Americans.

10 Cooper in Lauter (1994) p. 782. Cooper's radical thinking is summed up in the lines 'the world needs to hear her voice. It would be subversive of every human interest that the cry of one-half the human family be stifled. Woman in stepping from the pedestal of statue-like inactivity . . . to undertake to shape, mold, and direct the thought of her age, is merely completing the circle of the world's vision' (p. 797).

11 Michel Foucault (1977) uses the term in his *Language, Counter-Memory, Practice; Selected Essays and Interviews*, Ithaca, NY, Cornell University Press. The process described here by Lipsitz can be closely related to the work of Toni Morrison and to her use of the term 're-memory' as a necessary means of revising and rethinking history. Morrison (1988) has said 'We live in a land where the past is always erased . . . The past is absent or it's romanticised. This culture doesn't encourage dwelling on, let alone coming to terms with, the truth about the past. That memory is much more in danger now than it was 30 years ago.'

12 Again, this is a phrase borrowed from Foucault's *Discipline and Punish*, but a term which has been echoed in Taylor's own comments (1977, p. 404) and in critical comments by the black feminist June Jordan (in Russell, 1990, p. 2), to describe the intention of white discourse to reduce African-Americans to passivity.

13 See also Frances Harper's poem 'Learning to Read' published in Lauter (1994).

14 The tradition of infantilization of African-Americans is well established as a mechanism of dehumanization and control. It is ably demonstrated in Ellison, (1952):

> Yes! Yes! YES! That was all anyone wanted of us, that we should be heard and not seen, and then heard only in one big optimistic chorus of yassuh, yassuh, yassuh! (p. 410)

15 The complex positions of Washington and Du Bois cannot be fully discussed here in any detail, and I intend to suggest only a broad difference between their ideas so as to underline my own argument about a duality as central to African-American concepts of what constitutes education.

16 It is an interesting extension of my arguments that in these texts, as well as others, especially Alice Walker's *Meridian*, that the community 'voice' emerges as essential to the development of the protagonist, like the resurrection of Toni Morrison's concept of the 'village ancestor', 'advising, benevolent, protective, wise . . . the

matrix' (1981, p. 39) in the form of the village speaking out against the prevalent discourse.

17 Maya Angelou in an interview (1988) Chamberlain, *Writing Lives*.
18 James Baldwin, review of Alex Haley's *Roots* in *The Price of the Ticket*.

References

ANGELOU, M. (1969) *I Know Why the Caged Bird Sings*, London, Virago.

ANGELOU, M. (1986) *All God's Children Need Travelling Shoes*, London, Virago.

BAKER, H. (1972) *Long Black Song*, Chapel Hill, NC, University of Virginia Press.

BALDWIN, J. (1972) *No Name in the Street*, New York, Dial Press.

BALDWIN, J. (1981) *The Fire Next Time*, Harmondsworth, Penguin.

BALDWIN, J. (1985) *The Price of the Ticket: Collected Non-fiction, 1948–1985*, London, Joseph.

BALL S.J. (Ed) (1990) *Foucault and Education: Discipline and Knowledge*, London, Routledge.

BENSTON, K. (1984) 'I yam what I am: The topos of (un)naming in Afro-American fiction', in GATES, H.L. (Ed) *Black Literature and Literary Theory*, London, Routledge.

CARBY, H.V. (1987) *Reconstructing Womanhood: The Emergence of the Afro-American Woman Novelist*, Oxford, Oxford University Press.

CHAMBERLAIN, M. (Ed) (1988) *Writing Lives: Conversations Between Women Writers*, London, Virago Press.

CLAYTON, J. (1993) *The Pleasures of Babel: Contemporary American Literature and Theory*, New York, Oxford University Press.

CLIFFORD, J. and MARCUS, G. (Eds) (1986) *Writing Culture: The Poetics and Politics of Ethnography*, Berkeley, CA, University of California Press.

COUZENS, H.D. (Ed) (1986) *Foucault: A Critical Reader*, Oxford, Blackwell.

DAVIS, T. (1992) *1959*, Harmondsworth, Penguin.

DOUGLASS, F. (1845) *The Narrative of the Life of Frederick Douglass, An American Slave*, Harmondsworth, Penguin.

DU BOIS, W.E.B. (1961) *The Souls of Black Folks*, New York, Fawcett.

DU BOIS, W.E.B. (1970) *Speeches and Addresses 1920–1963*, London, Pathfinder.

EARLY, G. (Ed) (1933) *Lure and Loathing: Essays on Race, Identity and the Ambivalence of Assimilation*, London, Allen Lane.

ELLISON, R. (1952) *Invisible Man*, Harmondsworth, Penguin.

FOUCAULT, M. (1977) *Discipline and Punish: The Birth of the Prison* (trans Sheridan, A.) Harmondsworth, Penguin.

GATES, H.L. (Ed) (1984) *Black Literature and Literary Theory*, London, Routledge.

GATES, H.L. (Ed) (1990) *Reading Black, Reading Feminist: A Critical Anthology*, New York, Meridian.

HOOKS, B. (1991) *Yearning: Race, Gender, and Cultural Politics*, London, Turnaround.

LAURET, M. (1994) *Liberating Literature: Feminist Fiction in America*, London, Routledge.

LAUTER, P. (Ed) (1994) *The Heath Anthology of American Literature Vol. 1 & 2*, Lexington, KY, DC, Heath.

LEVINE, L. (1977) *Black Culture and Black Consciousness*, New York, Oxford University Press.

LIPSITZ, G. (1990) *Time Passages*, Minneapolis, MI, University of Minnesota.

MacPherson, D.A. (1991) *Order Out of Chaos: The Autobiographical Works of Maya Angelou*, London, Virago.

Morrison, T. (1970) *The Bluest Eye*, London, Chatto and Windus.

Morrison, T. (1981) 'City limits, village values: Concepts of the neighbourhood in black fiction', in Jaye, M.C. and Chalmers Watts, A. (Eds) *Literature and the Urban American Experience*, Manchester, Manchester University Press.

Morrison, T. (1987a) *Beloved*, London, Picador.

Morrison, T. (1987b) 'The site of memory', in Zinsser, W. (Ed) *Inventing the Truth: The Art and Craft of Memoir*, Boston, MA, Houghton Mifflin.

Morrison, T. (1988) 'Living memory', *City Limits*, 31 March–7 April, pp. 10–11.

Morrison, T. (1989) 'Unspeakable things unspoken: The Afro-American presence in American literature', *Michigan Quarterly Review*, **28**, winter, pp. 1–34.

Munslow, A. (1992) *Discourse and Culture: The Creation of America 1870–1920*, London, Routledge.

Peim, N. (1993) *Critical Theory and the English Teacher: Transforming the Subject*, London, Routledge.

Rushdy, A.H.A. (1992) 'Daughters signifyin(g) history: The example of Toni Morrison's *Beloved*', *American Literature*, **64**, 3 September, pp. 567–97.

Russell, S. (1990) *Render Me My Song: African-American Women Writers from Slavery to the Present*, London, Pandora.

Said, E. (1978) *Orientalism: Western Conceptions of the Orient*, Harmondsworth, Penguin.

Said, E. (1993) *Culture and Imperialism*, London, Vintage.

Sims, R. (1982) *Shadow and Substance: Afro-American Experience in Contemporary Children's Fiction*, National Council of Teachers of English, Urbana, IL.

Storey, J. (1993) *An Introductory Guide to Cultural Theory and Popular Culture*, London, Harvester Wheatsheaf.

Taylor, M.D. (1976) *Roll Of Thunder, Hear My Cry*, Harmondsworth, Penguin.

Taylor, M.D. (1977) 'Newberry award acceptance speech', *The Horn Book Magazine*, **53**, August, pp. 401–9.

Walker, A. (1976) *Meridian*, London, Women's Press.

Walker, A. (1984) *In Search of Our Mothers' Gardens*, London, Women's Press.

West, C. (1993) *Keeping Faith: Philosophy and Race in America*, London, Routledge.

Williams, R. (1958) *Culture and Society 1780–1950*, Harmondsworth, Penguin.

Wisker, G. (Ed) (1993) *Black Women's Writing*, London, MacMillan.

Wright, R. (1945) *Black Boy*, London, Longman.

Wright, R. (1989) *Uncle Tom's Cabin*, New York, Harper and Row.

X, M. (1965) *The Autobiography of Malcolm X*, Harmondsworth, Penguin.

Appendix

Class Activities: Analyzing Power

Exploring the Meanings of Discourse

1 One way of gaining some sense of this concept in a way that might be useful here is to relate it to a familiar institution and its particular 'language' and 'unwritten rules', such as the school and the classroom.
2 The class might discuss the unwritten rules that operate within this framework (a discourse of the classroom).
   (a) the arrangement of the room is important in establishing a set of positions, rules, hierarchies — how?
   (b) certain things are acceptable and encouraged in the classroom, certain things are not — what are they? Include speech, writing, behaviour in this discussion.
   (c) what is the role, authority, position of the teacher in this situation? Are they governed by the same rules or different rules, and does this give them greater power? Why is this?
   (d) what is the relationship of the teacher to the room's appearance, the points raised in (b)? Do they 'set the tone' and control the boundaries of the class's language? Limit and contain the extent of the activity?
   (e) do different types of subjects demand a different kind of 'language' and do different rules apply? Compare, for example, an English language oral class with a science laboratory in which experiments are being undertaken.

* This sort of approach should stimulate a range of ideas and points.

Now add the questions:

(a) Is it the class and the teacher who set these 'rules' and establish these languages? If they don't, who does, and what connection and control do teacher and class have over the rules?
(b) If an inspector or governor were in the classroom, would that alter the rules, or change the way the class functioned? Why?

(c) If the class had a very important examination at the end of the month, would that influence the rules, language, tone of the class? Why?

Discourse, Power and Resistance in African-American literature

3   Use passages from the texts discussed in the chapter on African-American literature to examine how these texts explore the discourse of the classroom, its rules, languages, powers.

4   Go on to see how these particular texts are using a range of points to show how power works through discourse and that this has a wider significance for African-Americans whose very history has been controlled and channelled by a dominant set of rules and accepted attitudes of racism and prejudice.

5   As discussed in the chapter, I would use two parallel passages:
    (i)   Mildred Taylor, *Roll of Thunder, Hear My Cry* pp. 148–50
    (ii) Thulani Davis, *1959* pp. 150–2

6   How is the discourse of the classroom (teacher and class) altered by the intrusion of a third force onto the scene? What does this tell us about the nature of power, that is, who is in control here and how do they exercise their power?

7   The two passages comment on the book/lesson being given. Why do the third parties wish to 'adjust' the messages coming from the teacher? Why don't they seem to approve of the lesson?

8   In the Davis extract (p. 150) the inspector says 'That material has not been authorized by anyone'. Why is this such a big issue?

9   Likewise in the Taylor extract (p. 150) the inspector says 'This book's approved by the Board of Education and you're expected to teach what's in it'. How does this attitude seek to control what can and can't be said, discussed, learned?

10 This is a **discourse**, established and controlled with the aim of defining what is acceptable and what is not. It controls by limiting knowledge or channelling knowledge in particular directions. This helps unravel the ways in which power works in society. It also shows how this **power**, which runs through discourse, *positions the subject*, that is, shapes and defines the individual in relation to that discourse and power, telling them what they can be and say and do.

11 Why is this 'positioning of the subject' particularly relevant to the African-American? What is it related to historically? Think back to the way slavery functioned and controlled the individual.

12 In the passages, is there an indication of some efforts to work against those powers that seek to mould and shape the individual? What are they, and how successful are they? This is termed **resistance**, and demonstrates the ability to fight back and to question the norms established in a dominant, authorized environment, like a school.

13 Begin to examine other passages in the novel(s) towards planning an essay on education and school as a medium for the passing on of social roles, values and power.

14 Two difficult extracts might be offered at this point from Ralph Ellison (1952), *Invisible Man*, Harmondsworth, Penguin.

    (i)   The Battle Royal scene pp. 19–32 in which black boys are humiliated at the hands of powerful white business men as a mechanism of control.

    (ii) pp. 94–5, in which the young boys are reminded of their 'place' from within an educational institution. They are 'positioned' by the authority of a powerful white discourse. For example,

> This was our world, they said as they described it to us, this our horizon and its earth, its seasons and its climate . . . and this we must accept and love and accept even if we did not love. We must accept . . . (p. 95)

Section 3

Principles in Practice

Chapter 9

Towards 2000: Tomorrow's Books, Tomorrow's Readers

Ed Marum

> Merely teaching men to read and write does not work miracles; if there are not enough jobs for men able to work, teaching more men to read and write will not create them. (Freire, 1972a, p. 25)

As we approach the third millenium, there is a great deal to do to change 'official' views of literacy and the kind of schooling offered to pupils within the state system. In essence, what needs to be done is to unpick the elements that have come together since the 1970s and to replace the existing school system with a new one. The Conservative government has over the last sixteen years presided over a conscious dismantling of the educational structures which have previously held the state system in place. Their incremental, short-term tinkering with and revisions to the powers of local authorities, governors and headteachers has produced low morale, a cynicism towards politicians and their motivations, and continuing confusion for parents watching their children progress through a shifting and unclear educational framework to a world beyond school which is itself uncertain and often unwelcoming. It should come as no surprise, therefore, that many children, particularly those in inner-city environments, seem to have lost belief in the educational process by the time of their mid-teens. We have seen in recent years some of the social consequences of their disillusionment. In order to avert more serious problems in the future, we need to review our educational system as a matter of urgency.

Contributors to this book have shown, from a variety of perspectives, constructive and practical steps that English teachers might take to cushion some of the impact of government policy on the curriculum, particularly with respect to the requirements of the National Curriculum. But changing the curriculum will not in itself change the nature of schools. We must change our view of literacy, but we must also ensure that those wider changes that will offer greater hope and confidence for our future are also effected. Many of these changes, such as those I believe necessary to secure an improved state welfare and benefits system, a better coordinated housing policy, an effective long-term strategy on employment, etc., are beyond our brief here. We need to remember, however, that whatever happens in schools cannot alone change the social attitudes and values of a Britain which lacks a clear sense of international identity in an increasingly pluralist world environment. Those involved in education should certainly have a voice on such issues, as they affect both our own lives and those of future generations. English teachers in particular have by tradition been an effective body in expressing their concerns. It is important that they should continue to do so.

Within the schools context, the wider changes that I have suggested are necessary, need to encompass a revision of the organization, expectations and attitudes of teachers. Without such changes, it will be impossible to implement the broad curricular revision I am seeking. I should like to develop this point in a little detail.

First, there can be no doubt that the view of 'culture' enshrined in the Cox Report, even before its various amendments by government officers, was a limiting one. I agree with Jones's analysis of the situation which, published three years ago, seemed something of a lonely voice at that time:

> On the basis of positive, 'undialectical' understandings of 'Cox' arises a particular approach to the politics of English teaching, which centres on efforts to take advantage of the space the Report offers for the continuing development of 'progressive' approaches, and which defends it against the right. Only to the most rigorous purism can constructive engagement of this kind appear as some form of collaborationism; it is a necessary dimension of any response to 'Cox'. We want to suggest, though, that something has been lost in this process: a capacity not just to look at the space within 'Cox', but the ground beyond it. We have been told many times that 'Cox' has not ruled out anything, and that arguments like ours, by discussing the limits of the Report, have the effect of suggesting that radical practice can find no home within its programme. One of the problems with a case like this is that it is happier with the exploration of marginal opportunities, than with thinking about a future for English outside the Report's framework. It substitutes the pragmatics of constructive engagement for the work of developing alternative practices. (Jones, 1992, p. 126)

The revisions to practice which I am suggesting are necessary include a movement away from the rationale of the National Curriculum in English as it exists in its present form, as well as a clear shift in thinking about classroom work. At the intellectual level, we need to redefine our understanding of 'literacy' along the lines I have suggested; firstly, to encompass Meek's view, quoted earlier, that we should regard literature as 'simply the writing that people do'. This quite properly shifts our concern away from 'privileged' views of texts, such as those espoused in the notion of 'literary canons' or 'great' literary traditions, which are seen to somehow and immutably stand apart from all 'other' and therefore inferior literature, towards an understanding that literature, as one aspect of communications in the modern world, needs to be read and studied from a variety of perspectives which take account of historical, regional, class, gender and cultural standpoints of both writers and readers. This, I think, is what Meek is meaning in her statement that 'literacy is about reading and writing texts of all kinds and the entitlement of all'. She is also of course saying that literacy is about far more than books; that we are graphically literate before we read; that 'computer literacy' continues to prove a rapidly developing medium which is not seriously addressed in the great majority of schools (partly because many pupils are more literate than their teachers); that film and television studies have as important a place in English as do the written and spoken language in print. If an important task of English teachers is to develop intelligent 'critical readers', basic training of pupils in communications methodologies must become an essential part of the primary curriculum. The need to construct a developmental model which begins with the 'personal' — reading, writing and talk examining feelings, values, beliefs — and moves on to consider the 'non-personal' — the construction of different texts for diverse audiences, mechanical and technological communications systems and their methodologies — will finally become inescapable. All, in fact, that is involved in our everyday uses of 'reading', which range far wider than book use and which will be of such social significance in determining our future will, almost too late, gain future intellectual and academic status.

Changing Practice: Beyond 2000

In practice, what is required to be done demands a revision of the primary curriculum. What is understood by 'language and learning' must be reinterpreted: our rationale demands the development of interdisciplinary study across infant and junior age ranges, and the accompanying abandonment of subject-based organization such as that wrongheadedly required by the National Curriculum proposals. Beyond this, I set out here in brief my thoughts as to what is likely to happen in the coming years.

Literacy teaching will in future need to be multi-media in design and implementation and, by definition, truly cross-curricular. STORY will be generally acknowledged as the cultural centre for educational advance. This will entail structural, organizational and administrative changes in school management as well as in classroom practice.

At secondary level, future social needs will dictate that the National Curriculum will be scrapped as inadequate and ineffective in providing the broad, balanced and coherent curriculum necessary to prepare pupils for quality education at further and higher levels, as well as for the multi-media, networked communications world they will live in. Again, the curriculum model will be multidisciplinary and not traditionally subject-based. It will be constructed around areas of experience which all pupils study. These will be centred around the visual and practical arts; theory and practice in mathematics and science; literacy and design studies, and multicultural world studies.

At both stages, primary and secondary, there will be no system of national testing before the age of 14, as by the year 2000 the present system will have proved unworkable, as well as financially crippling, administratively cumbersome, and to no positive educational effect. At the age of 14, pupils will be tested within local areas by tests designed by their teachers and moderated by local panels of teachers. These tests will be criterion-referenced, and the results will be confidential to pupils, parents and schools. On the basis of these results, combined with their previous educational records, pupils will be counselled as to the elements of the 14–18 curriculum they will choose to pursue. This curriculum will be composed of an individually selected balance of the areas of experience they have previously pursued. In the 16–18 phase, all pupils will study, on the basis of a negotiated personal contract, towards the Certificate in Further Education. It is likely that this last phase of the programme will be modular in construction. Awards in language and literature will be based on a portfolio of coursework accumulated over the final two years of the course, moderated by groups of local teachers. This coursework element will have replaced unseen written examinations at 16 and 18. The certificate itself will replace all previous existing qualifications, such as the GNVQ, 'A' levels, etc., and will be the basis for determining the nature of the higher education route to be followed. It will simultaneously carry a national vocational qualification status.

Traditional school inspections, such as those mounted under OFSTED, will no longer take place, as the system currently in operation, like that for the national testing of pupils, will have proved totally impracticable. There will be a national system of school self-review and appraisal, linked to the setting of institutional annual targets. This will be accompanied by a considerable growth in curriculum and staff development training for in-service teachers.

Teacher-training will be completely overhauled, moving rapidly away from existing arrangements involving school-led training on site and proposed training agencies. Independent teacher training units will be established, on a contractual basis, to train groups of teachers, in partnership with named 'training' schools, financed for that purpose. These units will comprise a range of professionals with varying interests and experience. The training will be organized and coordinated by seconded practising advisory teachers, chosen and selected at local authority level and employed on a rotational basis through joint contracts between local authorities and training units.

In sum, the changing global communications environment will inevitably lead to major revisions in the structure, organization and teaching of literacies in schools over the next generation. STORY, in oral and written forms, will remain central to the developing curriculum, but as a distinct form among a broadening range of communication studies in which information technology, the diversified use of computing applications and information retrieval systems, as well as film, video and television, will be formally acknowledged within and beyond the profession. In the medium term, schools as we presently know them will need to undergo extensive reorganisation; in the longer term, of course, home-based, networked schooling systems will be set up. It is likely that these will gradually replace the school as an identifiable institution.

In a sense, therefore, it will no longer be possible for 'schooling' to regulate the social and cultural attitudes to and of childhood in the way it has done since the nineteenth century. Set against our probable future, the National Curriculum proposals seem woefully inadequate on this as on the other counts I have discussed. Again, Jones has already pointed this out very clearly:

> Claiming its relevance to all students, it (the National Curriculum) in fact neglects the specific conditions of their lives and the interests which motivate their learning. It presents to students a model of knowledge which, in its particular orientation towards their lives, is unlikely to be attractive. Thus its claim to deliver a better education is, and will continue to be, contested at the level of the classroom.'
> (*ibid.*, pp. 127–8)

Towards a Beginning

The concept of childhood is not quite dead. If the inevitable pressures upon young people will continue to accelerate their premature desires for the imagined worlds of adolescence and maturity, it will be all the more important that the formal education they receive should seek to directly address the 'specific conditions of their lives' from nursery to secondary schooling. If the other face of innocence is enquiry, educators must acknowledge and act upon the very real enthusiasm for learning that young people regularly, and often despite the odds, display. They must, above all, radically change their practice to retain and stimulate that enthusiasm through the years of formal schooling.

We need, in the first instance, a new generation of teachers who are 'multiliterate' in the sense I have identified, and who will be able and willing to inform and guide children and adolescents in the new kind of partnership learning requires. Our approach to the literacies of the future will both condition and reflect the kind of society we wish to be. We will need to acknowledge the truth about our condition, rather than to erect still more false windmills to tilt at. English teachers, above all others, must be able to stand in unity with Pennac:

> Man builds houses because he is alive, but he writes books because he knows he's mortal. He lives in groups because he is gregarious, but he reads because he knows he's alone. His reading keeps him company, but without replacing any other; rather no other company can

take its place. Reading offers him no definitive explanation of his fate, but weaves a tight network of correspondences between life and him. These correspondences, tiny and secretive, speak of the paradoxical good fortune of being alive, even while they're illuminating the tragic absurdity of life. The result is that our reasons for reading are quite as *strange* as are our reasons for living. And no one is charged to have us render an account of that intimate strangeness. (Pennac, 1994, pp. 177–8)

The first step that English teachers must now take is to acknowledge the situation they are in before they go on to change it. The first part of that process is not yet complete. The contributors to this book hope that they have helped to identify ways forward in the process of facing some of the problems that need to be addressed. This is not a new situation; nor is it a hopeless one:

Problem-posing education is revolutionary futurity. Hence it is prophetic (and, as such, hopeful), and so corresponds to the historical nature of man. (sic) Thus, it affirms men as beings who transcend themselves, who move forward and look ahead, for whom immobility represents a fatal threat, for whom looking at the past must only be a means of understanding more clearly what and who they are so that they can more wisely build the future. . . . The point of departure of the movement lies in men themselves. But since men do not exist apart from the world, apart from reality, the movement must begin in the 'here and now', which constitutes the situation within which they are submerged, from which they emerge, and in which they intervene. Only by starting from this situation — which determines their perception of it — can they begin to move. To do this authentically they must perceive their state not as fated and unalterable, but merely as limiting — and therefore challenging. (Freire, 1972b, p. 57)

The most important current challenge for English teachers is clear. A great deal depends on their response. Future literacies, as part of our understanding of 'cultures', are even now in the process of redefinition outside the classroom. Like the concept of 'literacy', that of 'culture' will 'come to have different meanings while it is still in use' (Scafe, 1989, p. 22).

Because literacies will become increasingly important in our understanding of future 'cultures', and because the latter will in a very real sense shape our understanding of our collective world future, we might do worse than to make a beginning by reminding ourselves of the words of Raymond Williams (1958):

The word culture cannot automatically be pressed into service as any kind of social or personal directive. Its emergence in its modern meanings marks the effort at total qualitative assessment, but what it indicates is a process not a conclusion. (p. 285)

References

FREIRE, P. (1972a) *Cultural Action for Freedom*, Harmondsworth, Penguin Books.

FREIRE, P. (1972b) *Pedagogy of the Oppressed*, Harmondsworth, Penguin Books.

JONES, K. (1992) *English and the National Curriculum: Cox's Revolution?*, London, Kogan Page.

PENNAC, D. (1994) *Reads Like A Novel* (trans Gunn, D.) London, Quartet Books.

SCAFE, S. (1989) *Teaching Black Literature*, London, Virago Press.

WILLIAMS, R. (1958) *Culture and Society*, Harmondsworth, Penguin Books.

Notes on Contributors

Neil Campbell trained as a secondary school teacher, worked in a sixth-form college in Leicestershire and now teaches American Studies at the University of Derby. His current research interests are in youth culture and African-American literature, areas on which he has also published. He is presently writing a book on American cultural studies to be published by Routledge in 1995.

Christine Hall is a Lecturer in Education at the University of Nottingham. She has taught English in a variety of comprehensive schools and has recently been involved in editing three collections of short stories published by Heinemann: *Nineteenth Century Short Stories* (1993), *Classic Short Stories* (1994) and *Short Stories by Women* (1995). She teaches with Mick Saunders on the Master's degree programme in Children's Literature at the University of Nottingham.

Ed Marum is Head of the Division of Humanities at the University of Derby, where he is also the programme leader in Children's Literature. He has taught in a variety of schools and has also been English Adviser for Liverpool and a General Inspector in London. He is currently working on another book with Falmer Press, *Children and Books in the Modern World: An International Perspective on Literacy*.

Jenny Marum is County Adviser for English in Humberside. She has worked in a variety of primary and secondary schools and has also been an Advisory Teacher for Language Development and Head of an English Department in a comprehensive school. She has a particular interest in children's literature, equal opportunities issues and in-service training for English teachers.

James Pattenden has been Head of English at Eckington School, Derbyshire, for over ten years. During this period, he has led his department through a range of curricular innovations, including the introduction of GCSE, the National Curriculum and 'A' level English language. Currently, he regrets the cessation of 100 per cent coursework in English and awaits its eventual return. He is a member of the North-East Derbyshire Four Counties Syllabus Group.

Mick Saunders is Course Director for the PGCE at the School of Education, University of Nottingham. He has taught in primary and secondary schools and is interested in language development generally and children's literature in particular. His publications include *Developments in English Teaching* (Open Books), *Into Books* (Oliver and Boyd), and, with Christine Hall and Sallyanne Greenwood, *Focus on Fiction* (Heinemann).

Liz Slater is Curriculum Adviser for Primary English for the County of Essex Development and Advisory Service and is a Director of the Essex Reading Project. She has taught in primary and secondary schools, and was a Deputy Headteacher in an Essex primary school before becoming a primary language advisory teacher. She is particularly interested in the implications of group learning in the classroom, information texts, language in the environment and writing in primary schools.

Index